Devil-Worship in France

with Diana Vaughan and the Question of Modern Palladism

Devil-Worship in France

with Diana Vaughan and the Question of Modern Palladism

A. E. Waite

with an introduction by R. A. Gilbert

WeiserBooks
Boston, MA/York Beach, ME

First published in 2003 by
Red Wheel/Weiser, LLC
York Beach, ME

With offices at:
368 Congress Street
Boston, MA 02210
www.redwheelweiser.com

Introduction and *Diana Vaughan and the Question of Modern Palladism* copyright © 2003 R. A. Gilbert

All rights reserved. No part of this publication may be reproduced or transmitted in any form or by any means, electronic or mechanical, including photocopying, recording, or by any information storage and retrieval system, without permission in writing from Red Wheel/Weiser, LLC. Reviewers may quote brief passages. *Devil-Worship in France* first published by George Redway, London, 1896.

Library of Congress Cataloging-in-Publication Data

Waite, Arthur Edward.
Devil-worship in France with Diana Vaughan and the question of modern palladism / A.E. Waite ; with an introduction by R.A. Gilbert.
p. cm.
Includes bibliographical references and index.
ISBN 1-57863-286-2 (alk. paper)
1. Satanism—France—History. 2. Occultism—France—History. I. Title.
BF1548.W2 2003
133.4'22'0944—dc21 2003011390

Typeset in the United States
Printed in the United States
Printer: The Maple-Vail Book Manufacturing Group
10 09 08 07 06 05 04 03

8 7 6 5 4 3 2 1

The paper used in this publication meets the minimum requirements of the American National Standard for Information Sciences-Permanence of Paper for Printed Library Materials Z39.48-1992 (R1997).

CONTENTS

DIANA VAUGHAN AND THE QUESTION OF MODERN PALLADISM

INTRODUCTION

ON THE EVENING of 19 April 1897, a large and expectant audience filled the hall of the *Société Géographique* in Paris. They had come to see the first public appearance of Diana Vaughan, ex-Satanist and Catholic convert, whose sensational *Mémoires* had variously appalled and delighted them for almost two years. Their expectations were not met: in place of Diana Vaughan they were faced with another supposed convert, the journalist Leo Taxil.

Miss Vaughan, he told them, would not be appearing. Indeed, she could not for she did not exist. She and the Palladium—the satanic-masonic organisation from which she had supposedly escaped—were myths of his own creation, part of a gigantic hoax to discredit the Church and to discomfit the freemasons. They should not be disappointed, Taxil told them, for just as he had promised, Palladism had been destroyed—by its creator. "I have committed infanticide," he said. "Palladism is now dead and dead forever. Its father has just killed it." During the uproar that followed, Taxil quietly walked off the stage. And that, it seemed, was that.

Even before this dénouement the more sober critics of Taxil's fantastic and salacious tales of debauchery and black magic had condemned their "gross inaccuracy," noted that they were "too absurd for sober contemplation,"[1] and commented on the credulity and naïveté of those Catholic writers who insisted that they were true. G. R. S. Mead, who was disposed to see sexual depravity all around him, looked on the "Masonic Satanism" furore in Paris as one of the "bye-ways of credulity and immorality in France" and summed it up as a strange combination of "blind faith, fanaticism, and charlatanry, proceeding from ignorance and immoderate desire, curiosity and conceit."[2] With the benefit of a century of hindsight, it is difficult to dissent from his view, but however absurd the whole affair appears to us to be, Taxil was wrong. He may have killed his child, but fanatic minds, more devious even than his, have brought it back to life, and it is because of their actions that Waite's study of "The Question of Lucifer" is still important.

---

1. See, *e.g.*, reviews of *Devil-Worship in France* by David Gow, in *The Two Worlds*, 31 July 1896; and by W. T. Stead, in *Borderland*, 1896.

2. G. R. S. Mead, Review of *Devil-Worship in France, Lucifer,* Vol. 18, August 1896, p. 436.

The whole sorry tale of so-called "Palladian Freemasonry" began not in the 1890s, but in 1867, when the fourteen-year-old Gabriel Jogand[3] (who was to become "Leo Taxil") borrowed a book on Freemasonry from a school friend. Jogand was born at Marseilles in 1853 and educated at Jesuit schools, where he displayed a rebellious streak. He was fascinated by what he read, but the Catholic Church was anti-masonic and the book was confiscated. Reacting to this, Jogand turned against the Church and drifted into free thought and radical politics. After the Revolution of 1871, he began a career in journalism, contributing to and editing radical and anti-clerical periodicals, under the pen name of Leo Taxil.

His interest in Masonry was also rekindled, partly because French Freemasonry had become virulently anti-clerical (to the extent that in 1877 the Grand Orient de France had removed the requirement that its members should believe in God, an act that resulted in its repudiation as a regular masonic body by almost every Grand Lodge in the world). Early in 1881, Gabriel Jogand was initiated at Paris in the Lodge *Les Amis de l'Honneur Français,* but he never progressed beyond the first degree, and in August that year he was expelled from the Grand Orient for the "crimes" of literary theft and publishing pornography.

Although rejected by the freemasons, and by many of his former colleagues who had felt the barbs of his scabrous wit,

---

3. His surname is frequently given as Jogand-Pagès, his mother's maiden name having been Pagès.

Leo Taxil—as he was now known to friends and enemies alike—remained almost hysterically anti-clerical and sought for a new way of attacking the Church. He found it by putting his masonic expulsion to good use. In 1885, Taxil made a public rejection of his beliefs, announced his conversion to the faith and began to publish increasingly sensational anti-masonic works. These included *Les Soeurs Maçonnes (The Masonic Sisters)* of 1886, an exposure of the "secret ceremonies" of Lodges for women. Five years later, a new edition of this book, renamed *Y-at-il des Femmes dans la Franc-maçonnerie? (Are there women in Freemasonry?)*, included a startling account of his own invention: the Palladian Order.

This Palladian Masonry was allegedly for both men and women, and Taxil printed its supposed rituals, exciting his readers with descriptions of blasphemy, devil worship and thinly veiled debauchery, and with highly entertaining illustrations. Delighted to have such a well-informed convert to write for their cause, the Church's own flock of anti-masonic "authorities" put Taxil's tales to good use in their own publications. An eager public lapped them up, and Taxil promptly proceeded to gild his lily.

In addition to the horrors of female Freemasonry, Taxil had fed the anti-masons with dreadful stories of masonic murders (*Les assassinats maçonniques,* 1889), and for his planned magnum opus, he conflated the two. He did not work alone but sought the help of a fellow anti-clerical writer, Charles Hacks, who supplied some of the text and an assumed name: Dr. Bataille. Their joint work, *Le Diable au XIXe Siècle (The Devil in the Nineteenth Century),* appeared in weekly parts between 1893 and 1895 and was also available bound up in two volumes. It is an enormous work, fully illustrated and with many spurious documents to support its claims. These were varied, but were based on the alleged existence of a secret governing body—the Palladian Order—that lay behind and controlled all of Freemasonry around the world. It was presided over—until his death in 1891—by the prominent American mason, Albert Pike; it admitted women; it engaged in orgiastic and blasphemous ceremonies at which demons appeared and miracles happened; and it sought the overthrow of the Catholic Church and of the established social order. In a word, it was Satanism—which, for the Church, was synonymous with both Freemasonry and Spiritualism. It was also, of course, utter nonsense, but the French public lapped it up.

Central to the Palladian thesis was the existence of a leading lady, one Diana Vaughan, who—like her creator, Leo Taxil—had repented of her ways and converted to the Catholic Church. But unlike Taxil, she had not had an interview with the Pope and no one had ever seen her. This, however, was no barrier to belief. She wrote (in her *alter ego* of Taxil's secretary, and at his dictation) letters to clerical authors who championed her cause and gladly vouched for her reality and her *bona fides*. And then, as *Le Diable* drew to its conclusion, she began to publish her *Mémoires*.[4] No less sensational than the work of Dr. Bataille—which is hardly

---

4. The *Mémoires d'une Ex-Palladiste* were published in Paris in twenty-four monthly parts, between July 1895 and June 1897.

surprising, given that they have the same author—the memoirs piled yet more horrors at the masonic door. The cause of anti-masonry blossomed, hundreds of hysterical books and pamphlets appeared in the wake of *Mémoires d'une Ex-Palladiste,* and an Anti-Masonic Congress was planned for 1896, to be held at Trent in northern Italy. This was the high point of the whole affair; Leo Taxil was present but Diana Vaughan was not, although he had promised to produce her. The delegates fell into opposing camps of believers and non-believers, and Palladism began to totter.

But while all this was going on, what was happening in the masonic camp? French masons denounced Taxil's works, but to little effect, for they preached only to the converted: non-masons, whether Catholic or not, had no interest in masonic affairs and much preferred salacious revelations to the truth. In England, the masonic authorities did as they have always done: utterly ignored the whole affair and remained silent. Much the same course was followed by the rest of the English-speaking masonic world—until names of living masons began to tumble from the pages of Dr. Bataille's weekly parts.

The more august of these—the titled rulers of Freemasonry in England, for example—maintained a dignified silence, but the less exalted expressed their alarm. Some of them, such as Wynn Westcott and John Yarker, were well known in occult circles and deeply resented the satanic slur on their good names. Albert Pike had died in 1891, before *Le Diable* appeared, but his office of Sovereign Grand Commander of the Southern Jurisdiction of the Ancient & Accepted Scottish Rite in the U.S.A. had been defamed together with his name. He was alleged to have issued a set of "Instructions" on 14 July 1889—Bastille Day, it may be noted; 4 July would have been more appropriate for the U.S.—which included a statement that "Lucifer is God," and asked rhetorically,

> If Lucifer were not God would Adonay (the God of the Christians) whose deeds prove his cruelty, perfidy and hatred of man, barbarism and repulsion for science, would Adonay and his priests calumniate him?[5]

The freemasons under attack clearly needed a champion. They found one, unasked, in the person of A. E. Waite.

At the time when he began to examine and analyse the whole question of Palladian Masonry, Waite was not a mason (he was not initiated until 1901), but he *was* a member of the Hermetic Order of the Golden Dawn. He knew Westcott, Yarker and many other freemasons; he was fluent in the French language; and he had a growing reputation as an authority on most aspects of occultism. In addition, he had been raised as a Catholic, and although he had lapsed from the faith, he retained an affection for the Church and possessed an understanding of the attitudes and mindset of its anti-masonic hierarchy.

---

5. The alleged "Instructions" were printed by A. C. de La Rive in his book *La Femme et l'Enfant dans la Franc-Maçonnerie universelle, d'après les documents de la secte (1739-1893),* Paris, 1894. He drew them entirely from the works of Leo Taxil.

Waite differed from most of his contemporaries in the field of occult literature in his scrupulous attention to factual detail. He was thus the ideal champion for Freemasonry: impartial, familiar with the subject matter, and known as an authority upon it. But he was not the first to question Leo Taxil and his fellow travellers; that honour belongs to the unorthodox Christian mystic, C. C. Massey.[6]

By 1895, there were references to anti-masonry in English Catholic periodicals, but it was not until the announcement of the Anti-Masonic Congress, in the *Tablet* for 17 August 1895, that Diana Vaughan made an appearance. This spurred Massey to write a full account of Palladian Masonry, as presented in *Le Diable,* for the spiritualist journal, *Light,* which printed his five articles between September and November of that year. They sparked a flurry of letters, comments and other articles variously denouncing the anti-masons (who were of necessity, also anti-spiritualists) and hinting darkly that Satanism did lurk in unsuspected places.

Waite first entered the debate on 7 December 1895 to dispute the absurd claims of "Diana Vaughan" to be a descendant of Thomas Vaughan the alchemist. He also notes that while the two volumes of *Le Diable*

> contain much which can only be adequately dealt with by high-grade Masons, there are at the same time a

6. Charles Carleton Massey (1838–1905) was an Idealist philosopher, theosophist (in the sense of a follower of Jacob Boehme), spiritualist and mystic.

> multitude of points open to the investigation of any thorough student, and it is on these that [Dr. Bataille's] general credibility or otherwise will largely depend.[7] (pp. 593–594)

When he next referred to Dr. Bataille's credibility it was to state that "he is a Munchausen of masonry who writes penny dreadfuls in Paris" (*Light,* Vol.16, p. 152). He had returned to the fray earlier, on 4 January 1896, and while criticising "Miss Vaughan's version of Rosicrucian history," he gave notice that he was writing a full, critical study: "and I do not think it will stand the searching investigation which I propose to give it elsewhere" (*Light,* Vol. 16, p. 12).

What he does not say is why he intends to carry out his "investigation." Certainly he was irritated by gross errors of fact in published works on occultism—his reviews demolished many nonsensical theories of the day—but he also felt his honour to be impugned by attacks upon the Golden Dawn. These were not made directly by Taxil and his crew, but obliquely by those spiritualists who believed in the myth of the Palladium. The most notable was Arthur Lillie, who suggested that "a light has been shed on certain mysterious pacts and incantations said to be going on in modern

7. In this he was not alone. Westcott publicly stated that he knew nothing of Diana Vaughan, while letters by both Isabelle de Steiger and W. A. Ayton condemning Palladian nonsense appeared in the columns of *Light.* Ayton's letter is pseudonymous but includes his obligatory tirade against the Jesuits.

London" (*Light,* Vol. 16, p. 242). After Waite criticised his comments on Eliphas Lévi,[8] and implicitly included Lillie among those witnesses to Palladism whom he described as "paste-pot compilers of books, who are not Masons, and have no source of knowledge" Lillie challenged him to be open about the Golden Dawn.

Referring to Waite, he wrote:

> He belongs, I am told, to the occult society that formerly had Eliphas Lévi for a head. Let him assure us that the society knows nothing of goat's heads with ray-darting foreheads, and that Eliphas Lévi libelled it when he said that the Initiates of Occult Science (meaning its members) "still adore" Baphomet. Let Mr. Waite write this in sober English and we will believe him. (*Light,* Vol. 16, p. 287)

Waite responded in the issue of 4 July, writing:

> I can, however, truthfully state that the occult society with which I am connected makes no mention of Baphomet, nor does it use either his head or his tail in its symbolism. Further, no goat's head and no reversed pentagram have ever been seen therein.

---

8. Taxil incorporated Lévi's illustration of the Baphomet in the bloodthirsty pictorial cover to *Les Mystères de la Franc-Maçonnerie* (1887). This led Lillie to associate Lévi with Satanism.

Lillie, he notes, misquoted and now misapplies the relevant passage from Lévi.

Quite apart from its relevance to the Taxil affair, Waite's letter is of extraordinary interest in the further comment he makes about Lévi's membership of the "society" (i.e., The Hermetic Order of the Golden Dawn). Waite writes,

> I may also say that Eliphas Lévi, though he did belong to this society, was never its chief, so that in this respect Mr. Lillie is quite wrongly informed. Lévi reached half-way up the grades, and was then discarded and excluded because his books were found to contain so much matter borrowed from the society's MSS.

None of this is to be found in the surviving "official" history of the G. D. given to its members. It thus seems likely that Waite was quoting from the original version of the history that was abruptly withdrawn without reason during the 1890s, and of which no copy is known to have survived.

The other significant point Waite makes in this letter is the impossibility of obtaining the truth about the Palladium from a freemason:

> Nor . . . is the denial of the ordinary mason of any value; it is made in good faith, but also in ignorance of the facts. On the other hand, also by the hypothesis, the perfect initiate, who does know, will presumably deny all the same, at least until he is converted.

Which, of course, makes the non-mason Waite the ideal person to answer "The Question of Lucifer." And leads us to the third reason for his writing *Devil-Worship in France.*

George Redway, the publisher of the book, had resumed independent publishing in October 1895 and was eager to have books by Waite on his list. He was also a freemason[9] and a book about the Taxil affair would have an added appeal: not only would it have the cachet of Waite as author, but it would strike back against those who impugned the good name of Freemasonry. With his flair for an ear-catching phrase, it seems probable that Redway was also responsible for the book's title.

Waite began to write *Devil-Worship in France* in January 1896 and had evidently completed the final draft within four months, as it was published in June. This was little enough time for a careful investigation, even allowing for his familiarity with the sources, and it is a tribute to his energy and acumen that he could produce such a well-rounded and devastating critique. Inevitably, there were errors. Waite states that Eliphas Lévi was not a freemason (which he was) and denies that Albert Pike had written a book entitled *Sepher h'Debarim (The Book of the Words)* although this had been printed in 1878. But these are very minor flaws and the book lives up to the claims made for it in the prospectus that Redway issued (and probably wrote). According to these, Waite has "unveiled the mass of fraud, falsehood and for-

9. George William Redway was initiated into the Elthorne and Middlesex Lodge on 12 December 1892.

gery" contained in the many depositions of alleged witnesses to this "extraordinary conspiracy against the fraternity." This is undeniable, but Redway was guilty of hyperbole when he also claimed that the author's work "constitutes perhaps the most curious contribution which has been ever made to the literature of Masonry."

The book *was* well received, even by the Catholic press. The *Tablet* referred to it as "the clever but not convincing book of an honourable opponent," and while remaining hostile to Freemasonry, felt able to "commend the book as a temperate and conscientious endeavour to clear [Masonry] from a hideous stigma." Spiritualist and masonic periodicals praised Waite, as might have been expected, but the secular press did also. Thus for the *Literary World,* it was "a lucid and timely work," while the *Contemporary Review* found it to be "a clear, condensed, and, on the whole, fair account of the controversy," and for the *Echo* "Mr. Waite has brilliantly vindicated Freemasonry." All well and good, but praise did not translate into buoyant sales, indicating that the great general public, at least in England, had little interest in either Masonry or Satanism.

In October the Anti-Masonic Congress was held at Trent, but neither that nor Taxil's dénouement of the following April kindled public enthusiasm, and Redway declined to publish the sequel, *Diana Vaughan and the Question of Modern Palladism*. Why, then, publish it today? The answer is not simply that the book is interesting on account of its author (although it *is* so), or that *Devil-Worship* is now very rare—sixty-five years ago Waite wrote that it "is so utterly scarce that it is never seen in a catalogue"—but that both works are relevant to contemporary hysteria about Satanism. Folly dies hard, and there are those in the world today who batten on that folly to promote unsavoury agendas of their own.

The long, anonymous review of *Devil-Worship in France* that appeared in *Light,* criticised Freemasonry for its unnecessary secrecy and for the anti-clerical attitudes of many European masons. As a consequence, the reviewer noted, "even some Protestant denominations in America have now taken the alarm, and are now forbidding Freemasonry to their members." This hostility had been in place for many years, but the Taxil affair exacerbated it and supplied specious ammunition to American anti-masons—of which they have made continuous use ever since. Nor did Catholic anti-masons remain idle.

Leo Taxil may have exploded his own myths, but belief in them survived. In 1902 Waite wrote a caustic review of an unpleasant but ephemeral anti-masonic work, *The X-Rays in Free Masonry,* by A. Cowan.[10] Waite commented on the author's reliance on dubious witnesses and noted also that similar contemporary works claimed to prove that he (Waite) himself was

> not merely Mason and Rosicrucian but Palladist and Satanist of the most pronounced kind. (*Light,* Vol. 22, p. 10)

10. This is a pseudonym: a "cowan" is a non-mason. The author was a Roman Catholic, Col. J. J. L. Ratton, who later wrote a more interesting commentary on the Revelation of St. John.

Many years afterwards, in 1938, Waite commented on the renewed use of Taxil's Palladian myths:

> Anti-Masonic reviews are again attempting in Paris to reap a lurid harvest from seeds of flagitious invention sown so far back, in regard not alone to Luciferian Freemasonry but to the vile Masonic strategy which compelled Taxil to make a false and fraudulent confession. (*Shadows of Life and Thought,* 1938, p. 144)

This was, of course, how the Parisian anti-masons had explained away Jogand's exposure of his myth. Leo Taxil—so they continued to name him—had been bribed, or threatened, by the wicked Palladian masons to deny that there was any truth in the stories he had told. Common sense would deny the truth of a crocodile demon obligingly playing the piano at a masonic soirée, but anti-masons rarely possess this attribute, and the myths have been endlessly recycled.

Jogand himself died in 1907, enabling the anti-masons to take his name in vain without fear of contradiction. This they did most effectively in 1934 in *Léo Taxil et la Franc-Maçonnerie, Lettres Inédites* (edited by L. Fry), the publication which was the subject of Waite's censure in his autobiography. It prints in full, but quite uncritically, the correspondence with various Catholic priests of Leo Taxil, A. C. de la Rive, and—Diana Vaughan! This would be merely amusing if it were not for the appendices of the book which make an insidious, organic link between Freemasonry and Judaism: both are seen as satanic and a threat to the established world order. The similarity between anti-Masonry and anti-

Semitism had been noted in the masonic press at the time of the Taxil affair, but the writer had not foreseen that one day they would fuse together. He wrote:

> The credulity with which the stories of some doubtful converts from Atheism have been received, and the encouragement that has been given to their extraordinary publications, resemble nothing so much as the anti-Semitic propaganda in Central Europe. (*Freemason's Chronicle,* 10 October, 1896)

Today the Catholic Church still disapproves of Freemasonry, but it does not link it with Satanism and does not attempt to instigate a latter-day witch hunt. That approach is now favoured by Protestant fundamentalists, whose anti-intellectual mindset prevents them from making an accurate analysis of suspect "evidence," or of entering into a dialogue with those of differing views. As a consequence, the fictitious "Instructions" of Albert Pike are used to endorse the lie that Freemasonry is founded on the worship of Satan. Taxil's invented "Instructions" now feature in *Spellbound* and *The Curse of Baphomet,* two crude but widely circulated—and frequently reprinted—comic books published in California by Jack Chick. This would be of little concern if it were not that these, and similar titles, have been translated into many other languages and distributed around the world, to be read and believed by large numbers of ill-educated and credulous people.

Nor are freemasons the only ones at risk from the potential consequences of such a hostile portrayal. The Palladium also embraced Eastern religions, Spiritualism and every form of occultism. Followers of all of these are also at risk because of the perpetuation of Leo Taxil's hoax. Waite's critical studies of the affair are a necessary weapon in the armoury of all who would oppose bigotry. Their reappearance is timely indeed.

R. A. Gilbert

Devil-Worship In France

or

The Question of Lucifer A Record of Things Seen and Heard in the Secret Societies According to the Evidence of Initiates

"The first in this plot was Lucifer."
—Thomas Vaughan

PREFACE

THE TERM Modern Satanism is not intended to signify the development of some new aspect of old doctrine concerning demonology, or some new argument for the personification of the evil principle in universal nature. It is intended to signify the alleged revival, or, at least, the reappearance to some extent in public, of a *cultus diabolicus*, or formal religion of the devil, the existence of which, in the middle ages, is registered by the known facts of the Black Sabbath, a department, however, of historical research, to which full justice yet remains to be done. By the hypothesis, such a religion may assume one of two forms; it may be a worship of the evil principle as such, namely, a conscious attempt on the part of human minds to identify themselves with that principle, or it may be the worship of a power which is regarded as evil by other religions, from which view the worshippers in question dissent. The necessity for this distinction I shall make apparent in the first chapter of this book. A religion of the darkness, subsisting under each of these distinctive forms, is said to be in practice at the present moment, and to be characterised, as it was in the past, by the strong evidence of miracles,—in other words, by transcendental phenomena of a very extraordinary kind, connecting in a direct manner with what is generically termed Black Magic. Now, Black Magic in the past may have been imposture reinforced by delusion, and to state that it is recurring at the present day does not commit anyone to an opinion upon its veridical origin. To say, also, that the existence of modern diabolism has passed from the region of rumour into that of exhaustive and detailed statement, is to record a matter of fact, and I must add that the evidence in hand, whatever its ultimate value, can be regarded lightly by those only who are unacquainted with its extent and character. This evidence is, broadly, of three kinds:—(*a*) The testimony of independent men of letters, who would seem to have come in contact therewith; (*b*) the testimony volunteered by former initiates of such secret associations as are dedicated to a *cultus diabolicus*; (*c*) the testimony of certain writers, claiming special sources of information, and defending some affected interests of the Roman Catholic Church.

My purpose in this book is to distinguish, so far as may be possible, what is true from what is false in the evidence, and I have undertaken the task, firstly, because modern mystics are accused, *en masse,* of being concerned in this cultus; secondly, because the existence of modern Satanism has given opportunity to a conspiracy of falsehood which is wide in its ramifications, and serious on account of its source; thirdly, because the question itself has awakened considerable interest both within and without transcendental circles, and it is desirable to replace hazy and exaggerated notions by a clear and formal statement.

I have connected the new diabolism with France in my title, because the evidence in each of its kinds has been filed by French writers, and we have no other source of information. So far as that evidence is sound, we have to thank France for producing it; but, on the other hand, should it prove that a whole city of invention has been constructed, "with all its spires and gateways," upon a meagre basis of fact, it is just that French imagination should have full credit for the decorative art which has adorned this Question of Lucifer.

The plan of my work had been sketched, and a number of chapters written, when I found myself to some extent preceded by a writer well known to occultists under the pseudonym of Papus, who has quite recently published a small brochure, entitled *Le Diable et L' Occultisme,* which is a brief defence of transcendentalists against the accusations in connection with Satanism. I gladly yield to M. Papus the priority in time, which was possible to a well-informed gentleman at the centre of the conspiracy. His little work, however, does not claim to be either a review or a criticism, and does not therefore, in any sense, cover the ground which I have travelled. It is an exposition and exoneration of his own school of mystic thought, which is that of the Martinists, and I have mentioned it in this connection in its proper place.

CHAPTER I

SATANISM IN THE NINETEENTH CENTURY

IF A SHORT TIME ago that ultimate and universal source of reference, the person of average intelligence, had been asked concerning Modern Diabolism, or the Question of Lucifer,—What it is? Who are its disciples? Where is it practised? And why?—he would have replied, possibly with some asperity:—"The question of Lucifer! There is no question of Lucifer. Modern Diabolism! There is no modern Diabolism." And all the advanced people and all the strong minds would have extolled the average intelligence, whereupon the matter would have been closed hermetically, without disquieting and unwelcome investigations like the present.

The Great Teacher of Christianity beheld Lucifer fall from heaven like lightning, and, in a different sense, the modern world has witnessed a similar spectacle. Assuredly the demon of Milton has been cast down from the sky of theology, and, except in a few centres of extreme doctrinal concentration, there is no place found for him. The apostles of material philosophy have in a manner searched the universe, and have produced—well, the material philosophy, and therein is no question of Lucifer. At the opposite pole of thought there is, let us say, the spiritualist, in possession of many instruments superior, at least by the hypothesis, to the search-lights of science, through which he receives the messages of the spheres and establishes a partial acquaintance with an order which is not of this world; but in that order also there appears to be no question of Lucifer, though vexed questions there are without number concerning "unprogressed spirits," to say nothing of the elementary. Between these poles there is the flux and reflux of multitudinous opinions; but, except at the centres mentioned, there is still no question of Lucifer; it has been shelved or dropped.

The revival of mystical philosophy, and, moreover, of transcendental experiment, which is prosecuted in secret to a far greater extent than the public can possibly be aware, has, however, set many old oracles chattering, and they are more voluble at the present moment than the great Dodonian grove. As might be expected, they whisper occasionally of deeds done in the darkness which look weird when exposed to the day. The terms Satanism, Luciferianism, Diabolism, and their equivalents, have been buzzed frequently, though with some indistinctness, of late, and in accents that indicate the existence of a living terror—people do not quite know of what kind—rather than an exploded superstition. To be plain, the Question of Lucifer has reappeared, and in a manner which must be eminently disconcerting to the average intelligence and the advanced and strong in mind. It has reappeared not as a speculative inquiry into the possibility of a personal embodiment of evil operating mysteriously, but after a wholly spiritual manner, for the propagation of the second death; we are asked to acknowledge that there is a visible and tangible manifestation of descending hierarchy taking place at the close of a century which has denied that there is any prince of darkness.

Now there are some subjects which impress one at first sight as unserious, but we come to regard them differently when we find that they are being taken seriously. We have been accustomed, with some show of reason, to connect the idea of devil-worship with barbarous rites obtaining among savage nations, to regard it, in fact, as a suitable complement of the fetish. It seems hypothetically quite impossible that there can be any person, much less any society or class of persons, who, at this day, and in London, Paris: or New York, adore the evil principle. Hence to say that there is Black Magic actively in function at the present moment; that there is a living cultus of Lucifer; that Black Masses are celebrated, and involve revolting profanations of the Catholic Eucharist; that the devil appears personally; that he possesses his church, his ritual, his sacraments; that men, women, and children dedicate themselves to his service, or are so devoted by their sponsors; that there are people, assumed to be sane, who would die in the peace of Lucifer; that there are those also who regard his region of eternal fire—a variety unknown to the late Mr Charles Marvin[1]—as the true abode of beat-

1. Charles Marvin (1854–1890) was the author of *The Region of the Eternal Fire*, 1886, a study of the Russian petroleum industry.

itude—to say all this will not enhance the credibility or establish the intelligence of the speaker.

But this improbable development of Satanism is just what is being earnestly asserted, and the affirmations made are being taken in some quarters *au grand sérieux*. They are not a growth of to-day or precisely of yesterday; they have been more or less heard for some years, but their prominence at the moment is due to increasing insistence, pretension to scrupulous exactitude, abundant detail, and demonstrative evidence. Reports, furthermore, have quite recently come to hand from two exceedingly circumstantial and exhaustive witnesses, and these have created distinctly a fresh departure. Books have multiplied, periodicals have been founded, the Church is taking action, even a legal process has been instituted. The centre of this literature is at Paris, but the report of it has crossed the Channel, and has passed into the English press. As it is affirmed, therefore, that a cultus of Lucifer exists, and that the men and women who are engaged in it are neither ignorant nor especially mad, nor yet belonging to the lowest strata of society, it is worth while to investigate the matter, and some profit is possible, whatever the issue.

If the devil be actually among us, then for the sake of much which has seemed crass in orthodox religion, thus completely exonerated; for the sake of the fantastic in fiction and the lurid in legend, thus unexpectedly actualised; and, further, as it may be, for the sake of our own souls, we shall do well to know of it. If Abaddon, Apollyon, and the Lord of Flies are to be understood literally; above all, if they are liable to confront us *in propria persona* between Free Mason's

Hall and Duke Street,[1] or between Duke Street and Avenue Road,[2] then the sooner we can arrange our reconciliation with the one Church which has consistently and invariably taught the one full-grown, virile doctrine of devils, and has the *bonâ-fide* recipes for knowing, avoiding, and at need of exorcising them, why the better will it be, more especially if we have had previously any leanings towards the conception of an universal order not pivoting on perdition.

If, on the other hand, what is said be of the category of Ananias, as distinguished from what alchemists call the Code of Truth, it will be well also to know that some portions of the old orthodoxies still wait for their deliverance from the bonds of scepticism, that the actual is to be discriminated from the fantastic by the old test, namely, its comparative stupidity, and that we may still create our universe about any pivot that may please us.

I am writing ostensibly for transcendentalists, of whom I am one; it is as a student of transcendentalism that I have been led to examine this modern mystery, equipped as it is with such portentous phenomena. Diabolism is, of course, a transcendental question, and black magic is connected with white by the same antinomy that connects light and darkness. Moreover, we mystics are all to some extent accused by the

---

1. The headquarters of the Supreme Council of the Ancient & Accepted Rite of Freemasonry in England and Wales is at Duke Street, London.

2. In 1896 the headquarters of the Theosophical Society in England was in Avenue Road, St. John's Wood, London.

accusations which are preferred in the matter of modern diabolism, and this is another reason for investigating and making known the result.

At the same time, the general question has many aspects of interest for that large class which would demur to be termed transcendental, but confesses to being curious.

The earliest rumour which I have been able to recall in England concerning existing occult practices to which a questionable purpose might be attributed, appeared in a well-known psychological journal some few years since, and was derived from a continental source, being an account of a certain society then existing in Paris, which was devoted to magical practices and in possession of a secret ritual for the evocation of planetary angels ; it was an association of well-placed persons, denying any connection with spiritualism, and pretending to an acquaintance with more effectual thaumaturgic processes than those which obtain at séances. The account passed unchallenged, for in the absence of more explicit information, it seemed scarcely worth while to draw attention to the true character of the claim. The secret ritual in question could not have been unknown to specialists in magical literature, and was certainly to myself among these; as a fact, it was one of those numerous clavicles of the goëtic art which used to circulate surreptitiously in manuscript some two centuries ago. There is no doubt that the planetary spirits with which the document was concerned were devils in the intention of its author, and must have been evoked as such, supposing that the process was practised. The French association was not therefore in possession of a secret source of knowledge, but as impositions of this kind are to be *à priori* expected in such cases by transcendentalists of any experience, I for one refrained from entering any protest at the time.

Much about the same period it became evident that a marked change had passed over certain aspects of thought in "the most enlightened city of the world," and that among the *jeunesse doreé,* in particular, there was a strong revulsion against paramount material philosophy; an epoch of transcendental and mystic feeling was, in fact, beginning. Old associations, having transcendental objects, were in course of revival, or were coming into renewed prominence. Martinists, Gnostics, Kabbalists, and a score of orders or fraternities of which we vaguely hear about the period of the French Revolution, began to manifest great activity; periodicals of a mystical tendency—not spiritualistic, not neo-theosophical, but Hermetic, Kabbalistic, and theurgic—were established, and met with success; books which had grievously weighted the shelves of their publishers for something like quarter of a century were suddenly in demand, and students of distinction on this side of the channel were attracted towards the new centre. The interest was intelligible to professed mystics; the doctrine of transcendentalism has never had but one adversary, which is the density of the intellectual subject, and wherever the subject clarifies, there is idealism in philosophy and mysticism in religion. Moreover, on the part of mystics, especially here in England, the way of that revival had been prepared carefully, and there could be no astonishment that it came, and none, too, that it was accompanied, as it is accompanied almost invariably, by much that does not belong to it in the way of transcendental phenomena. When, therefore, the rumours of Black Magic, diabolism, and the abuse of occult forces began to circulate, there was little difficulty in attributing some foundation to the report.

A distinguished man of letters, M. Huysman[s], who has passed out of Zolaism in the direction of transcendental religion, is, in a certain sense, the discoverer of modern Satanism. Under the thinnest disguise of fiction, he gives in his romance of *Là Bas*, an incredible and untranslatable picture of sorcery, sacrilege, black magic, and nameless abominations, secretly practised in Paris. Possessing a brilliant reputation, commanding a wide audience, and with a psychological interest attaching to his own personality, which more than literary excellence infuses a contagious element into private views and impressions, he has given currency to the Question of Lucifer, has promoted it from obscurity into prominence, and has made it the vogue of the moment. It is true that, by his vocation of novelist, he is suspected of inventing his facts, and Dr "Papus," president of the influential Martinist group in French occultism, states quite plainly that the doors of the mystic fraternities have been closed in his face, so that he can know nothing, and his opinions are consequently indifferent. I have weighed these points carefully, but unless the mystic fraternities are connected with diabolism, which Papus would most rightly deny, the exclusion does not remove the opportunity of first-hand knowledge concerning the practice of Satanism, and, "brilliant imagination" apart, M. Huysman[s] has proved quite recently that he is in mortal earnest by his preface to a historical treatise on "Satanism and Magic," the work of a literary disciple, Jules Bois. In a criticism, which for general soberness and lucidity does not leave much to be desired, he there affirms that a number of persons, not specially distinguished from the rest of the world by the mark of the beast in their foreheads, are "devoted in secret to the operations of Black Magic, communicate or seek to communicate with Spirits of Darkness, for the attainment of ambition, the accomplishment of revenge, the satisfaction of their passions, or some other form of ill-doing." He affirms also that there are facts which cannot be concealed and from which only one deduction can be made, namely, that the existence of Satanism is undeniable.

To understand the first of these facts I must explain that the attempt to form a partnership with the lost angels of orthodox theology, which attempt constitutes Black Magic, has, in Europe at least, been invariably connected with sacrilege. By the hypothesis of demonology, Satan is the enemy of Christ, and to please Satan the sorcerer must outrage Christ, especially in his sacraments. The facts are as follow:—(*a*) continuous, systematic, and wholesale robberies of consecrated hosts from Catholic Churches, and this not as a consequence of importing the vessels of the sanctuary, which are often of trifling value and often left behind. The intention of the robbery is therefore to possess the hosts, and their future profanation is the only possible object. Now, before it can be worth while to profane the Eucharist, one must believe in the Real Presence, and this is acknowledged by only two classes, the many who love Christ and some few who hate Him. But He is not profaned, at least not intentionally, by his lovers; hence the sacrilege is committed by his enemies in chief, namely, practisers of Black Magic. It is difficult, I think, to escape from that position; and I should add that sacramental outrages of this astonishing kind, however deeply they may be deplored by the Church, are concealed rather than paraded, and as it is difficult to get at the facts, it may be inferred that they are not exaggerated, at least by the Church; (*b*) The occasional perpetration of certain outrageous crimes, including murder and other abominations, in which an element of Black Magic has been elicited by legal tribunals. But these are too isolated in place and too infrequent in time to be evidence for Satanic associations or indications of a prevalent practice. They may therefore be released from the custody of the present inquiry to come up for judgment when called on; (*c*) The existence of a society of Palladists, or professors of certain doctrines termed Palladism, as demonstrated, *inter alia,* by the publication of a periodical review in its interests.

M. Huysman[s]'s facts, therefore, resolve into acts of sacrilege, indicating associations existing for the purpose of sacrilege, which purpose must, however, be regarded as a means and not an end, and the end in question is to enter into communication with devils. Independently of M. Huysman[s], I believe there is no doubt about the sacrilege. It is a matter of notoriety that in 1894 two ciboria, containing one hundred consecrated hosts, were carried off by an old woman from the cathedral of Notre Dame under circumstances which indicate that the vessels were not the objects of the larceny. Similar depredations are said to have increased in an extraordinary manner during recent years, and have occurred in all parts of France. No less than thirteen churches belonging to the one diocese of Orleans were despoiled in the space of twelve months, and in the diocese of Lyons the archbishop recommended his clergy to transform the tabernacles into strong boxes. The departments of Aude, Isère, Tarn, Gard, Nièvre, Loiret, Yonne, Haute-Garonne, Somme, Le Nord, and the Dauphiny have been in turn the scene of outrage. Nor are the abominations in question confined to France: Rome, Liguria, Salerno have also suffered, while so far off as the Island of Mauritius a peculiarly revolting instance occurred in 1895.

I am not able to say that the personal researches of the French novelist have proceeded beyond the statistics of sacrilege, which, however, he has collected carefully, and these in themselves constitute a strong presumption. M. Huysman[s] is exhaustive in fiction and reticent in essay-writing, yet he gives us to understand explicitly that the infamous Canon Docre of *Là Bas* is actually living in Belgium, that he is the leader of a "demoniac clan," and, like the Count de St Germain, is in frequent terror of the possibilities of the life to come. An interviewer has represented M. Huysman[s] as stating that his information was derived from a person who was himself a Satanist, but the revelations disturbed the sect, and the communication ceased, though the author had originally been welcomed "as one of their own." But it is clear to my own mind that for his descriptions of the orgies which take place at the assemblies of modern black magicians, M. Huysman[s] is mainly indebted to documents which have been placed in his hands by existing disciples of the illuminé Eugene Vintras, and the "Dr Johannes" of *Là Bas.* Vintras was the founder of a singular thaumaturgic sect, incorporating the aspirations of the Saviours of Louis XVII. ; he obtained some notoriety about the year 1860, and an account of his claims and miracles will be found in Éliphas Lévi's *Histoire de la Magie,* in the same writer's *Clef des Grands Mystères,* and in

Jules Bois' *Petites Religions de Paris.* He left a number of manuscripts behind him, recounting his life-long combats with the priests of black magic—a series of fervid narratives which savour strongly of hallucination, but highly picturesque, and in some quarters accepted quite seriously.

In like manner, concerning the existence of Satanic associations, and especially the Palladium, M. Huysman[s] admittedly derives his knowledge from published sources. We take it, therefore, that he speaks from an accidental and extrinsic acquaintance, and he is therefore insufficient in himself to create a question of Satanism; he indicates rather than establishes that there is a question, and to learn its scope and nature we must have recourse to the witnesses who claim to have seen for themselves. These are of two kinds, namely, the spy and the seceder—the witness who claims to have instigated the subject at first hand with a view to its exposure, and those who have come forward to say that they once were worshippers of Lucifer, worshippers of Satan, operators of Black Magic, or were at least connected with associations which exist for these purposes, who have now, however, suspended communication, and are stating what they know. In the first class we find only Doctor Bataille; in the second, Diana Vaughan, Jean Kostka, Domenico Margiotta, and Leo Taxil.

Finally, we have, as stated in the preface, some testimony from writers representing the interests of the Latin Church, in a special manner, and speaking with the authority of that Church. The most important of these is the late Archbishop Meurin. At the same time, M. Huysman[s] apart—who occupies much the same quasi-religious position as that which attached a fleeting interest to the personality of Mr W. H.

Mallock[1]—all writers and all witnesses are, or assume to be, at the present time, convinced and zealous Roman Catholics.

I have already stated that the purpose of Black Magic is simply and obviously to communicate with devils, and if we interrogate our sources of knowledge as to the object of such communication, it must be admitted that the response is vague. Perhaps the object will best be defined as the reinforcement of human ability by diabolical power and intelligence for the operation of evil along the lines of individual desire and ambition. For the fulfilment of what is good man aspires towards God, and to fulfil evil he attempts to conspire with Satan.

It must, however, be observed that modern devil-worship, as exposed by its French experts, has two aspects, corresponding to the distinction already laid down in my preface. There is (*a*) devil-worship pure and simple, being an attempt to communicate with evil spirits, admitting that they are evil; (*b*) the cultus of Lucifer, star of the morning, as distinguished from Satan, on the hypothesis that he is a good spirit. It will be seen very readily that the essence of diabolism is wanting in the second division, namely, the Satanic intention, so that it belongs really to another category, though the classification may be accepted for the moment to prevent dispute at the beginning of a somewhat complex inquiry. The first division is, in any case, Satanism proper, and its adepts are termed Satanists; those of the second division are, on the

1. William Hurrell Mallock (1849–1923), English novelist and popular political satirist.

other hand, Luciferians, Palladists & c. The two orders are further distinguished as unorganised and as organised diabolism. The cultus of Satan is supposed to be mainly practised by isolated persons or small and obscure groups; that of Lucifer is centralised in at least one great and widespread institution—in other words, the first is rare and sporadic, the second a prevalent practice. We accordingly hear little of the one, while the testimonies which have been collected are concerned exclusively with the other. It is possible, in fact, to dismiss Satanism of the primary division in a few words, because materials are wanting for its history. It is founded on orthodox Christianity; it acknowledges that the devil is a lost angel, but it affirms that the God of the Christians has deceived His believers, has betrayed the cause of humanity, has exacted the suppression of the nature with which He Himself has endowed it; they have therefore abandoned a cruel and tyrannical Master, and have gone over in despair to His enemy.

Satanism of the second division, its principles and its origin, will be described in the second chapter.

CHAPTER II

The Mask of Masonry

THE IDENTIFICATION of the cultus of Lucifer with devil-worship pure and simple is not, as we have seen, at first sight an entirely just proceeding, but at the same time it is inevitable. As already observed, the source of all our knowledge concerning Modern Diabolism exists within the pale of the Catholic Church; the entire literature is written from the standpoint of that church, and has been created solely in its interests. Some of that literature has been put forth with the special marks of high ecclesiastical approbation, and to some this guarantee is wanting, but the same spirit informs the whole. To insist on this point is important for many reasons which will become apparent at the close of our enquiry, and for one which concerns us now. It is impossible for the Catholic Church to do otherwise than brand the cultus of Lucifer as identical with that of Satan, because, according to her unswerving instruction, the name Lucifer is an equivalent of Satan, and, moreover, the Luciferian cultus is so admittedly anti-Christian that no form of Christianity could do otherwise than regard it as a worship of darkness and evil. While, therefore, the adoration of a good principle under this discredited name may in one of its aspects be merely an error of judgment, and not the worship of a devil, apart from other facts which destroy this consideration, we must all agree that from the standpoint of Christian and Latin orthodoxy the Luciferian is a diabolist, though not in the sense of the Satanist.

The doctrine of Lucifer has been tersely described by Huysman[s] as a kind of reversed Christianity—a Catholicism *à rebours.* It is, in fact, the revival of an old heresy founded on what we have most of us been accustomed to regard as a philosophical blunder; in a word, it is a Manichæan system having a special anti-Christian application, for while affirming the existence of two equal first principles, Adonaï and Lucifer, it regards the latter as the god of light and goodness, while the Christian Adonaï is the prince of darkness and the veritable Satan. It is inferred from the condition of the world at the present time that the mastery of the moment resides with the evil principle, and that the beneficent Deity is at a disadvantage. Adonaï reigns surely, as the Christian believes, but he is the author of human misery, and Jesus is the Christ of Adonaï, but he is the messenger of misfortune, suffering, and false renunciation, leading ultimately to destruction when the *Deus maledictus* shall cease to triumph. The worshippers of Lucifer have taken sides in the cause of humanity, and in their own cause, with the baffled principle of goodness; they co-operate with him in order to insure his triumph, and he communicates with them to encourage and strengthen them; they work to prepare his kingdom, and he promises to raise up a Saviour among them, who is Antichrist, their leader and king to come.

Such is the doctrine of Lucifer according to the testimony of witnesses who have come out from his cultus; it is not an instruction which *à priori* would seem likely to commend itself to a numerically powerful following, but the society which is concerned with its propagation is affirmed to have spread over the whole world, and to be represented in all its chief cities. It is that which we have already found mentioned by M. Huysman[s] as possessing a demonstrated existence and being a proof positive of modern Satanism, namely, the Palladian Order. Having broadly ascertained its principles, our next course is to discover its alleged history, and here it is necessary to admit that it is a matter of some difficulty to place the position in such an aspect that it will be a tolerable subject for inquiry among readers in England. The mystery of modern Diabolism and the Cultus of Lucifer is a part of the mystery of Masonry as interpreted by an Anti-Masonic movement now at work in France. The black magic, of which we hear so much, involves a new aspect of the old Catholic Crusade against the Fraternity of the Square and Compass, and by the question of Lucifer is signified an alleged discovery that Masons diabolise.

Now, we are all well acquainted with the historical fact that the Latin Church has long been hostile to Masonry, that popes have condemned the order, and have excommunicated its initiates. Having regard to the position of the brotherhood here in England, most of us have been content to infer in this respect that the ripe old age of the Church is passing into a second childhood; some, however, have concluded that there may be more in Continental Freemasonry than meets the English eye, and here the Church herself comes forward to assure them that the fraternity abroad is a hotbed of political propaganda, and is responsible for the most disastrous revolutions which have perplexed the modern world; that it is actually, as the exploded Robison described it, a conspiracy against crowned heads; and that it is at the present time the most potent, most secret enemy which checkmates and hinders herself.

It is now further affirmed that behind the Masonry of today—here in England posing as a benefit society, and political or not upon the Continent, but everywhere disclaiming any connection with a religious propaganda—there is affirmed to be another Masonry, of which the ordinary Mason knows nothing, secretly directing the order, and devoted to the cultus of Lucifer. This organisation, which has sprung up within recent years, is largely, though not exclusively, recruited from Masonry; it works through the powerful Masonic apparatus, and, according to the evidence which has been put in, it has obtained a substantial and masterful control over the entire Fraternity. It has focussed the raw material of Masonic hostility towards the Catholic Church; as it is anti-Christian in religion, so is it revolutionary in politics; and once more, it is called the Palladian Order.

This exceedingly grave and important accusation, together with its side issues, has perhaps all the more claim on our consideration because, apart from actual diabolism, which is in itself so paralyzing as almost to arrest discussion, it conflicts with all that we know or believe concerning the Masonic constitution. Let me briefly collect the points. (*a*) Masonry possesses a secret directing centre—which has been strenuously denied by the Fraternity. (*b*) It has a mission and a doctrinal propaganda—which also been invariably denied. (*c*) It is concerned with political objects—which, for the most part, is denied. (*d*) It has a transcendental teaching—which is generally denied, and (*e*) is concerned largely with transcendental practices and phenomena—which would be denied absolutely, had the question been seriously raised till this day. (*f*) It initiates women—which, except in a very secondary, occasional, and insignificant manner, is *in toto* and at all times denied. The last point is brought within the scope of our inquiry because the Palladium is an androgyne order.

Now, it will be fairly well known to many who are not within the ranks of the fraternity that the Grand Lodges of every country are supposed to be autonomous, and that there has been no previous impeachment of this fact; that, ostensibly at least, there is no central institution to which they are answerable in Masonry. Individual lodges derive from a single Grand Lodge and are responsible thereto, but Grand Lodges themselves are supreme and irresponsible. It will be known also that the Masonic system in England differs from that of France, that the French rite has always occupied a somewhat heterodox position, and that since the Grand Orient expunged the Grand Architect of the Universe, so to speak, from its symbolism, official communication has been suspended by the Grand Lodge of England. It will be known further that outside recognised Masonic systems many rites have arisen which are only Masonic to the extent that their point of departure is from the Master-grade. As a special instance may be cited the Supreme Oriental Rite of Memphis and Misraim. In England the Lodge meetings of these rites are never suffered to take place in the great central institution of Freemasons Hall; in France, the Grand Orient has consistently forbidden its members to participate in the Memphis system. To hold Masonry responsible for irregularities or abuses which from time to time may obtain in these fantastic developments from the parent institution, would be about as just and reasonable as to impeach the Latin Church on the score of corruptions now existing in the heresies which have separated from her.

Having established these points in view of the result of our inquiry, let us now trace the manner in which a supreme authority, frequently termed by the accusers Universal Masonry, is alleged to have grown up. Upon this subject not only the most complete information but the only formal narratives are provided by the later witnesses, so that the following account, while in no sense translation, is based exclusively upon the works of Domenico Margiotta and Dr Bataille.

On the 20th of May, 1737, there was constituted in France the Order of the Palladium, or Sovereign Council of Wisdom, which, after the manner of the androgyne lodges then springing into existence, initiated women under the title of Companions of Penelope. The ritual of this order was published by the Masonic archaeologist Ragon, so that there can be no doubt of its existence. At the same time, so far as I am aware, there are few materials forthcoming for its history. In some way which remains wholly untraceable this order is inferred to have been connected by more than its name with the legendary Palladium of the Knights Templars, well known under the title of Baphomet. In any case it failed to spread, and it is uncertain whether the New and Reformed Palladium, also an androgyne order, with which we shall presently be concerned, is a metamorphosis or reconstruction of the original institution, but a connection of some kind is affirmed. For a period exceeding sixty years we hear little of the legendary Palladium; but in 1801 the Israelite Isaac Long is said to have carried the original Baphomet and the skull of the Templar Grand Master Jacques de Molay from Paris to Charleston in the United States, and was afterwards concerned in the reconstruction of the Scotch Rite of Perfection and of Herodom under the name of the Ancient and Accepted Scotch Rite, which subsequently became widely diffused, and it is stated that the lodge of the thirty-third degree of the Supreme Council of Charleston has been the parent of all others, and is therefore, in this rite, the first supreme council of the entire globe.

Eight years later, on the 29th of December 1809, a man of great importance to the history of Freemasonry was born in the city of Boston. Albert Pike came of parents in a humble position, who, however, struggled with their difficulties and sent him to Harvard College, where he duly graduated, taking his degree as M.A. in the year 1829. He began his career as a schoolmaster, but subsequently led a romantic and wandering life, his love of untrodden ground leading him to explore the Rocky Mountains, then very imperfectly known. In 1833 he settled in Arkansas, and, drifting into journalism, founded the *Arkansas Advocate*, wherein his contributions, both prose and verse, but the latter especially, obtained him a reputation in literature. The admission of Arkansas into the confederation of the United States was in part his work, and from this period he began to figure in politics, becoming also the recorder of the Supreme Court in that state. One year after the civil war, in which he took active part, Pike removed to Memphis in Tennessee, where he again followed law and literature, establishing the *Memphis Appeal*, which he sold in 1868, and migrated to Washington. His subsequent history is exclusively concerned with unwearying Masonic labours.

Now, it was at Little Rock in Arkansas that Albert Pike was first initiated, and ten years later, that is, in 1859, he was elected Sovereign Commander Grand Master of the Supreme Council of Charleston.[1] Having extraordinary powers of organisation, he became a person of wide influence in the Ancient and Accepted Scotch Rite, and a high authority also on the ritual, antiquities, history, and literature of Masonry. Under his guidance, the Scotch Rite extended and became dominant. Hence, when the Italian patriot Mazzini is said to have projected the centralization of high grade Masonry, he could find no person in the whole fraternity more suited by his position and influence to collaborate with him. Out of this secret partnership there was begotten on September

---

1. The correct title is "Grand Commander of the Supreme Council for the Southern Jurisdiction of the United States. Later, the prefix "Sovereign" was added.

20, 1870—that is to say, on the very day when the Italian troops entered the Eternal City—a Supreme Rite and Central Organisation of Universal High Grade Masonry, the act of creation being signed by the American Grand Master and the Italian liberator, the two founders also sharing the power between them. A Supreme Dogmatic Directory was created at Charleston, with Pike at its head, under the title of Sovereign Pontiff of Universal Freemasonry. Mazzini took over the Supreme Executive, having Rome as its centre, under the title of Sovereign Chief of Political Action.

If we now recur to the statements that the genuine Templar Baphomet and the skull of Jacques de Molay had been deposited at Charleston for the space of seventy years, and that Albert Pike was Grand Master of the Supreme Council of the Ancient and Accepted Scotch Rite in that city, we shall understand why it was that the new institution was termed the New Reformed Palladian Rite, or the Reformed Palladium. Subsequently, five Central Grand Directories were established—at Washington for North America, Monte Video for South America, Naples for Europe, Calcutta for the Eastern World, and Port Louis in Mauritius for Africa. A Sovereign Universal Administrative Directory was fixed at Berlin subsequently to the death of Mazzini. As a result of this astute organisation, Albert Pike is said to have held all Masonry in the hollow of his hand, by means of a twofold apparatus—the Palladium and the Scotch Rite. During all his remaining days, and he lived to a great age, he laboured indefatigably in both causes, and the world at the present moment is filled with the organisation that he administered.

Four persons are cited as having been coadjutors in his own country—his old friend Gallatin Mackey, in honourable memory among masons; a Scotchman named Longfellow, whom some French writers have ludicrously confused with the poet; one Holbrook, about whom there are few particulars; and, finally, Phileas Walder, a native of Switzerland, originally a Lutheran Minister, afterwards said to have been a Mormon, but, in any case, at the period in question, a well-known spiritualist, an earnest student of occultism, as were also Holbrook and Longfellow, and, what is more to the purpose, a personal friend and disciple of the great French magus Éliphas Lévi. Albert Pike was himself an occultist, whether upon his independent initiative, or through the influence of these friends I am unable to say. Miss Diana Vaughan, who is one of the seceding witnesses, affirms that it was an early and absorbing passion. However this may be, the New Reformed Palladium was kept most rigidly separate from all other Masonry, the Scotch Rite included; that is to say, no initiate of even the highest grade had, as such, the right or opportunity of entrance into the occult order, which, at the same time, was chiefly recruited, as already stated, from the higher ordinary grades, but the recipients of the new light became silent from the moment that it was imparted. Now, it was exclusively in the Palladian order that Albert Pike and his confidants propagated transcendental religion, as it is said to have been understood by them. In other words, while the Scotch Rite continued to speculate, the Palladium betook itself to magic and succeeded so well that there was a perpetuity of communication between Charleston and the unseen world. It does not appear from the evidence either when or why Albert Pike and his collaborators transferred their allegiance from the God of the sages to Lucifer. The Catholic Church regards all magic as diabolism, and makes or tolerates no mystic distinction between the black and white departments of transcendental practice, but the specific character of the Palladian cultus is so clearly defined in the depositions that it cannot pass as a presentation of magical doctrine distorted by prejudice. It is almost stripped of correspondence with any existing school of occult teaching, and it is either the true statement of a system founded by Pike, or the deliberate invention of malice. The thaumaturgic phenomena tabulated in connection therewith are of an extremely advanced kind, including the real and bodily presence of Lucifer at frequent and regular intervals.

When Mazzini died he indicated to Albert Pike a possible successor in Adriano Lemmi, who became in due course the chief of the Executive Department, and when in the fulness of years the pontiff of Luciferian Freemasonry himself passed on to the higher life of fire, which is the Palladian notion of beatitude, and in the peace and joy of Lucifer, the sovereign pontificate itself, after resting for a short period upon incompetent shoulders in the person of Albert Gallatin Mackey, was transferred to the Italian; the seat of the Dogmatic Directory was removed to Rome; a split in the camp ensued, inspired by a lady initiate, since famous under the name of Diana Vaughan, and to this we owe most of the revelations. Furthermore, with the death of Albert Pike the cultus of Lucifer is said to have undergone a significant transfiguration. For him the conception of Satan was a blasphemous fiction, devised Adonaïte priestcraft to obscure the veridic lustre which inheres in the angel of the morning-star; but this view represented, as it is said, rather the private opinion of the Masonic pontiff, impressed by his strong personality on the lodges he controlled, and propagated by the instruction of his rituals. The more discerning among his disciples regarded it as the besetting weakness of their grand old man, and surreptitiously during his life-time the cultus of Satan pure and simple, that is, of devil-worship, the adoration of the evil principle as evil, was practised at numerous Palladian centres. After his death, it is said to have unmasked altogether, and Adriano Lemmi himself is depicted as an avowed Satanist.

Now, I believe it will fairly interpret the feeling of all readers to admit that when the authority of a great church has been brought into operation to crush a great institution by charges which most seriously discredit it—which represent it as diametrically and in all respects opposite in its internal nature to its ostensible appearance—we must by no means make light of the impeachment; we must remember the high position and the many opportunities of knowledge which are possessed by such an accuser; we must extend to that accuser at least the common justice of an impartial and full hearing; *à priori* considerations of probability and inferences from our previous knowledge, much less from opinions obtained at second-hand, must not be permitted to prejudice a case of so great importance; we must be prepared, if necessary, to admit that we have been egregiously deceived; and if the existence of Palladian Masonry can be proved an undoubted fact, we must assuredly do full honour to the demonstration, and must acknowledge with gratitude that the Church has performed a service to humanity by unveiling the true character of an institution which is imposing on a vast number of well-intentioned persons within its own ranks, who are admittedly unaware of the evil to which they are lending countenance and support. On the other hand, the same spirit of liberality and justice will require that the demonstration in question shall be complete; in support of such terrible accusations, only the first quality of evidence can obviously be admitted.

In the chapters which follow immediately, I shall produce in succession the evidence of every witness who has anything to tell us about Palladism, including those whose experience is of a personal kind and those whose knowledge is derived. Where possible, the testimony of each witness will be weighed as we proceed; what is unconvincing or irrelevant will be dismissed, while that which is important will be carried over to the final summary. In two cases only will it be found necessary to reserve examination for special and separate treatment.

CHAPTER III

The First Witnesses of Lucifer

That the witnesses of Lucifer are in all cases attached to the Latin Church, whether as priests or laymen, is no matter for astonishment when it is once realised that outside this Church there is no hostility to Masonry. For example, Robison's "Proofs of a Conspiracy" is almost the only work possessing, deservedly or not, any aspect of importance, which has ever been penned by a Protestant or independent writer in direct hostility to the Fraternity. Moreover, Catholic hostility varies in a vanishing direction with distance from the ecclesiastical centre. Thus, in England, it exists chiefly in a latent condition, finding little or no expression unless pressure is exercised from the centre, while in America the enforced promulgation of the *Humanum Genus* encyclical has been one of the serious blunders of the present pontificate as regards that country. The bibliography of Catholic Anti-Masonic literature is now, however, very large, nor is it confined to one land, or to a special epoch; it has an antiquity of nearly 150 years, and represents most of the European continent. That of France, which is nearest to our own doors, is naturally most familiar to us; it is also one of the most productive, and may be assumed to represent the whole. We are concerned with it in this place only during the period which is subsequent to the alleged foundation of the New and Reformed Palladium. During this period it falls obviously into two groups, that which preceded any knowledge of the institution in question and that which is posterior to the first promulgation of such knowledge. In the first we find mainly the old accusations which have long ceased to exert any conspicuous influence, namely, Atheism, Materialism, and revolutionary plotting. Without disappearing entirely, these have been largely replaced in the second group by charges of magic and diabolism, concerning which the denunciations have been loud and fierce. One supplementary impeachment may be said in a certain sense to connect both, because it is common to both; it is that of unbridled license fostered by the asserted existence of adoptive lodges. We shall find during the first period that Masonry was freely described as a diabolical and Satanic institution, and it is necessary to insist on this point because it is liable to confuse the issues. Before the year 1891 the diabolism identified with Masonry was almost exclusively intellectual. That is to say its alleged atheism, from the standpoint of the Catholic Church, was a diabolical opinion in matters of religion; its alleged materialism was a diabolical philosophy in matters of science; its alleged revolutionary plottings, being especially directed against the Catholic Church, constituted diabolical politics. Such descriptions will seem arbitrary enough to most persons who do not look forth upon the world from the windows of the Vatican, but they are undeniably consistent at Rome.

Of actual diabolism prior to the date I have named, there is, I believe, only the solitary accusation made by Mgr. de Ségur, and having reference to a long anterior period. He states that in the year 1848 there was a Masonic lodge at Rome, where the mass of the devil was celebrated in the presence of men and women. A ciborium was placed on an altar between six black candles; each person, after spitting and trampling on a crucifix, deposited in this ciborium a consecrated host which had been purchased or received in church. The sacred elements were stabbed by the whole assembly, the candles were extinguished at the termination of the mass, and an orgie followed, similar, says Mgr. de Ségur, to those of "Pagan mysteries and Manichæan re-unions." Such abominations were, however, admittedly rare, and the story just recited rests on nothing that can be called evidence.

During the years intervening between 1870 and 1891 we may search the literature of French Anti-Masonry in vain for any hint of the Palladium. In 1884 the collaboration of Louis D'Estampes and Claudio Jannet produced a work entitled "Freemasonry and the Revolution," which affirms that the immense majority of Masons, including those who have received the highest grades, do not enjoy the confidence of the true secrets, but the establishment of atheism in religion and socialism in politics as designs of the Fraternity are the only secrets intended.

The New and Reformed Palladium connects with the Order of the Temple by its supposed possession of the original Baphomet idol, but in 1882 this was entirely unknown to Mgr. Fava, who denies all the reputed connection between Templars and Masons, and traces the latter to Faustus Socinus as founder, following Abbé Lefranc in his "Veil raised for the Curious." A mystic and diabolic aspect of the Fraternity is so remote from his mind that in his "Secret of Freemasonry" the Bishop of Grenoble affirms that its sole project is to replace Christianity by rationalism.

The third and concluding volume of Père Deschamps' great compilation on "Society and the Secret Societies," supports, on the contrary, the hypothesis rejected by Fava. It recites much old knowledge concerning adoptive lodges, the Illuminés, the Orders of Philalethes, of Martinez Pasquales, and of Saint-Martin, on which subjects few writers indeed can say anything that is new; but while specially devoted to the political activity of the Fraternity all over Europe, Deschamps tells us nothing of the conspiracy which produced the New Palladium, though the alleged collaboration of Mazzini gave it a strong political complexion; of Pike nothing; of Diabolism still nothing. I may add that his work claims to be verified at all points.

In the year 1886 another ecclesiastic, Dom Benoit, published two formidable volumes on "Freemasonry and the Secret Societies," forming part of a vaster work, entitled "The City of anti-Christ in the Nineteenth Century." Like D'Estampes and Jannet, he distinguishes between a small number of initiates and a vast crowd of dupes who swell the ranks of the Fraternity. "Many Masons ascend the ladder of the grades without receiving the revelation of the mysteries." The highest functions of most lodges are said to be given to the dupes, while the ruling chiefs are concealed behind humble titles. It is further represented that in certain countries there are secret rites above the ordinary rites, and these are imparted only to the true initiates, which sounds like a vague and formless hint concerning a directing centre; but so far from supposing that such an institution may exist in Masonry, the author affirms that unity is impossible therein:—"Image of hell and hell anticipated, Masonry is the realm of hatred, and consequently of division. The leaders mutually despise and detest one another, and universally endeavour to deceive and supplant each other. A common hatred of the Church and her regular institutions alone unites them, and scarcely have they scored a victory than they fall out and destroy each other." The first seeds of the Manichæan accusation are found in the second volume, but the term is not used in the sense of Albert Pike's Luciferian transcendentalism, but merely as an equivalent of Protestantism coloured by the idea of its connection with the Socinian heresy. In conformity with this view, Dom Benoit attaches himself to the Templar hypothesis, saying that the Albigenses and the Knights of the Temple are the immediate ancestors of Masonry. But the point which is of most interest in connection with our inquiry is where Dom Benoit asserts that Satan is the god of Freemasonry, citing an obscure grade in which the ritual is connected with serpent-worship, and another in which the recipient is adjured "in the sacred name of Lucifer," to "uproot obscurantism." It is, however, only a loose and general accusation, for he says also that the Masonic deity is "the creature," that is, humanity, the mind of man, human reason; it is also "the infamous Venus," or the flesh; finally, "all divinities of Rome, Greece, Persia, India, and every pagan people, are the gods of Masonry." This is merely indiscriminate defamation which is without force or application, and the writer evidently knows nothing of a defined cultus of Lucifer existing in the Lodges of the Fraternity. So also when he elsewhere states that sexual excesses are sometimes accompanied in Masonry by Eucharistic profanations, he has only Mgr. de Ségur's out-of-date narrative to support him, and when he hints at magical practices, it is only in a general way, and apparently referring to acts of individual Masons. In one more significant passage he records, as a matter of report, that apparitions of the demon have occurred "recently" in Masonic assemblies, "where he is said even to have presided under a human form." While there is no mention of Palladism and none of Pike in his treatise, we may regard Dom Benoit as a herald of the coming accusation, speaking vaguely of things half heard.

Some time previous to 1888, Paul Rosen, a Sovereign Grand Inspector-General of the 33rd and last degree of the French rite, had come to the conclusion that the mysteries of Freemasonry are abominable, and in that year he published a work, entitled "Satan and Co.," suggesting that in this case a witness to the desired point had at last come forward, and, as a matter of fact, the writer does take us a few paces beyond the point reached by Benoit. So far as I am aware, he is the first French anti-Mason who mentions Albert Pike, with one exception, to be considered separately in the next chapter. He describes him as the Sovereign Grand

Commander of the Supreme Mother Council of every Supreme Council of the Ancient and Accepted Scotch Rite, and he tells the story of the foundation of that Rite, but he knows nothing of Isaac Long, the Palladium, or the skull. He cites also certain works which Pike wrote for the exclusive use of initiates, apparently of the higher grades of these rites, namely, "The Sephar H'Debarim," "Ethics and Dogmas of Freemasonry," and "Legenda Magistralia." But so far from accrediting the order with a supernatural aspect, he affirms that its war-cry is annihilation and anathema thereto. The end of Freemasonry is, in fact, social anarchy, the overthrowal of monarchical government, and the destruction of the Catholic religion. The Satanism imputed to Freemasonry by Paul Rosen is therefore of an arbitrary and fantastic order, having no real connection with this inquiry. Two years later the same author published a smaller volume, "The Social Enemy," which contains no material of importance to our purpose, but is preceded by a Pontifical Brief, conveying the benediction of Leo XIII. to the writer of "Satan and Co."

We pass now to the year of revelation 1891.

CHAPTER IV

Ex Ore Leonis

For over ten years past Leo Taxil, that is to say, M. Gabriel Jogand-Pages, has been the great accuser of Masonry, and he possesses an indistinct reputation in England as a man whose hostility is formidable, having strong points in his brief. During the entire period of his impeachment, which is represented by many volumes, he has uniformly sought to identify the Fraternity with the general purposes of Lucifer, but until the year 1891, it was merely along the broad and general lines mentioned in the last chapter. Now, in presence of such attributions as, for example, the Satanic character of tolerance in matters of religion, I, for one, would unconditionally lay down my pen, as there is no common ground upon which a discussion could take place.

From the vague imputation Leo Taxil passed, however, to an exceedingly definite charge—and it is beyond all dispute that by his work entitled "Are there Women in Freemasonry?"—he has created the Question of Lucifer in its connection with the Palladian Order. He is the original source of information as to the existence of that association; no one had heard of it previously, and it is therefore of the first importance that we should know something of the discoverer himself, and everything as to the particulars of his discovery, including the date thereof.

Previously to the year 1891 Leo Taxil knew nothing of the Reformed Palladium. He is the one Anti-Masonic writer named in the last chapter as preceding Paul Rosen with information about Albert Pike. This was in the year 1885, and in a work entitled, "The Brethren of the Three Points," which began the "complete revelations concerning Freemasonry" undertaken by this witness. Like Paul Rosen, he represents Pike merely as a high dignitary of the Ancient and Accepted Scotch Rite, but he does so under the incorrect title of Sovereign Commander Grand Master of the Supreme Council of the United States. He states further that the Grand Orient of France, as also the Supreme Council of the Scotch Rite of France, "send their correspondence" to the Grand Master of Washington. I conceive that no importance, as indeed no definite meaning, can be attached to this statement beyond the general and not very significant fact that there was some kind of communication between the three centres. In the year 1888 Pike was so little in harmonious relation with the French Grand Orient that by the depositions of later witnesses he placed it under the ban of his formal excommunication in virtue of his sovereign pontificate. For the rest, the "Brethren of the Three Points" contains no information concerning the New and Reformed Palladium, and this is proof positive that it was unknown at the time to the writer, for it would have been valuable in view of his purpose. The same observation applies to a second work published shortly after, "The Cultus of the Grand Architect." Had Leo Taxil been acquainted with a worship of Lucifer subsisting in Palladian Masonry he could not have failed to make use of it in a volume so entitled. The work in question is concerned, however, with the solemnities which obtain in Masonic temples, with the names and addresses of all French lodges, so that it is a directory as much as a revelation, with the political organisation of the Carbonari, with the Judge-Philosophers, and with certain official documents of Masonry.

But it may occur to those of my readers who are acquainted at first hand with the revelations of Leo Taxil that his knowledge was held over in view of his plan of publication, and that the Palladium would be disclosed in due course when he came to treat of androgyne or adoptive Masonry. Let us pass, therefore, to his next work, entitled, "Sister Masons, or Ladies' Freemasonry," which appeared in 1888, and in which we certainly meet with diabolism and also with Palladism, but not in connection with Albert Pike or the Charleston Central Directory. The reference in the first case is to practices which are alleged to obtain in the Egyptian Rite of Adoption, called the Rite of Cagliostro, and in the second to the Order of the Palladium as it was originally instituted in the year 1730. At the same time the information given is of serious importance, because it enables us to gauge the writer's method and credibility in the one case, and his knowledge at the period in the other. Once more, in the year 1886, Leo Taxil did not know of the Palladium as a reformed or revived institution; had he known he could not have failed to tell us.

I have not been able to trace all the sources of his information concerning the older Palladian Rite, but it comes chiefly from Ragon; he divides it into two systems:—(*a*) The Order of the Seven Sages, which was for men only, and appears as a banal invention with a ritual mainly derived from the "Travels of Anacharsis";[1] (*b*) The Order of the Palladium, composed of two masculine grades and one feminine grade, respectively, Adelphos and Companion of Ulysses for men, and Companion of Penelope for women. It pretends to have been founded by Fenelon, but at the same time claims an antiquity previous to the birth of the great Archbishop of Cambrai. Leo Taxil accuses it of gallantry, but the flirtations described in the ritual impress an impartial reader as a species of childish theatricals, a criticism practically exhausting the entire motive of the order, which, as I have already stated, lapsed into obscurity, and, so far as can be traced, into desuetude, though our witness uniformly refers to it in the present tense, and as if it were in active operation. However this may be, the description and summary of the ritual given by Leo Taxil place it outside the possibility of a connection with Templar Masonry, and also with the Baphomet Palladium in spite of what is alleged to the con-

1. *i.e.* J. J. Barthélemy, *Voyage de jeune Anarcharsis en Gréce*. Paris, 1788. It has no masonic content.

trary. Accepting the worst construction which is placed on its intention, it could have offered no point of contact with the alleged project of Albert Pike. So far, therefore, the information contained in Les Sœurs Maçonnes conflicts with the history of the New and Reformed Palladium as given in my second chapter.

It has been said, however, that Leo Taxil charges another Masonic order of the androgyne type with satanic practices. He divides the Egyptian Rite of Adoption into three grades; in that of apprentice, the discourse represents Adonaï as the Genius of Pride, and the serpent-tempter of Genesis as the eternal principle of goodness; in that of Companion, the symbolism of the ritual enforces the necessity of rehabilitating the character of the mystic serpent; in that of Egyptian Mistress, there is a pretended evocation of planetary spirits by means of a clairvoyante, and Leo Taxil affirms on his own authority that the Supreme Being referred to in the discourse at initiation is Satan. "According to the doctrine of the sect, the divinity is formed of two opposite principles, the genius of Being, who is Lucifer, and the genius of Destruction, who is Adonaï." This is so obviously the doctrine of the Luciferian Palladians that it is difficult to understand why the institution of Charleston is not connected, as to purpose, if not as to origin, with the Egyptian Adoptive Rite of Misraïmite Masonry.

At this point, however, it becomes my duty to state that there are some very curious facts in connection with the "Catechism of the Officiating Mistress," which is the source of information for the alleged Manichæan character of the third degree. The more considerable and essential portion of that document, so far from being referable to the supposed founder of the Rite, namely, Count Cagliostro, is a series of mutilated passages taken from *Éliphas Lévi's Dogme et Rituel de la Haute Magie,* and pieced clumsily together. That is to say, Leo Taxil, while claiming to make public for the first time an instruction forming an essential part of a rite belonging to the last century, presents to us in that instruction the original philosophical reflections of a writer in the year 1856, and, moreover, he distorts palpably the fundamental principle of that writer, who, so far from establishing dualism and antagonism in God, exhibits most clearly the essential oneness in connection with a threefold manifestation of the divine principle. I conceive that there is only one construction to be placed upon this fact, and although it is severe upon the documents it cannot be said that it is unjust. When, therefore, Leo Taxil terminates his study of the Egyptian Rite by "divulging some essentially diabolical practices of the Misraïm Lodges," namely, evocations of the elementary spirits, we shall not be surprised to find that the ritual of the proceedings is taken bodily from the same author who has been previously taxed for contributions. The reader need only compare *Les Sœurs Maçonnes,* pp. 323 to 330, with the "Conjuration of the Four" in the fourth chapter of the *Rituel de la Haute Magie.* It will be objected that this conjuration is derived by Lévi himself from a source which he does not name, and as a fact part of it is found in the *Comte de Gabalis.* Quite so, but my point is, that it has come to the Taxil documents through Éliphas Lévi. The proof is that part of the exorcisms are given in Latin and part in French, by the author of the *Rituel,* for arbitrary and unassignable reasons, and that

Les Sœurs Maçonnes reproduces them in the same way. It is evident, therefore, that we must receive Leo Taxil's "divulgations" with severe caution. I may add that the proceedings of the Holy Inquisition in the trial of Count Cagliostro were published at Rome by order of the Apostolic Chamber, and they include some particulars concerning the Egyptian Rite, of which Cagliostro was the author. These particulars in part correspond with the documents of the "Sister-Masons," but offer also significant variations even along the lines of correspondence.

Having established, in any case, that Leo Taxil knew nothing of the Reformed Palladium in the year 1886, we may pass over his next work, which reproduces a considerable though selected proportion of some of his previous volumes, because precisely the same observation applies to "The Mysteries of Freemasonry," and we may come at once to the year 1891. Some time subsequently to the third of August, our witness published a volume entitled "Are there Women in Freemasonry?" which, so far as one can see, bears the marks of hurried production. It is, in fact, "The Sister Masons" almost *in extenso*—that work being still in circulation—with the addition of important fresh material. The bulk of the new matter is concerned with the rituals of the New and Reformed Palladium, consisting of five degrees, conformable, as regards the first three, with the somewhat banal but innocent grades of the Modern Rite of Adoption, and passing, as regards the two final, into pure Luciferian doctrine. How did Leo Taxil become possessed of these rituals? He informs us quite frankly that by means of arguments *sonnants et trébuchants,* that is to say, by a bribe, he persuaded an officer of a certain Palladian Grand Council located at Paris to forget his pledges for the time required in transcribing them. That was not a very creditable proceeding, but in exposing Freemasonry ordinary ethical considerations seem to be ruled out of court, and it is idle to examine methods when we are in need of documents. By these documents, and by the editorial matter which introduces and follows them, Leo Taxil, as already observed, created the Question of Lucifer. Premising that a dual object governed the institution of androgyne lodges, namely, the opportunity for forbidden enjoyments, and the creation of powerful unsuspected auxiliaries for political purposes, he states that the latter part of this programme was specially surrendered to the old Palladian Masonry. Now it is clear that the rituals of the order which he published in 1886 bear no such construction as he here, and for the first time, imputes; they connect with part one of the programme, and he was content at the time with their impeachment on the ground of sexual disorder. Why has he changed the impeachment? No assignable reason appears from his subsequent remarks, but he goes on to allege that, under the auspices of Albert Pike and his group, the original order developed the New and Reformed Palladian Rite, in which the political purpose was itself subordinated to "Satanism pure and simple." Originating in the United States, it has invaded Europe, where it propagates with truly unheard of rapidity, so that in Paris alone there are three active lodges—that of the Lotus, founded in 1881, and situated in the Faubourg Saint-Germain, which has in turn created the lodges of St James, 1884, and of St Julian, 1889. The Lotus itself was preceded "by the organisation of some Areopagites of the Kadosch Grade of the French Rite and of the Ancient and Accepted Scotch Rite," who practised theurgy under the direction of Ragon and Éliphas Lévi, both of whom are represented as given over, body and soul, to all the practices of lawless diabolism, the latter being apparently the leader, after whose death the association met only infrequently, until it was revived by Phileas Walder, the friend, as we have already seen, of Albert Pike. It was he who imported the New and Reformed Palladium from America into France, and, assembling the disciples of Lévi, founded the Mother-Lodge of the Lotus.

The ritual obtained by Leo Taxil was printed in Latin and English, with an interleaved French version in manuscript. As presented by its discoverer, there is no doubt that it is an execrable production, involving the practice in open lodge of obscenity, diabolism, and sacrilege. Passing over the first three grades, and beginning "at the point of bifurcation," we find it stated in the ritual of the fourth degree of Elect that the New and Reformed Palladium has been instituted "to impart a new force to the traditions of high-grade Masonry," that the Palladium which gives its name to the order was presented to the fathers of the order by Eblis himself, that it is now at Charleston, and that Charleston is the first supreme Council of the globe. Thus it will be seen that the Palladian ritual confuses the Palladium Order with the Ancient and Accepted Scotch Rite. For the rest, the legend of the fourth degree is the first part of what is termed a blasphemous life of Jesus, representing Baal-Zeboub as his ancestor, Joseph as his father, according to physical generation, and Mirzam as his mother, who is highly honoured as the parent of many other children. Adonaï is the principle of evil, and Eblis, otherwise Lucifer, the good God. But the ritual of the fourth grade is innocent in its character when compared with the abominations of the fifth degree of Templar-Mistress. The central point of the ceremonial is the resurrection of Lazarus, which is symbolically accomplished by the postulant suffering what is termed the ordeal of the Pastos, that is to say, by means of public fornication. The purpose of this ordeal is to show that the sacred act of physical generation is the key to the mystery of being. The life of Jesus begun in the previous grade is completed in the present, and it will be sufficient for my purpose to indicate that it represents the Saviour of Christianity, who originally "began well," passing over from the service of the good god Lucifer, and making a pact with the evil Adonaï, in sign of which he ceased indiscriminate commerce with the women who followed him and pledged himself to live in chastity, for which he was abandoned by Baal-Zeboub, and is cursed by Palladists. "The duty of a Templar-Mistress is to execrate Jesus, anathematise Adonaï, and adore Lucifer." The rite concludes by the recipient spitting on a consecrated host and the whole assembly piercing it in turn with stilettos.

So far the sole testimony to the actual operation, as indeed to the existence, of these infamous ceremonies, is Leo Taxil, and it is once more my duty to state that the documents are in no sense above the suspicion of having been fraudulently produced by some one. It seems scarcely credible, but the instruction of the Elect Grade incorporates Masonic references *literatim* from the scandalous memoirs of Cassanova. That is a fact which sets open a wide door to skepticism.

Again, the instruction of the fifth degree contains more plagiarisms from Lévi, and in a section entitled "Evocations," Leo Taxil again reproduces the "Conjuration of the Four" which he has previously fathered on the Rite of Memphis and Misraim, and now states to be in use among Palladists. Once more, he prints a long list of the spirits of light which Palladians recommend for evocation, and this list is a haphazard gleaning among the eighty-four genii of the twelve hours given in Lévi's interpretation of the "Nuctemeron according to Apollonius." But these latter points are not arguments which necessarily reflect upon Leo Taxil, for, seeing that the New and Reformed Palladium was constituted in 1870, it is obvious that the author of the rituals may have drawn from the French magus, and Leo Taxil does connect the Palladium, as others have connected it, with Alphonse Louis Constant, partly through Phileas Walder his disciple, and partly by representing Constant as the leader of an occult association of Knights Kadosch. But when he represents Constant as himself a Mason we have to remember that Éliphas Lévi explicitly denied his initiation in his *Histoire de la Magie.*[1]

I should add that Leo Taxil in one of the illustrations represents a lodge of the Templar-Mistress Rite, wherein the altar is over-shadowed by a Baphomet which is a reduction in facsimile of the frontispiece to Lévi's *Rituel,* and all reasonable

1. Shortly after the publication of *Histoire de la Magie* in 1860, Lévi was initiated into Freemasonry. He was made a mason in the lodge *Rose du Parfait Silence* on 14 March 1861.

limits seem to be transgressed when he quotes from Albert Pike's "Collection of Secret Instructions," an extended passage which swarms with thefts from the same source, everyone of which I can identify when required, showing them page by page in the originals. Leo Taxil tells us that the "Collection" was communicated to him, but by whom he does not say. We are evidently dealing with an exceedingly complex question, and many points must be made clear before we can definitely accept evidence which is so mixed and uncertain in character.

If we ask the author of these disclosures what opportunities he has had to become personally acquainted with Masonry, we shall find that they are exceedingly few, for he was expelled from the order after receiving only the first degree. I do not say that this expulsion reflects in any sense discreditably upon him as a man of honour, but it closed his Masonic career almost as soon as it had begun, so that his title to speak rests only on his literary researches and other forms of derived knowledge, good enough, no doubt, in their way, but not so exhaustive as could be wished in view of the position he has assumed. It was shortly after this episode that Leo Taxil returned to the Catholic Church and attached himself to the interests of the clerical party. Previously to this his literary history must be for him a painful memory. He was a writer of anti-clerical romances and the editor of an anti-clerical newspaper—legitimate occupations in one sense, but in this instance too frequently connected with literary methods of a gravely discreditable kind. A catalogue of the defunct *Libraire Anti-Cléricale* is added to one of the romances, and advertises, among other productions from the same pen, the following contributions made by Leo Taxil to the literature of sacrilege and scandal:—1st, a Life of Jesus, being an instructive and satirical parody of the Gospels, with 500 comic designs; 2nd, The Comic Bible *(Bible Amusante)*; 3rd, The Debaucheries of a Confessor, a romance founded on the affair of the Jesuit Girarde and Catherine Cadière; 4th, a Female Pope, being the adventures and crimes of Pope Joan, written in collaboration with F. Laffont; 5th, The Pope's Mistresses, a "grand historical romance," written in collaboration with Karl Milo; 6th, Pius the Ninth before history, his life political and pontifical, his debaucheries, follies, and crimes, 3 vols.; 7th, The Poisoner Leo Thirteenth, an account of thefts and poisonings committed with the complicity of the present pontiff; 8th, Contemporary Prostitution, a collection of revolting statistics upon, *inter alia,* the methods, habits, and physical peculiarities of persons who practice pæderasty.

It will be seen that since his conversion our author has changed his objects without altering his methods. As in the past he unveiled the supposed ill-doings of popes and priests, as he exposed the corrupt practices of the Parisian police in the matter of crying social evils, so now he divulges the infamies of Masonic gatherings in the present. He claimed then to be actuated by a high motive and he claims it now. We must not deny the motive, but we certainly abhor the proceeding. In some very curious memoirs which have obtained wide circulation Leo Taxil acknowledges that he was gravely mistaken then, and he may be mistaken now. It must also be respectfully stated in conclusion that few persons who have contributed to lubricity in literature have ever failed to speak otherwise than from an exalted standpoint. When a short time ago M. Huysman[s] went in search of a type to which he could refer Luciferian "blasphemies" and outrages, he could find nothing more suitable to his purpose than Leo Taxil's "Bouffe Jesus." We do not refuse to accept him as a witness against Masonry because of these facts, but we must ask him as an honourable gentleman not to insist that we should do so on trust, and at the present moment the only opportunities which he has given us to check his statements do not wholly encourage us to accept them. It will be seen therefore that the knowledge of Palladian Masonry was first brought to light under circumstances of a debatable kind.

CHAPTER V

The Discovery of M. Ricoux

By the year 1891 Masonic revelations in Paris had become too numerous for one more or less to fix the volatile quality of public interest unless a new horror were attached to it. Passwords and signs and catechisms, all the purposes and the better half of the secrets—everyone outside the Fraternity who concerned themselves with Masonry and cared for theoretical initiation knew these, or was satisfied by the belief that he did. The literature of Anti-Masonry became a drug in the market, failing some novelty in revelation. The last work of Leo Taxil was eminently a contribution towards this missing quantity. He was already in a certain sense the discoverer of "Female Freemasonry," that is to say, he was the only equipped person who seriously maintained that the exploded androgyne system was worked in modern France, and when he added the development of the Palladium as the climax to the mystery of iniquity, it is small wonder that his book achieved notoriety to the extent of five thousand copies. He was assailed as a venal pamphleteer and his past achievements in literature were freely disinterred for his own benefit and for public instruction, but he was more than compensated by the approbation of Mgr. Fava, bishop of Grenoble, with whose opinions upon Satanism in Masonry we have previously made acquaintance. The Church indeed had all round agreed to overlook Leo Taxil's early enormities; she forgot that she had attempted to prosecute him and to fine him a round sum of 60,000 francs; the supreme pontiff forgave him the accusation of poisoning, and transmitted his apostolical benediction; he was complimented by the cardinal-vicar of Rome; and he is in the proud position of a man who has received felicitations and high approval from eighteen ecclesiastical dignitaries, whether cardinals, archbishops, or bishops. With his back against the *turris fortitudinis,* he faced his accusers stoutly and returned them blow for blow. Nor did he lack his lay defenders, one of whom, by the mode which he adopted, became himself, somewhat unexpectedly, a witness of Lucifer.

To those who disbelieve in the existence of Female Freemasonry, Leo Taxil had offered two pieces of wise advice: Go to the Bibliothèque Nationale, search the files of the Masonic organ *La Chaine d'Union,* and you will find proof positive of your mistake. Next proceed to the Maison T——, there is no need to reproduce the address, but it is given by Leo Taxil in full, and obtain their current price-list of lodge furniture, insignia, and other accessories, and you will find particulars of aprons for sisters, diplomas for sisters, garters for sisters, jewels for sisters. Except upon the signs of initiation, the catalogue is not surrendered, but in view of the literature of revelation the signs are no longer secret, &c.

All this is clearly outside the subject of Satanism, but it leads up, notwithstanding, to the discovery of M. Ricoux. As to this gentleman himself there are no particulars forthcoming; he has promised an account of his adventures during four years as an emigrant in Chili; and he has promised a patriotic epic in twelve cantos, but so far as my information goes they remain in the womb of time. But he has a claim on our consideration because it occurred to him that he would put in practice the advice of Leo Taxil, which he did accordingly in the autumn of 1891, and demonstrated to his own satisfaction that "Are there Women in Freemasonry?" is a book of true disclosure, and a question that must be answered in the affirmative. He performed thereupon a very creditable action; he wrote a pamphlet entitled "The Existence of Lodges for Women: Researches on this subject," &c., in which he stated the result of his investigation, collected the controversy on the subject which had been scattered through the press of the period, and defended Leo Taxil with the warmth of an *alter Ego.* But he had not limited his researches to the directions indicated in his author. Encouraged by the success which had attended his initial efforts, he determined upon an independent experiment in bribery, and after the same manner that Leo Taxil procured the "Ritual of the New and Reformed Palladium," so he succeeded in obtaining the "Collection of Secret Instructions to Supreme Councils, Grand Lodges, and Grand Orients," printed at Charleston in the year 1891. "This collection," he tells us, "is certainly a document of the first order; for it emanates from General Albert Pike, that is to say, from the 'Pope of the Freemasons.'" On this document he bases the following statements:—(*a*) Universal Freemasonry possesses a Supreme Directory as the apex of its international organisation, and it is located at Berlin. (*b*) Four subsidiary Central Directories exist at Naples, Calcutta, Washington, and Monte Video. (*c*) Furthermore, a Chief of Political Action resides at Rome, commissioned to watch over the Vatican and to precipitate events against the Papacy. (*d*) A Grand Depositary of Sacred Traditions, under the title of Sovereign Pontiff of Universal Freemasonry, is located at Charleston, and at the time of the discovery was Albert Pike.

Some of these statements, it will be observed, require rectification, in the light of fuller disclosures made by Palladian initiates, from whom the material of my second chapter has been chiefly derived, but it will be seen that it is substantially correct. M. Ricoux further states that "Albert Pike reformed the ancient Palladian Rite, and imparted thereto the Luciferian character in all its brutality. Palladism, for him, is a selection; he surrenders to the ordinary lodges the adepts who confine themselves to materialism, or invoke the Grand Architect without daring to apply to him his true name, and under the title of Knights Templars and Mistress Templars, he groups the fanatics who do not shrink from the direct patronage of Lucifer."

The most serious mistake which has been made in the use of the material is an unconscious attempt to read into the "encyclicals" of Albert Pike a proportion of Leo Taxil's material, for which the long citations given by M. Ricoux do not afford a warrant. What he really appears to have obtained is the instructions of Pike as Supreme Commander Grand Master of the Supreme Council of the Mother-Lodge of the Ancient and Accepted Scotch Rite of Charleston to the Twenty-three Supreme Confederated Councils of the Globe. And the Scotch Rite is, by the hypothesis, apart from the Palladium. In other respects, the information comes to much the same thing. The long document which the pamphlet prints *in extenso* exhibits Albert Pike preaching Palladism in the full foulness of its doctrine and practice—the "resolution of the problem of the flesh" by indiscriminate satisfaction of the passions; the multiplication of androgyne lodges for this purpose; the dual nature of the Divine Principle; and the cultus of Lucifer as the good God. The most curious feature of the performance is that here again it is from end to end a travesty of Éliphas Lévi, slice after slice from his chief writings, combined with interlineal additions, which give them a sense diametrically opposed to that of the great magus. Now, it is impossible that two persons, working independently for the production of bogus documents, should both borrow from the same source; hence Leo Taxil and M. Ricoux, if they have been guilty of imposition, must certainly have collaborated. It is unreasonable, however, to advance such an accusation in the absence of any evidence, and if we accept the contribution of M. Ricoux as made in perfect good faith, we must acknowledge that it exonerates Leo Taxil from the possible suspicion of himself adapting Lévi; and then the existence of a theurgic society, based on Manichæan principles, instituted by Albert Pike, and possessing a magical ritual taken in part from Lévi, wears a more serious aspect than when it rested on the unsupported assurance of one witness. The discovery of M. Ricoux is obviously of the first importance, and it is certainly to be regretted that he has not substantiated it by depositing the "Collection of Instructions" in the National Library, supposing it to be in his possession, or by photographing instead of transcribing, supposing he was pledged to its return.

CHAPTER VI

Art Sacerdotal

Some few months after the first testimonies to Palladism appeared, under the signatures of the witnesses whom we have already examined, a fresh contribution was made to the literature of Diabolism in its connection with Masonry, by a work entitled "Freemasonry, the Synagogue of Satan." The exalted ecclesiastical position of the author, Mgr. Léon Meurin, S.J., Archbishop of Port Louis in Mauritius, gave new impetus and an aspect of increased importance to accusations preferred at the beginning, as we have seen, by comparatively obscure or directly suspected writers. The performance, moreover, was apparently so learned, in some respects so unlooked for, and withal so methodical, that it became subsequently a source of universal reference in anti-Masonic literature. To this day M. Huysman[s] remains dazzled, and to those in search of reliable information on the subject, he says:—"If you would be saved from the excesses of unseated reason, and from narratives of Dunciad dulness, try Mgr. Meurin; read the Archbishop on Palladism." Within certain limits the advice is well-grounded; the art sacerdotal in its application to Anti-Masonry may leave much to be desired, but as a specimen of the superior criticism obtaining upon this subject in higher circles, it offers a strong contrast to the general tone and touch among the rank and file of the accusers. We are, in fact, warranted upon every consideration, in expecting a valuable contribution to our knowledge; but, I may say at once, that this expectation is unfortunately not realised. With a keen philosophical anticipation one turns the pages of "Freemasonry, the Synagogue of Satan," admires their beautiful typography, lingers with delight over the elaborate appendix of allegorical engravings, and experiences a brief sense of intellectual inferiority in the presence of such formidable sections, and so portentous a table of contents. It should be impossible to speak of the Archbishop without a mental genuflexion, but it remains true that our expectation is not realised. It will become us, at the same time, to speak as tenderly as possible of a pious and learned prelate who has now passed where Masons cease from Satanising and the thirty-three degrees are at rest. But it must be said plainly that the contents of his very large volume offer little to our purpose.

By the nature of his episcopal charge Mgr. Meurin had special facilities for ascertaining how men diabolise; the island of Mauritius has enjoyed many privileges of Infernus. There we lose sight of the Rosicrucians on the road to India; there the Comte de Chazal initiated Dr Bacstrom, and all this, of course, is diabolical from the standpoint of Anti-Masonry. Moreover, it must not be forgotten that Mgr. Meurin, in a series of wonderful conferences, has exhibited the superstitions of Mauritius, and, accepting the test of M. Huysman[s], the existence of Black Magic in this French colony is proved to hilt and handle by wholesale Eucharistic depredations, the sacrifice of cats at midnight upon the altars of rifled churches, and the discovery of the blood of the victims in the chalices used for the elements. The Church does not stir in the matter; it deplores and prays, which seems, in some respects, an ineffectual method of protecting the *latens Deitas.* If the Eucharist be liable to profanation, why reserve the Eucharist? Surely the negligence which makes such profanations possible is the offer of opportunity to Deicide, and great carelessness is cousin to condonation. However this may be, Mgr. Meurin seems to have been quite the authority to whom one would naturally refer for specific information upon devil-worship as it obtains within his own diocese, even if apart from Masonry. But he is too erudite to concern himself with individual facts, and he so far transcends diocesan limitations as to forget Mauritius completely. Another witness, who perhaps never visited Port Louis, affirms that the Central Directory of the Palladium for Africa is established in that place, but the prelate of Port Louis, from whom the information would have been precious, seems acquainted with nothing of the kind. The weapon of the mitred warrior is, at the same time, a sufficiently portentous thesis, as follows:—that Freemasonry is connected with Satanism by the fact that it has the Jews for its true authors, and the Jewish Kabbalah for the key of its mysteries; that the

Kabbalah is magical, idolatrous, and essentially diabolical; that Freemasonry, considered as a religion, is therefore a judaized devil-worship, and considered as a political institution, it is an engine designed for the attainment of universal empire, which has been the dream of the Jews for centuries.

My readers will be inclined to consider that such a hypothesis, though it may square with the Satanism of Adriano Lemmi, who, as we shall see, is accused of circumcision, can hardly he brought into harmony with the universal Masonry of Albert Pike, as the latter was neither Jew nor Judaiser. But common hatred of the Catholic Church is, in the opinion of Mgr. Meurin, a sufficient bond to identify the interests of both parties. Let us start, therefore, with the archbishop's own hypothesis, which he compresses into a single sentence: "To encircle the brow of the Jew with the royal diadem, and to place the kingdom of the world at his feet—such is the true end of Freemasonry." And again: "The Jewish Kabbalah is the philosophical basis and Key of Freemasonry." Once more: "The end of Freemasonry is universal dominion, and Freemasonry is a Jewish institution."

Accepting these statements as points that admit of being argued with deference to the rules of right reason, let us establish in turn two positions which do not admit of being argued because they are evident in themselves: (*a*) Where the significance of symbols is uncertain, it is easy to interpret falsely; (*b*) When a subject is obscure and difficult, no person is qualified to speak positively if his knowledge be obtained at second-hand. Now, have we good reason to suppose that Mgr. Meurin is possessed of first-hand knowledge, and is consequently in a position to interpret truly upon the difficult subject he has undertaken, namely, the esoteric doctrines of the Kabbalah? If not, we are entitled to dismiss him without further examination. As a fact, in this preliminary and essential matter the archbishop can stand no test. The antiquity of the Kabbalah is necessary to work his hypothesis, and he assumes it as if unaware that its antiquity had ever been impugned. There may be much to be said upon both sides of this hotly-debated question, but there is nothing to be said for a writer who seems ignorant that there is a question. And hence my readers will in no way be astonished to learn that his information is obtained at second-hand, or that his one authority is Franck. This fact is the key to his entire work, and the sole credit that is due to him is the skilful appearance of erudition which he has given to a shallow performance, and the natural mental elegance which has prevented him from being noisy and violent.

Our inquiry into modern devil-worship does not warrant us in discussing the position of writers who choose to assume that the Kabbalah, Gnosticism, and other systems are *à priori* diabolical, because assumptions of this kind are unreasonable. There are writers at this moment in France who argue that the English word God is the equivalent of Lucifer, but one does not dispute with these. For the satisfaction of my readers, it may, however, be as well to state that the voluminous treatise of Mgr. Meurin has come into existence because he has discovered, as one might say, accidentally, that the number 33, which is that of the degrees in French Freemasonry, is the number of the divinities in the Vedas, thus creating a presumption that the mysteries of Freemasonry connect with those of antiquity. Of course they connect with antiquity, for the simple reason that there is a solidarity between all symbolisms, and, moreover, it is perfectly clear that Masonry has either inherited from the past by a perpetuated tradition, or has borrowed therefrom. Mgr. Meurin had therefore as little reason to be astonished at the correctness of his presumption when he came to work it out as he had to be delighted with the inference which prevails throughout his inquiry, namely, that the mysteries of pagan antiquity were delusions of the devil, and that modern mysteries which connect with those are also diabolical delusions. Indeed he is so continually making discoveries which are fresh to himself and to no one acquainted with the subject, that one would be pleasantly diverted by his simplicity if it were not for the bad faith which underlies his assumptions. For example, every one who knows anything of Goëtic literature is aware that the rituals of black magic incorporate heterogeneous elements from Kabbalistic sources, but to Mgr. Meurin this fact comes with the force of a surprise.

His Masonic erudition is about as great and as little as his proficiency in Kabbalah; he quotes Carlyle as "an authority," applies the term orthodox to French Freemasonry exclusively, whereas the developments of the Fraternity in France have always had a heterodox complexion, while his tripartite classification of the 33 degrees of that rite and of the Ancient Accepted Scotch Rite is made in an arbitrary manner to suit a preconceived theory, and entirely effaces the importance inherent in the first three grades, which are themselves the sum of Masonry. Moreover, the classification in question is presented as a most secret instruction imparted in some fastness of Masonry outside the 33 degrees, but no authority is named.

Such being the qualifications and such the methods of the archbishop, I do not propose to accompany him through the long course of his interpretations, but will supply instead, for the economy of labour on the part of those who may wish to follow in his footsteps, a skeleton plan of procedure by which they will be able to prove learnedly anything they please in Freemasonry.

It is well known that the Fraternity makes use of mystic numbers and other symbols. Take, therefore, any mystic number, or combination of numbers, as *e.g.*, 3 × 3 = 9. You will probably be unacquainted with the meaning which attaches to the figure of the product, but it will occur to you that the 9 of spades is regarded as the disappointment in cartomancy. Begin, therefore, by confidently expecting some thing bad. Reflect upon the fact that cards have been occasionally denominated the Devil's Books. Conclude thence that Freemasonry is the Devil's Institution. Do not be misled by the objection that there is no traceable connection between cards and Masonry; anticipate an occult connection or secret *liaison*. The term last used has probably occurred to you by the will of God; do not forget that it describes a questionable sexual relationship. Be sure, therefore, that Freemasonry is a veil of the worst species of moral license. You have now reached an important stage in the unmasking of Masonry, and you can sum it as follows:—Freemasonry is the cultus of the Phallus. If you know anything of ecclesiastical Latin, the words *noctium phantasmata* may perhaps occur to you, and the whole field of demonology in connection with the Fraternity will open before you. But if you would confine yourself to the region of lubricity, recollect that our first parents went naked till the serpent tempted them, and then they wore aprons. Hence the apron, which is a masonic emblem, has from time immemorial been the covering of shame. Should it occur to you—vide *Genesis*—that God made the aprons, dismiss it as a temptation of the devil, who would, if possible, prevent you from unveiling him. By this time it will be well to recur to the number 9; your chain of reasoning has established that it possesses a horrible significance. Now take the number and follow it through the history of religions by means of some theological ready-reckoner, such as a cheap dictionary by Migne. You will be sure to find something to your purpose—*i.e.,* something sufficiently bad. Place that significance against the use of that number in Masonry. Repeat this process, picking up anything serviceable by the way, and continue so doing till your volume has attained its required dimensions. You will never want for materials, and this is how Masonry is unveiled.

There is no exaggeration in this sketch; Mgr. Meurin is indeed by far more fatuous. On the 26th of May 1876 the Supreme Council of Sovereign Grand Inspectors General of the 33rd Degree of the Ancient and Accepted Scotch Rite are said to have issued a circular, dated from 33 Golden Square, London. Will my readers believe their own eyes or my sincerity when I say that the most illustrious of the French Anti-Masonic interpreters, member of the Society of Jesus, and Archbishop of Port Louis, solemnly enjoins us to "remark the No. 33 and the square of gold, which signify the supreme place in the world assigned to the liberty of gold"? By thus commenting on a significant number attaching to a real address, situated, as everyone knows, in the most central district of this city, Archbishop Meurin believes that he is not descending from pleasant comedy into screaming farce of interpretation, but that he is acting seriously and judiciously, has a right to look wise, and to believe that he has hit hard!

No person who is acquainted with the Kabbalah, even in its historical aspects, much less the ripe scholar, M.A. Franck, from whom the materials are derived, will tolerate for a moment the theory that this mystical literature of the Jewish nation is capable of a diabolical interpretation. In particular it lends itself to the crude Manichæan system attributed to Albert Pike about as much and as little as it does to atheistic materialism. The reading of Mgr. Meurin may be compared with that of Mirandola, who discovered, not dualism, but the Christian mystery of the Trinity contained indubitably therein, who regarded it with more reason as the bridge by which the Jew might ultimately pass over to Christ, who infected a pontiff with his enthusiasm, and it will be seen that the Catholic Archbishop looks ridiculous in the lustre of his derived erudition. To insist further on this point is, however, scarcely to our purpose. The Kabbalah does not possess that integral connection with Masonry which is argued by Mgr. Meurin, and if it did, does not bear the interpretation which he assigns it, while his anti-Semitic thesis is demolished with the other hypothesis. But these things are largely outside the question which concerns us most directly. Over and above these points, does the witness whom we are examining contribute anything to our knowledge on the subject of the New and Reformed Palladium, otherwise Universal Masonry? The reply is perfectly clear. His one source of knowledge is Adolphe Ricoux; by some oversight he has not even the advantage of the rituals published by Leo Taxil. He may, therefore, be dismissed out of hand. The Satanism which he exhibits in Masonry is an imputed Satanism, and as to any actual Devil-Worship he reproduces as true the clever story of *Aut Diabolus, aut Nihil,*[1] which appeared originally in "Blackwood's Magazine," and has since been reprinted by its author, who states, what most people know already, that it is entirely fictitious.

In parting with the writer of "Freemasonry, the Synagogue of Satan," as with a witness whose evidence has broken down, it must be repeated that he has, by his exalted position, elegance of method, and show of learning, been a chief pillar of the Satanic hypothesis.

1. (Julian Osgood Field), *Aut Diabolus aut Nihil, and other tales* by X. L. 1894.

CHAPTER VII

The Devil and the Doctor

§ 1. Le Diable au XIXe Siècle

Although the New and Reformed Palladium is said to have been founded so far back as the year 1870, it will be seen that at the close of the year 1891 very little had become public concerning it. It is difficult to conceive that an institution diffused so widely should have remained so profound a secret, when the many enemies of the Fraternity, who in their way are sleepless, would have seized eagerly upon the slightest hint of a directing centre of Masonry. Moreover, an association which initiates ladies is perhaps the last which one would expect to be unknown, for while the essential matter of a secret is undeniably safe with women, it is on condition that they are known to possess it.

When the first hint was provided in 1891, Leo Taxil certainly lost no time, and Mgr. Meurin must have written his large treatise almost at fever speed. On the 20th of November in the same year, another witness came forward in the person of Dr Bataille, who speedily made it apparent that he was in a position to reveal everything about Universal Masonry and diabolism in connection therewith, because, unlike those who had preceded him, he possessed first-hand knowledge. If he had not himself beheld Lucifer in all his lurid glory, he had at least seen his messengers; he was an initiate of most secret societies which remotely or approximately are supposed to connect with Masonry; he had visited Charleston; he had examined the genuine Baphomet and the skull of Jacques de Molay; he was personally acquainted with Albert Pike, Phileas Walder, and Gallatin Mackey; he was, moreover, an initiate of the Palladium. He was evidently the missing witness who could unveil the whole mystery, and it would be difficult to escape from his conclusions. Finally, he was not a person who had come out of Masonry by a suspicious and sudden conversion; believing it to be evil, he had entered it with the intention of exposing it, had spent ten years in his researches, and now stepped forward with his results. The office of a spy is not usually clean or wholesome, but occasionally such services are valuable, and in some cases there may be certain ends which justify the use of means which would in other cases be questionable, so that until we can prove the contrary, it will be reasonable to accept the solemn declaration of this witness that he acted with a good intention, and that what he did was in the interests of the church and the world.

But, unfortunately, Dr Bataille has seen fit to publish his testimony in precisely that form which was most calculated to challenge the motive; it is a perfervid narrative issued in penny numbers with absurd illustrations of a highly sensational type; in a word, *Le Diable au XIXe Siècle,* which is the title given to his memoirs by the present witness, connects in manner and appearance with that class of literature which is known as the "penny dreadful." Some years ago the slums of London and Paris were inundated with romances published in this fashion and continued so long as they maintained a remunerative circulation; in many cases, they ended abruptly, in others they extended, like *Le Diable au XIXe Siècle* to hundreds of issues; they possess special characteristics which are known to experts in the by-ways of periodical literature, and all these are to be found in the narrative of Dr Bataille. No one in England would dream of publishing in this form a work which was to be taken seriously, nor am I acquainted with any precedent for it abroad. It is therefore a discreditable and unfortunate choice, but seeing that a section of the clerical press in France has agreed to pass over this point, and to accept Dr Bataille as a credible witness, and seeing also that he has been followed by other writers who must be taken into account and stand or fall with him, we must not regard his method as an excuse for refusing to hear him. Apart from him and his adherents there is indeed no first-hand evidence for Palladian Masonry. The present chapter will therefore contain a summary of what was seen and heard by Dr Bataille in the course of his researches.

§ 2. WHY SIGNOR CARBUCCIA WAS DAMNED.

In the year 1880, Dr Hacks, who makes, I believe, no attempt to conceal himself under the vesture of Dr Bataille, was a ship's surgeon on board the steam-boat *Anadyr,* belonging to the *Compagnie des Messageries Maritimes,* and then returning from China with passengers and merchandise. On a certain day in the June of the year mentioned, he was to the fore at his post of duty—that is to say, he was extended idly over the extreme length of a comfortable deck-chair, and the *hotel flottant* was anchored at Point-de-Galle, a port at the southern extremity of Ceylon, and one of the reputed regions of the terrestrial paradise. While the doctor, like a good Catholic, put a polish on the tropical moment by a little gloss of speculation over the mystery of Eden, some passengers presently came on board for the homeward voyage, and among them was Gaëtano Carbuccia, an Italian, who was originally a silk-merchant, but owing to Japanese competition, had been forced to change his *métier,* and was now a dealer in curiosities. His numerous commercial voyages had made them well acquainted with each other, but on the present occasion Carbuccia presented an appearance which alarmed his friend; a *gaillard grand et solide* had been metamorphosed suddenly into an emaciated and feeble old man. There was a mystery somewhere, and the ship's doctor was destined to diagnose its character. After wearing for a certain period the aspect of a man who has something to tell, and cannot summons courage to tell it—a position which is common in novels—the Italian at length unbosomed himself, beginning dramatically enough by a burst of tears, and the terrific information that he was damned. But the Carbuccia of old was a riotous, joyful, foul-tongued, pleasure-loving atheist, a typical commercial traveller, with a strain of Alsatia and the mountain-brigand. How came this red-tied scoffer so far on the road of religion as to be damned? Some foolish fancy had made the ribald Gaëtano turn a Mason. When one of his boon companions had suggested the evil course, he had refused blankly, apparently because he was asked, rather than because it was evil; but he had scarcely regained his home in Naples than he became irreparably initiated. The ceremony was accomplished in a street of that city by a certain Giambattista Pessina, who was a Most Illustrious Sovereign Grand Commander, Past Grand Master, and Grand Hierophant of the Antique and Oriental Rite of Memphis and Misraïm, who, for some reason which escapes analysis, recognised Carbuccia as a person who deserved to be acquainted with the whole physiology and anatomy of Masonry. It would cost 200 francs to enter the 33rd grade of the sublime mystery. Carbuccia closed with this offer, and was initiated there and then across the table, becoming a Grand Commander of the Temple, and was affiliated, for a further subscription of 15 francs annually, to the Areopagite of Naples, receiving the passwords regularly.

Impelled by an enthusiasm for which he himself was unable to account, he now lent a ready ear to all dispensers of degrees; Memphis initiates of Manchester allured him into Kabbalistic rites; he fell among occult Masons like the Samaritan among thieves; he became a Sublime Hermetic Philosopher; overwhelmed with solicitations, he fraternised with the Brethren of the New Reformed Palladium, and optimated with the Society of Re-Theurgists, from whom he ultimately received the veritable initiation of the Magi. Everywhere lodges opened to him, everywhere mysteries unveiled; everywhere in the higher grades he found spiritism, magic, evocation; his atheism became impossible, and his conscience troubled.

Ultimately his business led him to revisit Calcutta, where his last unheard-of experience had overwhelmed his whole being, just eight days previously to his encounter with Doctor Bataille. He had found the Palladists of that city in a flutter of feverish excitement because they had succeeded in obtaining from China the skulls of three martyred missionaries. These treasures were indispensable to the successful operation of a new magical rite composed by the Supreme Pontiff of Universal Freemasonry and Vicegerent of Lucifer, General Albert Pike. A séance was about to be held; Brother George Shekleton of immortal memory, the hero who had obtained the skulls, was present with those trophies; and the petrified quondam atheist took part, not because he wished to remain, but because he did not dare to go. The proceedings began, the skulls were placed on the tables; Adonaï and his Christ were cursed impressively, Lucifer as solemnly blessed and invoked at the altar of Baphomet. Nothing could be possibly more successful—result, shocks of earthquake, threatened immediate demolishment of the whole place, confident expectation of being entombed alive, terrific burst of thunder, a brilliant light, an impressive silence of some seconds, and then the sudden manifestation of a being in human form seated in the chair of the Grand Master. It was an instantaneous apparition of absolute bodily substance, which carried its own warrant of complete *bona fides.* Everyone fell on their knees; everyone was invited to rise; everyone rose accordingly; and Carbuccia found that he had to do with a male personage not exceeding eight and thirty years, naked as a drawn sword, with a faint flush of Infernus suffusing his skin, a species of light inherent which illuminated the darkness of the salon—in a word, a beardless Apollo, tall, distinguished, infinitely melancholy, and yet with a nervous smile playing at the corners of his mouth, the apparition of *Aut Diabolus aut Nihil* divested of evening dress. This Unashamed Nakedness, who was accepted as the manifestation of Lucifer, discoursed pleasantly to his children, electing to use excellent English, and foretold his ultimate victory over his eternal enemy; he assured them of continued protection, alluded in passing to the innumerable hosts which surrounded him in his eternal domain, and incited his hearers to work without ceasing for the emancipation of humanity from superstition.

The discourse ended, he quitted the daïs, approached the Grand Master, and eye to eye fixed him in deep silence. After a pause he passed on, without committing himself to any definite observation; yet there seems to have been a meaning in the ceremony, for he successively repeated it in the case of every dignitary congregated at the eastern side, and finally of the ordinary members. When it came to the turn of Carbuccia, he would have given ten years of his life to have been at the Galleys rather than Calcutta, but he contrived to pull through, without, however, creating a favourable impression, for *adversarius noster diabolus* passed on with contracted brow, and when the disconcerting inquiry was over, returned to the centre of the circle, gave a final glance around, approached Shekleton, and civilly requested him to shake hands. The importer of missionary skulls complied with a horrible yell; there was an electric shock, sudden darkness, and general *coup-de-théâtre.* When the torches were rekindled, the apparition had vanished, Shekleton was discovered to be dead, and the initiates crowding round him, sang: "Glory immortal to Shekleton! He has been chosen by our omnipotent God." It was too much for the galliard merchant, and he swooned.

Now, this is why Signor Carbuccia concluded that he was damned, which appears to have been precipitate. He has contrived, by the good offices of his lay confessor, to square matters with the hierarchy of Adonaï, who belongs to the Latin persuasion; he has changed his name, adopted a third profession and is so safe in retreat that his friends are as unlikely to find him as are the enemies who thirst for his blood.

Doctor Bataille, faithful to his rôle of good Catholic, perceived at once that the Merchant's Story of these new Arabian Nights was characterised by extreme frankness, was devoid of a sinister motive, and was not the narrative of a maniac. A physician he adds sententiously, is not to be deceived. He determined thereupon that he himself would descend into the abyss, taking with him a mental reservation in all he said and did as a kind of discharge in full. The Church and humanity required it. Behold him then presently at Naples, making acquaintance with Signor Pessina, and outdoing Carbuccia by expending 500 francs in the purchase of the 90th Misraïm grade, thus becoming a Sovereign Grand Master for life! "I will be the exploiter and not the accomplice of modern Satanism," said the pious Doctor Bataille.

§ 3. A Priestess of Lucifer.

Fortified with the purchase of his Memphis sovereignty, and the possession of various signs and passwords communicated by Carbuccia, which, by some interposition of Providence, must be assumed to have remained unchanged in the intervening period, Dr Bataille entered on his adventurous mission, bedewed with many tears, and sanctified by many blessings of an old spiritual adviser, who, needless to say, was at first hostile to the enterprise, and was afterwards as inevitably disarmed by the eloquence and enthusiasm of his disciple. Having regard to the fact that Masonry and Diabolism abound everywhere, according to the hypothesis, it obviously mattered little at what point he began the prosecution of his design; all roads lead to Rome, and the statement is equally true of the Rome of Masonry and the Vatican of Lucifer. As a fact, he started where Carbuccia may be said to have left off, namely, at Point-de-Galle in Southern Ceylon. There he determined to acquaint himself with Cingalese Kabbalism, a department of transcendental philosophy, about as likely to be met with in that reputed region of the Terrestrial Paradise as a cultus from the great south sea in the back parts of Notting Hill. Signor Pessina, however, had provided him with the address of a society which operated something that the doctor agrees to term Kabbalah, after the same manner that he misnames most subjects. But he was not destined to Kabbalize.

Repairing to the principal hotel, he there witnessed, through one of those fortuitous occurrences which are sometimes the mask of fate, a sufficiently indifferent performance by native jugglers, the chief of whom was exceedingly lean and so dirty as to suggest that he was remote from godliness. During the course of the conjuring this personage held the doctor by a certain meaning glance of his glittering eye, and when all was over the latter had a private information that Sata desired to speak with him. The naïve mind of the doctor regarded the name as significant in view of his mission; Sata was assuredly a Satanist. He consented incontinently, and was greeted by the juggler with certain mysterious signs which showed that he was a Luciferian of the sect of Carbuccia, though, by what device of the devil he divined the doctor's adeptship, the devil and not the doctor could alone explain at the moment.

A miscellaneous language is apparently spoken by the Cingalese jugglers—Tamil, including a little bad French, not less convenient than needful in the present case. It was made clear by some brief explanations that the medical services of Dr Bataille were solicited at the death-bed of a personage named Mahmah, for which purpose the two entered a hired conveyance, while the rank and file of the jugglers followed at a brisk trot. In this manner they traversed a frightful desert, plunged into a forest of brushwood, finally forded a stream, and after two hours arrived at an open clearing, in the centre of which was a hut. An ape occupied the threshold, a vampire bat hung from a convenient beam, a cobra was curled underneath, and a black cat welcomed them with arched back. The ape spoke Tamil freely and then marched off, reflecting upon which circumstance, the doctor thought that it was quite the strangest thing in the world.

The hut was the covering of a species of well, down which, with some quakings for the safety of limbs and body, our adventurer was persuaded to follow his guides, and they reached, at the end of a long flight of steps, an immense mortuary chamber. There, on a bed of cocoa-nut fibre, he found his patient, from whose mummified and hideous appearance he at once concluded that she was entirely given over to Satan and had long been a lost soul. As spiritually, so also physically, she was past all human aid; indeed she seemed dead already, and he gave his medical opinion to that effect. The countenance of this opinion was apparently the warrant required for the proceedings which immediately followed, and it is difficult to understand why fakirs in league with Satan—for such we are told they were—and possessed, no doubt, both of ordinary native and occult methods of diagnosis, could not have discovered this for themselves, more especially as the lady, who seems to have been a pythoness by profession, and commerced with a familiar spirit, had already reached the ripe age of 152 years.

To shorten a long and peculiarly noisome story, the astounded doctor ultimately beheld the dying woman revive suddenly, and crawl to the end of the chamber, where there was an elaborate altar surmounted by a figure of Baphomet; the fakirs crowded round her; the ape, the bat, the snake, the cat, all appeared on the scene; a brilliant illumination was produced by means of eleven lamps suspended from the ceiling; the woman drew herself into an erect position; the fakirs piled resinous branches round her; amidst invocations, mysterious chants, and yells, she permitted herself to be burned to death, her body slowly blackening, her face turning scarlet in the flames, her eyes starting from her head, and so she passed into ashes.

Why was the doctor privileged to be present at these proceedings? Because an agent of the fakirs had previously investigated his portmanteau on the hotel premises, and had discovered his Memphis insignia, which they returned to him in the mortuary chamber. As to the Baphomet, it is very fully described, and is identified with similar images of Masonic lodges in America, India, Paris, Rome, Shanghai, and Monte Video. The doctor says that it is the god of the occultists. The venerable Sata quoted Latin as intelligently as the ape spoke Tamil; he overwhelmed his benefactor with acknowledgments, and instead of a fee presented him with a winged lingam, by means of which he would be received among all worshippers of Lucifer in India, China,—in fact, as Sata said, *partout, partout*.

So did Dr Bataille make his first acquaintance with practical occultism, and these things being done, he returned to his hotel and departed thankfully to bed.

§ 4. A HOUSE OF ROTTENNESS.

Who would possess a lingam which was an *Open Sesame* to devildom and not make use thereof? By effecting an exchange with another ship's doctor, the exploiter of Lucifer found himself presently at Pondicherry, with three months of comparative freedom before him to explore the mysteries of the oriental peninsula. Need I say that he had scarcely landed at the French seaboard town when he at once made acquaintance with the very person who of all others was most suitable to his scheme? This was Ramassamiponnotamly-palé-dobachi—quite a short name, he assures us, for the natives of this part. All

Pondicherry more or less abounded in lingams and Lucifer, but as he carried his right hand clenched, the doctor at once suspected the half-naked Ramassam to be more than commonly devoted to the persuasion of perdition; nor was he mistaken, for the latter promptly inquired: "What is your age?" "Eleven years," said the doctor. "Whence do you come?" "From the eternal flame." "Whither do you go ?" "To the flame eternal." And to their mutual satisfaction they agreed the sacred name of Baal-Zeboub, the doctor producing his winged lingam, at which the other fell down in the open streets and adored him. The exhibition of the patent of a Sovereign Grand Master *ad Vitam* of the Rite of Memphis inspired further respect; it was evidently a document with which Ramassam had long been familiar; and he began to talk glibly of tyling. Like the horrors of Udolpho, the explanation was of course very simple: Mr John Campbell, an American, had instituted a lodge of the York Rite at Pondicherry which, in the most natural manner, admitted the Luciferian Fakirs as visitors, the Luciferian Fakirs admitted the members of the York Rite to their conventions, and they all bedevilled one another.

It would be idle to suppose that F∴ Campbell was not at Pondicherry on business when the doctor chanced to arrive, and in the course of the afternoon the latter was taken by Ramassam to a house of ordinary appearance, into which they were admitted by another Indian, who, of course, like the guide, spoke good French. Through the greenery of a garden, the gloom of a well, and the entanglement of certain stairways, they entered a great dismantled temple devoted to the service of Brahma, under the unimpressive diminutive of Lucif. The infernal sanctuary had a statue of Baphomet, identical with that in Ceylon, and the ill-ventilated place reeked with horrible putrescence. Its noisome condition was mainly owing to the presence of various fakers, who, though still alive, were in advanced stages of putrefaction. Most people are supposed to go easily and pleasantly to the devil, but these elected to do so by way of a charnel-house asceticism, and an elaborate system of self-torture. Some were suspended from the ceiling by a rope tied to their arms, some embedded in plaster, some stiffened in a circle, some permanently distorted into the shape of the letter S; some were head downwards, some in a cruciform position. It was really quite monstrous, says the doctor, but a native grand master explained, that they had postured for years in this manner, and one of them for a quarter of a century.

Fr∴ John Campbell proceeded to harangue the assembly in ourdou-zaban, but the doctor comprehended completely, and reports the substance of his speech, which was violently anti-Catholic in its nature, and especially directed against missionaries. This finished, they proceeded to the evocation of Baal-Zeboub, at first by the Conjuration of the Four, but no fiend appeared. The operation was repeated ineffectually a second time, and John Campbell determined upon the Grand Rite, which began by each person spinning on his own axis, and in this manner circumambulating the temple in procession. Whenever they passed an embedded fakir, they obtained an incantation from his lips, but still Baal-Zeboub failed. Thereupon the native Grand Master suggested that the evocation should be performed by the holiest of all the fakirs, who was produced from a cupboard more fetid than the temple itself, and proved to be in the following condition:—(*a*) Face eaten by rats; (*b*) one bleeding eye hanging down by his mouth; (*c*) legs covered with gangrene, ulcers, and rottenness; (*d*) expression peaceful and happy.

Entreated to call on Baal-Zeboub, each time he opened his mouth his eye fell into it; however, he continued the invocation, but no Baal-Zeboub manifested. A tripod of burning coals was next obtained, and a woman, summoned for this purpose, plunged her arm into the flames, inhaling with great delight the odour of her roasting flesh. Result, *nil*. Then a white goat was produced, placed upon the altar of Baphomet, set alight, hideously tortured, cut open, and its entrails torn out by the native Grand Master, who spread them on the steps, uttering abominable blasphemies against Adonaï. This having also failed, great stones were raised from the floor, a nameless stench ascended, and a large consignment of living fakirs, eaten to the bone by worms and falling to pieces in every direction, were dragged out from among a number of skeletons, while serpents, giant spiders, and toads swarmed from all parts. The Grand Master seized one of the fakirs and cut his throat upon the altar, chanting the satanic liturgy amidst imprecations, curses, a chaos of voices, and the last agonies of the goat. The blood spirted forth upon the assistants, and the Grand Master sprinkled the Baphomet. A final howl of invocation resulted in complete failure, whereupon it was decided that Baal-Zeboub had business elsewhere. The doctor departed from the ceremony, fraternising with Campbell, and kept his bed for eight-and-forty hours.

§ 5. THE SEVEN TEMPLES AND A SABBATH IN SHEOL.

It was in the month of October 1880 that, in the course of his enterprise, Doctor Bataille reached Calcutta. Freemasonry, he informs us, invariably affects the horrible, and as he invests Calcutta with the sombre hues of living death and universal putrefaction, it naturally follows that the Indian city is one of the four great directing centres of Universal Freemasonry. Everywhere the pious Doctor discovered the hand of Lucifer; everywhere he beheld the consequences of superstition and Satanism; cataclysms, floods, tornados, typhoons, plagues, cholera, representing the normal state of health and habit, and the consequences of universal persuasion in favour of the fiend. A corpse, he testifies, is met with at every step, the smoke of burning widows ascends to heaven, and the plain of Dappah, in immediate contiguity to the city, is a vast charnel-house where innumerable multitudes of dead bodies are flung naked to the vultures. The English Mason will at once recognise that of all places in the world Calcutta is most suited to be a Mecca of the Fraternity and the capital of English India. The Kadosch of the Scotch Rite, the Sublime Chosen Master of the Royal Arch, the Commander of the White and Black Eagle of the rite of Herodom, the perfectly initiated Grand Inspector of the Scotch Philosophical Rite, the Elect Brother of the Johannite Rite of Zinnendorf, and the Brother of the Red Cross of Swedenborg, a thousand other dignitaries of a thousand illuminations, gather in the Grand Masonic Temple, and, as the Doctor gravely tells us, are employed in cursing Catholicity. By a special conjunction of the planets, the Doctor, on reaching headquarters, had immediate intelligence that the great Phileas Walder had himself recently arrived on a secret mission from Charleston. There also he made acquaintance with another luminary of devildom, by name Hobbs, who presided at the important proceedings which resulted in the damnation of Carbuccia. Brother Hobbs, possessed of much experience in Lucifer, gave many assurances concerning the incessant apparitions of The Master of Evil to all worthy persons. Now the Doctor, by virtue of his Misraïm patent, was as much a priest for ever according to the Melchisedeck of Masonry, as if he had been born without father or mother, but at the moment he had not received the perfect initiation of the Palladium; technically, therefore, he had no right to participate in the Supreme Mysteries. However, it is needless to say that he had arrived in the nick of time to be present at a ceremony which takes place only once in ten years, provided that he was willing to undergo the trifle of a preliminary ordeal.

On the same evening a select company of initiates proceeded in hired carriages through the desolation of Dappah, under the convoy of initiated coachmen, for the operation of a great satanic solemnity. At an easy distance from the city is the Sheol of the native Indians, and hard by the latter place there is a mountain 500 feet high and 2000 long, on the summit of which seven temples are erected, communicating one with another by subterranean passages in the rock. The total absence of pagodas makes it evident that these temples are devoted to the worship of Satan; they form a gigantic triangle superposed on the vast plateau, at the base of which the party descended from their conveyances, and were met by a native with an accommodating knowledge of French. Upon exchanging the Sign of Lucifer he conducted them to a hole in the rock, which gave upon a narrow passage guarded by a line of Sikhs with drawn swords, prepared to massacre anybody, and leading to the vestibule of the first temple, which was filled with a miscellaneous concourse of Adepts, from officers and tea-merchants even to tanners and dentists. In the first temple, which was provided with the inevitable statue of Baphomet, but was withal bare and meagrely illuminated, the doctor was destined to pass through his promised ordeal, for which he was stripped to the skin, placed in the centre of the assembly, and at a given signal one thousand odd venomous cobra de capellos were produced from holes in the wall and encouraged to fold him in their embraces, while the music of flute-playing fakirs alone intervened to prevent his instant death. He passed through this trying encounter with a valour which amazed himself, persisted in prolonging the ceremony, and otherwise proved himself a man of such extraordinary metal that he earned universal respect and received the most flattering testimonials even from Phileas Walder. That the serpents were undoubtedly venomous was afterwards proved upon the person of one of the natives present who, delivered to their fury, fell, covered with apparently mortal bites, but was subsequently treated by native remedies and carried before the altar of Baphomet to be cured by the special intervention of the good God Lucifer. This ceremony was accomplished by the intervention of a lovely Indian Vestal, by the prayers of the Grand Master, a silk-mercer by commercial persuasion, and by the mock baptism of a serpent, after which the sufferer rose to his feet and the inconvenient venom spurted of itself out of his wounds. From the Sanctuary of the Serpents the company then proceeded, with becoming recollection, into the second temple or Sanctuary of the Phœnix.

The second temple was brilliantly illuminated and ablaze with millions of precious stones wrested by the wicked English from innumerable conquered Rajahs; it had garlands of diamonds, festoons of rubies, vast images of solid silver, and a gigantic Phœnix in red gold more solid than the silver. There was an altar beneath the Phœnix, and a male and female ape were composed at the altar steps, while the Grand Master proceeded to the celebration of a black mass, which was followed by an amazing marriage of the two engaging animals, and the sacrifice of a lamb brought alive into the temple, bleating piteously, with nails driven through its feet. This was intended to symbolize an illuminated reprobation of celibacy and an approval of the married state, or its less expensive substitutes.

The third temple was consecrated to the Mother of fallen women, who, in memory of the adventure of the apple, has a place in the calendar of Lucifer; the proceedings consisted of a dialogue between the Grand Master and the Vestal which the becoming modesty of the doctor prevents him from describing even in the Latin tongue.

The fourth temple was a Rosicrucian Sanctuary, having an open sepulchre, from which blue flames continually emanated; there was a platform in the midst of the temple designed for the accommodation of more Indian Vestals, one of whom it was proposed should evaporate into thin air, after which a fakir would be transformed before the whole company into a living mummy and be interred for a space of three years. These were among the events of the evening, and were accomplished with great success without much disturbing the mental equilibrium of the doctor, though he confessed to a certain impression when the Fakir introduced his performance by suspension in midair.

The fifth temple was consecrated to the Pelican and was used by an English officer to deliver a short discourse on masonic charity, which the doctor regarded as vulnerable from a moral point of view and suggestive of easy virtue.

The sixth temple was that of the Future and was devoted to divinations, the oracles being given by a Vestal in a hypnotic condition, seated over a burning brazier. The doctor was accommodated with a test, but another inquirer who had the temerity to be curious as to what was being done in the Vatican received a severe rebuff; in vain did the spirit of the Clairvoyante strive to penetrate the "draughty and malarious" palace of the Roman Pontiff, and Phileas Walder, mortified and maddened, began to curse and to swear like the first Pope. The experiment disillusionized the assembly and they thoughtfully repaired to the seventh temple, which, being sacred to Fire, was equipped with a vast central furnace surmounted by a chimney and containing a gigantic figure of Baphomet; in spite of the intolerable heat pervading the entire chamber, this idol contrived to preserve its outlines and to glow without pulverising. A ceremony of an impressive nature occurred in this apartment; a wild cat, which strayed in through an open window, was regarded as the appearance of a soul in transmigration, and, in spite of its piteous protests, was passed through the fire to Baal.

And now the crowning function, the Magnum Opus of the mystery, must take place in the Sheol of Dappah; a long procession filed from the mountain temples to the charnel-house of the open plain; the night was dark, the moon had vanished in dismay, black clouds scudded across the heavens, a feverish rain fell slowly at intervals, and the ground was dimly lighted by the phosphorescence of the general putrefaction. The Adepts went stumbling over dead bodies, disturbing Rats and Vultures, and proceeded to the formation of the magic chain, which consisted in high-grade Masons, provided with silk hats, sitting down in a vast circle, every Adept embracing his particular corpse. The ceremony included the recitation of certain passages borrowed from popular grimoires, the object in view being the wholesale liberation of Spirits wandering in the immediate neighbourhood of their bodies. This closed the proceedings and the doctor confesses that the distractions of the evening occasioned him a disturbed sleep accompanied by nightmares.

§ 6. A PALLADIAN INVITATION.

Before leaving Calcutta our adventurer purchased from Phileas Walder, for the sum of two hundred francs, the serviceable dignity of a Palladian Hierarch, "fortified with which he would be enabled to penetrate everywhere." Regarding all English possessions as peculiarly productive in the Dead Sea fruit of diabolism, Singapore was the next scene of his curious researches. The English as a nation are criminal, but Singapore is the yeast-house of British wickedness, where vice ferments continually; there man masonifies naturally and most Masons palladise. The doctor states plainly that one thing only has preserved the place from the doom of the cities of the plain, and that is the presence of certain good Christians, otherwise Catholics, in what he terms the accursed city. For himself he tarried only to witness the initiation of a Mistress-Templar according to the Palladian rite, which took place in a Presbyterian Chapel, the Presbyterian persuasion, as he tells us, being one of the broad roads leading to avowed Satanism. The password was appropriately the name of the first murderer, and the doctor was greeted to his great astonishment by an old acquaintance, an English pastor, whom he had frequently seen upon his own magnificent steam-boat, who also rejoiced in the nick-name of the Reverend Alcohol, being, like the majority of Englishmen, almost invariably drunk. The ceremony of initiation, which is described at great length in the narrative, is a variation from that of Leo Taxil; the doctor, in mercy to his readers, suppressing a part of the performance. Speaking generally, it was concerned, as we have previously seen, with an anti-Christian version of Gospel history and some commonplace outrages of the Eucharistic elements, during which proceedings our witness perspired freely. So, as he tells us, did one more Protestant pass over to the worship of Lucifer.

The operations of the ritual were followed by a "divine solemnity," which had something of the character of an ordinary spiritual séance, supposing it to have been held in a mad-house. I need only say that when the lights were turned up at the end, every article of furniture, including a large organ, was discovered hanging from the ceiling. As a final phenomenon, the Master of the Ceremonies detached his shadow from his substance, arranged it against the wall in the shape of a demon, and it responded to various questions by signs. There was a burst of loud applause, the proceedings terminated, and the Masonic Temple became once more a Presbyterian Chapel.

§ 7. THE SAN-HO-HEI.

The doctor informs us that China is the gate of Hell, and that all its inhabitants are born damned; child-like and bland in appearance, the Chinaman is invariably by disposition a Satanist, having tastes wholly diabolical. As to the religion of Buddha, it is simply Satanism *à outrance*. Chinese occultism is centralised in the San-Ho-Hei, an association "parallel to high grade Masonry," having its head-quarters at Pekin, and welcoming all Freemasons who are affiliated to the Palladium. It does not, however, admit women, and has only one degree. Its chief occupation is to murder Catholic missionaries. When a Palladian Mason seeks admission for the first time to one of its assemblies, he betakes himself to the nearest opium den, carrying on his person the documents which prove his initiation; he places his umbrella head downwards on his left side, and stupefies himself with the divine drug. He is then quite sure that he will be transported in a comatose condition to the occult reunion. When the doctor reached Shanghai, he experienced some hesitation before he attempted an adventure so uncertain in its issue. He remembered, however, that he was possessed of a miraculous medal of St Benedict, which he regarded as his trump card, a species of passport or return ticket, available at any date and by any line of Devildom. He determined to get drunk accordingly; but even as he entered Masonry with a becoming reservation of conscience, so he entered the drug-shop with a reservation as to the degree of his drunkenness, in spite of which he fell, however, into a deep sleep, and awoke in the assembly of The Secret Avengers, one of whom, to facilitate proceedings, had a good knowledge of English, and a perfect familiarity with all Charleston passwords. The Baphomet, of course, presided, but it appears that the Chinese have certain conscientious scruples on the subject of Goats, and hence a Dragon's head was substituted for that of the ordinary image. The doctor was not the only European present at the proceedings of the celestial assembly; but while he was the sole representative of his own nation, it goes without saying that there was a fair sprinkling of the abominable British.

So complete is the unanimity which obtains between the initiates of China and Charleston that the bulk of the proceedings takes place in the English language; but for this disposition of Providence, the doctor would have been at a serious disadvantage. The first object of the company was to encompass the destruction of missionaries, and for this purpose a coffin was presently brought in, containing the skeleton of a deceased brother, who had so far diverged from duty that he had entered in league with the Jesuits, and had dared to act as a spy upon the august proceedings of the Sublime Society of Avengers. The first act may be regarded as somewhat bizarre in character; it consisted in evoking an evil spirit to animate the skeleton, and to answer certain questions. This was accomplished with absolute success. The bones of the departed brother had, however, been so consecrated by his

Jesuitical proclivities that, even when animated by a devil, they discovered extreme reluctance in disclosing the number and quality of certain Franciscan zealots who had just started from Paris to convert the Empire. Ultimately, however, it was admitted that they were now on the high seas, which information given, the bony oracle could no longer contain its rage, but pursued an English Mason of the 33rd degree from end to end of the assembly, and succeeded in inflicting some furious bites and blows. The second act commenced by uncovering a species of exaggerated baptismal font, filled to the brim with water, and representing the great ocean over which the missionaries were passing. The assembly crowded round it, and by means of magic rods and other devices, succeeded in evoking a minute figure of a steam-ship containing the adventurers. Their magic also raised up a perfect tempest of wind in the closed apartment, but by no device could they effect the slightest disturbance upon the placid bosom of the water. The ceremony had, in fact, to be abandoned as a failure in its desired intention. Too well did the Spirit Yesu protect His missionaries. The assembly accordingly repaired into a second apartment. There the officiating dignitaries assumed the vestments of Catholic priests. They produced a wax figure, designed to represent a missionary, amused themselves with a mock trial, inflicted imaginary tortures, and returned the dummy to a cupboard, after which they proceeded to the crucifixion of a living pig. The third act was an agonising experience for the doctor, being nothing less than the sacrifice of one of the brethren, the selection being determined by lot. The doctor, in his quality of visitor, was, it is true, spared the chance of being himself the victim, but he nearly became executioner. One of the Chinese adepts having been chosen, to his intense satisfaction, and approved by some mechanical movements on the part of the dragon-headed Baphomet, permitted his limbs to be removed, and then earnestly invoked the assistance of the "Charleston brother" for the purpose of severing his head. It was an honour invariably accorded to the visitor of the highest grade. The doctor, who could not bring himself to the point, was saved at the last moment by the miraculous levitation of Phileas Walder from an immense distance, this occult personage having become transcendently cognisant of what was going forward in China, and being anxious to interrogate the severed head as to the possible recovery of his daughter, who was then seriously ill. In virtue of his superior dignity, he claimed the privilege of the execution, and the doctor modestly retired.

Such were the adventures of our witness in the assembly of Holy Avengers. He enumerates at great length the evidence against hallucination as a result of his excess in opium, but I suggest to observing readers that there is a more obvious line of criticism.

§ 8. THE GREAT CITY OF LUCIFER.

It was in March of the year 1881 that Doctor Bataille proceeded for the first time to Charleston, to make acquaintance at headquarters with the universal Masonry of Lucifer and its Pontiff Albert Pike. Charleston is the Venice of America, the Rome of Satan, and the great City of Lucifer. Always enormously prolix, and adoring the details which swell the flimsy issues of cheap periodical narratives, our witness describes at great length the city and its Masonic temple, with the temple which is within the temple and is consecrated to the good God. My second chapter has already provided the reader with sufficient information upon the persons alleged to be concerned in the foundation of Universal Freemasonry and in the elaboration of its cultus. Nor need I dwell at any length upon the personal communication which passed between Doctor Bataille, Albert Pike, Gallatin Mackey, Sophia Walder, Chambers, Webber, and the rest of the Charleston luminaries. Miss Walder explained to him the great hope of the Order concerning the speedy advent of anti-Christ, the abolition of the papacy, and the destruction of the Christian religion. She also related many of her private experiences with the infernal monarchy, being acquainted with the exact number of demons in the descending hierarchy, and with all their classes and legions. She confidently expected to be the great grandmother of anti-Christ, and in the meantime possessed the transcendental faculty of becoming fluidic at will. Mr Gallatin Mackey exhibited his *Arcula Mystica*, one of seven similar instruments existing at Charleston, Rome, Berlin, Washington, Monte Video, Naples, and Calcutta. To all appearance it resembled a liqueur-stand, but it was really a diabolical telephone worked like the Urimm and Thummimm, and enabling those who possessed it to communicate with each other, whatever the intervening distance. The Doctor, in his quality of initiate, was, of course, taken over the entire premises; he examined the head of the great templar Molay, deciding by his anthropological knowledge that the relic was not genuine, and that it was not the skull of a European. As to the templar Baphomet, situated in the Sanctum Regnum, and before which Lucifer is supposed to appear, it is sufficient to say that Doctor Bataille, who invariably treads cautiously where it is easy for other steps to follow him, has no personal testimony to furnish upon the subject of the apparition, and the relations of other persons do not concern us at the moment.

§ 9. TRANSCENDENTAL TOXICOLOGY.

The memorials of Charleston are not entirely favourable to the true strength of our witness; it was requisite to "lie low" in America, but the Doctor bristles in Gibraltar; he is once more upon British soil. Does not the Englishman, consciously or otherwise, put a curse on everything he touches? Doctor Bataille affirms it; indeed this quality of malediction has been specially dispensed to the nation of heretics by God himself; so says Doctor Bataille. Since the British braggart began to embattle Gibraltar, having thieved it from Catholic Spain, a wind of desolation breathes over the whole country. An inscrutable providence, of which our witness is the mouthpiece, has elected to set apart this rock in order that the devil and the English, who, he says, are a pair, may continue their work of protestantising and filling the world with malefice. To sum the whole matter, the Britisher is an odious usurper "who has always got one eye open." Now, having regard to the fact that out of every tribe and tongue and people and nation a proportion to be numbered by millions is given over to devil-worship and Masonry, and that consequently there is an enormous demand for Baphomets and other idols, for innumerable instruments of black Magic, and for poisons to exterminate enemies, it is obviously needful that there should be a secret central department for the working of woods and metals and for Transcendental Toxicology. To Charleston the dogmatic directory, to Gibraltar the universal factory. But so colossal an output focussed at a single point could scarcely proceed unknown to Government at a given place, and any nation save England might object to this class of exports. The cause of Masonry and the devil being, however, dear to the English heart, it would, of course, pass unchallenged at Gibraltar, and at this point an anglo-phobe with a remnant of reason would have remained satisfied. Not so our French physician, who affirms that the exports in question do not merely escape inquisition at the hands of civil authority but are in fact a government industry.

> "Bluish 'mid the burning water, full in face Trafalgar
> lay;
> In the dimmest north-east distance dawned Gibraltar,
> grand and gray—
> Here and here did England help me, how can I help
> England, say?"

These are the words of Browning, and his question has well been answered by the institution of the secret workshops and the secret laboratory; as in most other cases England has helped herself, unless, indeed, it should occur to the doctor that the poet was a Satanist, like Pike, who himself was a poet, and had a chief finger in the pie.

Now the great historic rock is tunnelled by innumerable caverns, which, our deponent witnesses, have never been explored by the tourist, and in the most impracticable portions of the great subterranean maze, whosoever has the audacity to penetrate will discover for himself the existence of the industrial department of diabolism, but he must not expect to come back unless he be a Sovereign Grand Master *ad vitam*, and an initiate of Lucifer. The doctor has explored these caverns, has seen the factory in full working order, has exhaustively described the way in, has returned from the gulf like Dante, and has given away the whole mystery. Possessed of his key to the labyrinth the wayfaring man shall not err therein, and it will, no doubt, be a new curiosity for the more daring among Cook's tourists. The workshops are supplied with mechanics by a simple expedient; hopeless specimens of English malefactors, condemned to penal servitude for the term of their natural life, are relegated to this region, a kind of grim humour characterising the selection. The most hideous convicts are chosen, and those most corresponding in outward appearance to the favourite devils of the hierarchy, under whose names they pass in the workshops, where they commonly communicate with each other in the language of Volapuk. The reason given is that this language has been adopted by the Spœeic Rite, which I confess that I had not heard of previously, but I venture to think that the doctor has concealed the true reason, and that Volapuk has been thus chosen because it is a diabolical invention; a universal language prevailed previously to the confusion of Babel, and the new language is an irreligious attempt to produce *ordo ab chao* by a return to unity of speech.

The Toxicological Department is worked by a higher class of criminals, as for example, absconding trustees, who are there comfortably settled in life, enjoying many modern conveniences. It produces poisons which usually cause death by cerebral hemorrhage; but each has its special antidote, possessed of which the initiated poisoner can eat and drink with his victim; on this subject the doctor pursues, however, a policy of masterly reticence. But such, in brief, is the deep mystery of Gibraltar, such is the Toxicological department of universal Freemasonry.

§ 10. THE DOCTOR AND DIANA.

It would be impossible to follow the doctor through the entire course of his memoirs, not that they are wholly biographical, exclusively concerned with modern diabolism, or with the great conspiracy of masons against God, Man, and the universe; one of his subsidiary and yet most important objects is to fill space, in which respect he has almost eclipsed the great classics of the penny dreadful in England. I must pass with a mere reference over his dealings in spiritualism; it is needless to say that in this branch of transcendental investigation he witnessed more astounding phenomena than falls commonly to the lot of even veteran students. His star prevailed everywhere, and the world unseen deployed its strongest forces. At Monte Video, for example, falling casually into a circle of spiritualists, he was seated, surrounded by a family of these unconscious and amateur diabolists, before an open window at night time; across the broad mouth of the river a great shaft of soft light from the lamp of the lighthouse opposite shone in mid-air, over the bosom of the water, and as it fell upon their faces he discerned, floating within the beam itself, the solid figure of a man. It was not the first time that the apparition, under similar circumstances, had been seen by the rest of the household, but for him it bore a message of deeper mystery than for these uninitiated spiritualists; although in man's clothes, his observant eye recognised the face of the spirit; terrible and suggestive truth, it was the face of the vestal Virgin, who, far off in Calcutta, had fluidified in the third temple, and he uttered a great cry! He has now decided to void the virginity of the vestal, and to assume that she was in reality a demon, and not a being of earth. At the same time, my readers must thoroughly understand that the doctor, when he meddles in spiritualism, is a man who is governed in his narratives by an intelligent faculty of criticism which borders on the purely sceptic; he delights in the display of instances where an element of trickery may be detected; no one better than himself can distinguish between bogus and bogey, and he takes pleasure in directing special attention to his extraordinary good judgment and sound common-sense in each and all these matters. Hence no one will be surprised to hear that at the house of a lady in London, an ordinary table, after a preliminary performance in tilting, transformed suddenly into a full-grown crocodile, and played touchingly on the piano, after which it again changed into a table, but the gin, the whisky, the pale ale, and the other intoxicants which are indispensable at séances in England, had been entirely consumed by the transcendental reptile to fortify him on his return journey to the mud-banks of the Nile. Nor has the spontaneous apparition been wanting to complete the experiences of Dr Bataille. He was seated in his cabin at midnight pondering over the theories formulated in natural history by Cuvier and Darwin, who diabolised the entire creation, when he was touched lightly on the shoulder, and discovered standing over him, in his picturesque Oriental costume, like another Mohini, the Arabian poisoner-in-chief of the Gibraltar Toxicological Department, who, after some honourable assurances that the Bible was not true, departed transcendentally as he came. This personage subsequently proved to be the demon Hermes. Even when he merely masonified, the doctor had unheard-of experiences in magic. For example, at Golden Square, in the west central district of this wicked city, an address which we have heard of before, at the conclusion of an ordinary Lodge meeting, there was an evocation of the demon Zaren, who appeared under the form of a monstrous three-headed dragon completely cased in steel, and, endeavouring to devour his evoker, was restrained by the magical pentagram, ultimately vanishing with the peculiar odour of Infernus.

In connection with various marvels the doctor has much to tell us concerning two sisters in Lucifer who have long been at daggers drawn, and considering their supernatural attributes, it is incomprehensible in a high degree that they have not destroyed one-another like the Magician and the Princess of a more credible narrative of wonders in the "Arabian Nights." Diana Vaughan, much heard and little seen, has since become famous by her conversion to the Catholic faith. Honoured with her acquaintance for a considerable period, the doctor invariably testifies the utmost respect for this wealthy, beautiful, and high-placed Palladian lady, so long protected by a demon, of the superior hierarchy, and enjoying what he somewhat obscurely terms an obsessional guardianship. On the 28th of February, 1884, at a theurgic séance of Templar Mistresses and Elect Magi of Louisville, the ceiling of the temple was riven suddenly, and Asmodeus, genius of Fire, descended to slow music, having in one hand a sword, and in other the long tail of a lion. He informed the company that there had just been a great battle between the leaders of Lucifer and Adonaï, and that it had been his personal felicity to lop the Lion's tail of St Mark; he directed the members of the eleven plus seven triangle to preserve the trophy carefully, and, that it might not be a lifeless relic, he had thoughtfully informed it with one of his minor devils until such time as he himself should intervene to mark his omnipotent favour towards a certain predestined virgin. The vestal in question was Diana of the Charlestonians, elect sister in Asmodeus, who at that time was not affiliated to Palladism. When the doctor subsequently drew her on the subject of this history, she replied, after the manner of the walrus, "Do you admire the view?" For himself, the good doctor dislikes the narrative, not because it does violence to possibility, but because it did violence to St Mark; there is evidently an incomplete dignity about a tail-less evangelist. As to the tail itself, he has no personal doubt that it was the property of an ordinary lion, and that it has since become possessed of a devil.

At the risk of offending Miss Vaughan, the doctor expatiates on her case, and learnedly demonstrates that her possession is of so uninterrupted a kind that it has become a second nature, and belongs to the 5th degree; however this may be, he establishes at great length one important point in her favour, which has occasioned all French Catholics to earnestly desire her conversion. I have stated already that the grade of Templar-Mistress is concerned partly with profanations of the Eucharist. For example, the aspirant to this initiation is required to drive a stiletto into the consecrated Host with a becoming expression of fury. When Miss Vaughan visited Paris in the year 1885, where Miss Walder had sometime previously established herself, she was invited to enter this grade, and accepted the offer. A séance for initiation was held accordingly, but Miss Vaughan would have none of profanation, and refused blankly to stultify her liberal intelligence by the stabbing of a wheaten wafer. She did not believe in the Real Presence, and she did not wish to be childish. A great sensation followed; her initiation was postponed; appeal was made to Charleston; and the formality was dispensed with in her case by the intervention, as it was supposed at the moment, of Albert Pike's authority, even as her Father's intervention had excused her beforehand from another ordeal which could not be suffered with propriety. This episode implanted in the breast of Sophia Walder an extreme form of Palladian hatred for the Diana of Philalethes. Now, Sophia was in high favour with all the hosts of perdition, yet her rancorous relations with her sister Adept did not make Diana less a *persona grata* to the peculiar intelligence which governs the descending hierarchy. In the Mammoth Cave of Kentucky the Palladian Magi and the Mistress Templars decided one day to have a little experiment with the Undines, so they shouldered their magical instruments; but the eager elementaries, habiting the dark abysses, did not wait to be evoked; the water bubbled in the Lake, the roof was constellated with stars, and who should appear but Asmodeus, on the bank opposite, in all his infernal glory! With open arms he loudly called on Diana, and that lady, suddenly transfigured, walked calmly over the water, and kissed the feet of her demon, who incontinently vanished. Inspired by a sense of deficiency, the doctor says that the visit to the Mammoth Cave terminated without any further incident. He was not an ocular witness of what he relates in this instance, but he received it from the lips of Diana, and the lips of Diana, in the opinion of all honourable men, would be preferable to the eyes of the doctor.

But the doctor had the testimony of his eyes upon another occasion; it is known that Miss Vaughan's celebrity began with her hostility to the Italian Grand Master, Adriano Lemmi. When the seat of the Sovereign Pontificate, as deponents testify, was removed from Charleston, the great city of Lucifer, even unto the Eternal City, and many adepts demissioned, there was a doubt in the rebel camp as to the continued protection of Lucifer. If Diabolus had gone over to Lemmi, they were indeed bereft. Miss Vaughan, however, remained calm and sanguine:—"I am certain of the celestial protection of the Genii of Light," said Diana, and, producing her talisman, she bent her right knee to the ground, turned a complete somersault without falling, flung her tambourine into the air, which descended gently and remained suspended a yard from the ground, while she herself, passing into a condition of ecstasy, also rose into the air in a recumbent posture. She remained in this state for the space of fifteen minutes, the silence being only broken by the distant rumbling of thunder. Many of the spectators could not believe their eyes. At length very gently her body assumed a vertical position, head downwards, but as a concession to polite feeling the remaining laws of gravity were suspended, like herself, and her skirts were not correspondingly inverted. Slowly the ecstatic lady continued to circulate, the assembly stood at gaze "like Joshua's moon in Ajalon," and presently she was in the vertical position of a swimmer, the phenomenon concluding by her restoration to *terra firma*. This wonder was accomplished by the magic power of a diabolical Rose which the lady carried in her bodice.

On yet another occasion the doctor witnessed the prodigy of the bilocation of Diana by the assistance of a simple magical process, when to his most certain knowledge she was hundreds of leagues away; but the recitations of Doctor Bataille have reduced bilocation to a banality, and a mere reference will suffice.

A monograph of Miss Vaughan's miracles would, however, be incomplete if it failed to exhibit her in her capacity as a breaker of spells; whatsoever has been bound by devildom can be loosed by Diana. At the height of the commotion occasioned by her persistent refusal to participate in sham sacrilege, there was one member of the Paris Triangle who manifested peculiar acrimony in demanding the expulsion of a delinquent who had dared to impeach the ritual. As a punishment for his own presumption, and in the presence of the assembled adepts, his head was suddenly reversed by an unseen power, and for the space of one and twenty days he was obliged to review the situation face backwards. This severe judgment dismayed all present; Miss Walder had recourse to an evocation and discovered that it had been inflicted by Asmodeus, the protector of her rival, who furthermore would not scruple to visit with violent disaster any person who discovered an evil design against so elect a sister as Diana. If the present culprit desired to be set free from his grotesque position, he must humbly have recourse to her. Miss Vaughan was in America at the moment, but she generously came to his rescue as soon as steam could carry her, and restored him his lost front view by a jocose imposition of hands. I should add that on the very day when this misadventure took place at Paris, Miss Vaughan was defending her standpoint in person before the Triangle of Louisville; opinion was divided about her, and the result appeared uncertain, when the demoniac tail of St Mark, evacuating the minor devil, who had hired it on a repairing lease, accepted Asmodeus as a tenant, and violently circumambulating the apartment belaboured all those whose voices had been raised against his Vestal. Finally the tassel of the tail turned into the head of the demon and vowed his devotion to Diana so long as she remained unmarried; did she dare, however, to desert him for an earthly consort, he was commander of fourteen legions, and he would strangle the man of clay.

It would be unkind to Miss Sophia Walder if I let it be supposed for a moment that the palm of prestige is borne away by her rival. I have already noted that this lady occasionally fluidifies to the satisfaction of a select audience, but, like the materialising medium, she finds it a depleting performance which usually confines her to her room, and her price, therefore, is five thousand francs. She is first Sovereign in Bitru, and is defined by the doctor to be in a state of latent possession, having a semi-diabolical nature and the gift of substitution. It was possibly at Milan that he witnessed the most persuasive test of her occult powers. She took him confidentially apart and explained to him that she had been in a condition of "penetration" for about three hours. "At dinner the food of which I partake becomes volatile in my mouth; wine evaporates invisibly the moment it makes contact with my lips; I eat and drink in appearance, but my teeth masticate the air." Now this was due, not to the voracity of Bitru, but to the keen appetite of Baal-Zeboub; the magnetic lady did not, however, explain this point after the common method of speech; she fixed her blazing orbs upon the doctor, and he saw flames everywhere; a moment more and her feet were free from earth; she stretched out her left hand, and on the open palm he beheld the successive apparitions in characters of flame of the ten letters which constitute the great name. With a touch of internal collapse he commended himself to the Virgin Mary, the ecstatic paroxysm passed, and they wandered down another lane, for they were in the midst of leafy umbrage. Presently a tree gracefully arranged a portion of its branches in the form of a fan, and bowed with profound reverence. Still more fantastic, a paralysed branch produced a living human hand, which in the accompanying engraving is ornamented with an immaculate cuff, and that hand presented a bouquet to Sophia. By reason of these matters the doctor became pensive.

A Palladian séance followed. The litany of Lucifer was chanted, and the prodigy of "substitution" was effected. The ceremony took place in a grotto with a stalactite roof; Miss Walder produced from a basket the serpent which was an inseparable companion of all her travels; it immediately genuflected in front of her, swarmed the wall, and assumed a pendant position attached to one of the stalactites. It was a reptile of no ordinary kind, for it began to develop an interminable length of coils till it had spread itself circlewise over the entire ceiling, and its head was joined to its tail. The doctor says that he was now prepared for anything. The serpent gave forth seven horrible hisses, and in the dim light, for the torches which illuminated the place were successively giving out of themselves, each person became conscious of an unseen entity blowing with burning breath in their faces. When at length there was complete darkness, Sophia herself became radiant, and brilliantly illuminated the grotto with an intense white light; five enormous hands could then be seen floating in space, also intensely luminous, but emitting a green lustre; each hand went wandering in search of its prey, ultimately seizing a brother, whom it drew irresistibly forward in the direction of Sophia. Moved by a mysterious influence, two of them grasped her arms, two clutched her by the shoulders, one placed his hand on her head. The serpent again hissed seven significant times, and in place of the solid Sophia the third Alexander of Macedon was substituted in phantom guise. When he faded Sophia reappeared and continued going and coming with a phantom between each of her appearances, so that she was in turn replaced by Luther, Cleopatra, Robespierre, and others, concluding with the Italian patriot Garibaldi, who eclipsed all the others, for his bust was converted into a bronze urn from which red flames burst forth. The flames took a human form, and gave back Sophia to the assembly.

Such is the gift of substitution, which follows penetration, and such is the substance of the memoirs of M. Bataille, ship's doctor, who, in the year 1880, undertook to exploit Freemasonry and has come forth unsinged from Diabolism. There is one maxim of the Psalmist which the experience of most transcendentalists has taught them to lay to heart, and to repeat without the qualifications of David when certain aspects of supernatural narrative are introduced—*Omnis homo mendax!* But lest I should appear to be discourteous, I should like to add a brief dictum from the Magus Éliphas Lévi. "The wise man cannot lie," because nature accommodates herself to his statement. In a polite investigation like the present, there is, therefore, no question whether Doctor Bataille is defined by the term *mendax,* which is forbidden to literary elegance; it is simply a question whether he is a wise man, or whether nature blundered and did not conform to his statement.

The credibility, in whole or in part, of Dr Bataille's narrative will involve some extended criticism, and I purpose to postpone it till the remaining witnesses have been examined. We shall then be in a position to appreciate how far later revelations support his statements. Setting aside the miraculous element, which is tolerably separate from what most concerns our inquiry, namely, the existence of Palladian Masonry attached to the cultus of Lucifer, it may be stated that the most sober part of Dr Bataille's memoirs is the account of his visit to Charleston; here the miraculous element is entirely absent. He confirms by alleged personal investigations the existence of the New and Reformed Palladium; he is the first witness who distinguishes clearly between the Luciferian Order and the Supreme Council of the Ancient and Accepted Scotch Rite of Charleston. That distinction is made, however, at one expense; it assumes that the Supreme Council preserved the Baphomet idol as well as the reputed skull of Molay for nearly seventy years, and then surrendered it to another order with which it had no official acquaintance. Under what circumstances and why did it do that? The Ancient and Accepted Scotch Rite is connected by its legend with the Templars, and for the Charleston Supreme Council to part with the trophies of the tradition seems no less unlikely than for a regiment to surrender its colours.

CHAPTER VIII

Dealings with Diana

The philosophy of Horatius is supposed to represent incompletely the content of heaven and earth, but neither earth nor heaven, as at present constituted, would be capable of enclosing the entire content of Dr Bataille's memoirs. Miss Diana Vaughan, with whose history we are next concerned, comes before us under a different aspect. I have failed to ascertain under what circumstances she first became known in France. *Le Diable au XIXe Siècle* may have constituted her earliest introduction; she was certainly unknown to Leo Taxil when he published the Palladian rituals, or she would not have escaped mention in the account he there gives of Miss Sophia Walder. However this may be, we have made her acquaintance in the course of the previous chapter, but I am constrained to state that she has, up to the present, shown herself exceedingly circumspect in substantiating the evidence of her precursor.

The whole world is aware, and I need not again repeat, that Miss Diana Vaughan was converted to the Catholic Church some time after Dr Bataille completed his astounding narrative. A Palladist of perfect initiation, comprehending the mysteries of the number 77, and doing reverence to the higher mystery of 666, Grand Mistress of the Temple, Grand Inspectress of the Palladium, and according to him who, in a sense, has prepared her way and made straight her paths, a sorceress and thaumaturge before whose daily performances the Black Sabbath turns white, Miss Vaughan quarrelled, as we have seen, with a sister initiate, Sophia Walder, and conceived for the Italian Grand Master, Adriano Lemmi, the charity of the evil angels, which is hatred. When the Supreme Dogmatic Directory of Universal Freemasonry was removed from Charleston to Rome and the pontificate passed over to Lemmi, as the revelations allege, Miss Vaughan closed her connection with the Triangles, carrying her colours to a vessel equipped by herself, and founded a new society under the title of the Free and Regenerated Palladium, incorporating the Anti-Lemmist groups, and soon after began a public propaganda by the issue of a monthly review, devoted to the elucidation of the doctrines of the Lucifer cultus and to the exposure of the Italian Grand Master. To hoist the black flag of diabolism, as Miss Vaughan would now term it, thus in the open day, naturally elicited a strong protestation from the Palladist Federation, so that she was in embroilment not only with Lemmi but also with the source of the initiation which she still appeared to prize. At the same time she exhibited no indications of going over to the cause of the Adonaïtes. Becoming known to the Anti-Masonic centres of the Catholic Church only through her hostility to Lemmi, she was always a *persona grata* whose conversion was ardently desired, but on several public occasions she advised them that their cause and hers were in radical opposition, and that, in fact, she would have none of them, being outside any need of their support, sympathy, or interest. She would cleave to the good God Lucifer, and she aspired to be the bride of Asmodeus. At length the long-suffering editor of the *Revue Mensuelle,* weary of his refractory protégé, would also have none of her, though he surrendered her with evident regret to be dealt with by the prayers of the faithful. One month after, M. Leo Taxil, through the medium of the same organ, announced the conversion of Miss Vaughan, and in less than another month, namely, in July, 1895, she began the publication of her "Memoirs of an ex-Palladist," which are still in progress, so that, limitations of space apart, my account of this lady will be unavoidably incomplete.

Her memoirs are, unfortunately, not a literary performance; and their method, if such it can be called, is not chronological. Beginning with an account of her first introduction to Lucifer, *vis-à-vis* in the *Sanctum Regnum* of Charleston, on April 8th 1889, they leap, in the second chapter, over all the years intervening to a minute analysis of the sentiments which led to her conversion, and of the raptures which followed it, above all on the occasion of her first communion. It is not till the third chapter that we get an account of her Luciferian education, or, more correctly, an introduction thereto, for the better part of five monthly numbers has not brought us nearer to her personality than the history of an ancestor in the seventeenth century. As the publisher is still soliciting annual subscriptions to the enterprise, and offering a variety of advantages after methods not unknown in England among the by-ways of periodical literature, the completion of the work is probably a distant satisfaction for those who take interest therein.

Now, having regard to the narrative of Dr Bataille, and having regard to the statements set forth in my second chapter, it is obvious that Miss Vaughan is a witness of the first importance as to whether there is a Masonry behind Masonry, which, more or less, manages, or attempts to manage, the entire society, unknown to the rank and file of its initiates, however high in grade; as to whether its seat is at Charleston, with Albert Pike for its founder, and as to whether its doctrine is anti-Christian, and its cultus that of Lucifer, supported by magical wonders, concerned with sacrilegious observances, and either a disguised Satanism, or drifting in that direction. As already hinted, the mythical and miraculous element,—in a word, that portion of Doctor Bataille's narrative which does violence to sense and reason,—Miss Vaughan has not at present imperilled her position by substantiating, but as to the points I have enumerated, she has most distinctly come forth out of Palladism to tell us that these things are so, and to reinforce what was previously stated by unveiling her private life.

It is therefore my duty and desire to do her full justice, and with this purpose in view, I propose to recite briefly the chief heads of her memoir, so far as it has been published up to date. I must, however, premise at the beginning that she does not come before us with one trace of the uncertainty of accent which might have been expected to characterise the newly-acquired language, not merely of Christian faith, but of its Roman dialect. We find her speaking at once, and to the manner born. Could anything, by possibility, be narrower than certain perished sections of evangelical religion in England, it would be certain sections of ultramontane religion in France; but Miss Vaughan has acquired all the terminology of the latter, all the intellectual bitterness, all the fatuities, as one might say, in the space of five minutes. When she has wearied of her memoirs at the moment, or has reached, after the manner of the novelist, some crucial point in her narrative, she breaks off abruptly, brackets *à suivre,* and proceeds to an account of the latest wonder-working image, or a diatribe against spirit manifestations in the typical manner of the French clerical press. To be brief, Miss Vaughan has adopted, body and soul, precisely those abuses which Catholics of intelligence earnestly desire to see expunged from their great religion. She has probably never heard of the Forged Decretals, but she would defend their authenticity if she had; she has probably never heard of the corrupted, or any version of the Epistles of St Ignatius, but she would accept the corruptions bodily upon the smallest hint that they savoured better with the hierarchy, and she would do all this apparently in good faith on the authority of a purblind party within the Church, which exists to keep open its wounds. Now, I submit that a *volte face* is possible, especially in religious opinions, but that a pronounced habit of religious thought cannot be acquired in a day, so that, in the history of Miss Vaughan's conversion, there is more than can be discerned on the surface. The precise nature of the element which eludes must be left to the judgment of my readers, but, personally, I reserve my own, out of fairness to an unfinished deposition.

There is a generic difference between Doctor Bataille and Miss Vaughan. He is an ordinary human being, and if we may trust the many pictures which represent him in his narrative, exceedingly unpretending at that. We have also some portraits of Miss Vaughan, who is aggressive and good to look at; but this is not the generic distinction. Doctor Bataille, poor man, is the scion of an ordinary ancestry within the narrow limits of flesh and blood. Miss Vaughan, on the contrary—I hope my readers will bear with me—has been taught from her childhood to believe that she was of the blood royal of the descending hierarchy, and I cannot gather from her vague mode of expression whether she has altogether rejected the legend of her descent, which is otherwise sufficiently startling.

The position of authority and influence occupied by Miss Vaughan in what she terms high Masonry is to be explained, as she modestly informs us, not by her personal qualities, but by a traditional secret concerning her family, which is known only to the Elect Magi. Miss Vaughan and her paternal uncle are the last descendants of the alchemist Thomas Vaughan, whom she terms a Rosicrucian, and identifies with Eirenæus Philalethes, author of "The Open Entrance to the Closed Palace of the King." On the 25th of March 1645, she tells us, on the authority of her family history, Thomas Vaughan, having previously obtained from Cromwell the privilege of beheading the "noble martyr" Laud, Archbishop of Canterbury—the title to nobility, in her opinion, seems to rest in the probability of his secret connection with Rome—steeped a linen cloth in his blood, burnt the said cloth in sacrifice to Satan, who appeared in response to an evocation, and with whom he concluded a pact, receiving the philosophical stone, and a guaranteed period of life extending over thirty-three years from that date, after which he was to be transported without dying into the eternal kingdom of Lucifer, to live with a glorified body in the pure flames of the heaven of fire.

After this compact, he wrote the "Open Entrance," the original MS. of which, together with its autograph Luciferian interpretation on the broad margins, is a precious heirloom in the family. Some two years later, in the course of his travels, he reached New England, where he dwelt for a month among the Lenni-Lennaps, and there in an open desert, on a clear night of summer, while the moon was shining in splendour, he was wandering in solitary meditation when the luminary in question, which was in the crescent phase, came down out of heaven, and proved to be an arched bed, very luminous and wonderful, containing a vision of sleeping female beauty. This was the nuptial couch of Thomas Vaughan and its occupant was Venus-Astarte, surrounded by a host of flower-bearing child-spirits, who conveniently provided a tent, and provided also delicious meals during a period of eleven days. Several curious particulars differentiated these Hermetic nuptials, undreamed of by Christian Rosencreutz, from those which govern more ordinary proceedings below the latitude of the Lenni-Lennaps. In the first place, goddess succubus, Astarte provided the ring, which was of red gold enriched with a diamond, and placed it on the finger of her lover; in the second place, transcendental gestation, celestial or otherwise, fulfils the mystery of generation with exceeding despatch, for Astarte was delivered of an infant on the eleventh day independently of medical assistance, whereupon she demanded the return of the nuptial ring, and vanished with tent and sprites astride of the crescent couch. The fruit of their union was left in the arms of Thomas, who was directed to trample on all sentiments of paternal affection, and to deliver the child into the charge of a tribe of fire-worshipping Indians. He does not appear to have sued for the restitution of conjugal rights, and cheerfully surrendered the human hybrid to a family of Lenni-Lennaps, together with his medallion portrait drawn by an artist from devildom, so that the daughter might recognise her father after the method which obtains among novelists. Thomas Vaughan placed the broad ocean between himself and the scene of his marriage, and he never re-visited his daughter, who, in spite of her miraculous origin, does not appear to have distinguished herself in any way, at least up to the point at present reached by the history.

Miss Vaughan says that all the Elect Magi do not accept this legend of the blood royal, and she admits her own doubts subsequent to her conversion. As an article of intellectual faith I should prefer the birth-story of Gargantua, but it satisfied Miss Vaughan till the age of thirty years, and her father and grandfather before her, even supposing that it was *fabriquée par mon bisaïeul James, de Boston,* as hazarded by elect Magi whom a remnant of reason hinders.

The "Memoirs of an Ex-Palladist" have not at present proceeded further than the translation of Thomas Vaughan into the paradise of Lucifer, but from the "Free and Regenerated Palladium" and from other sources the chief incidents of Miss Vaughan's early life may be collected and summarised briefly. We learn that she is the daughter of an American Protestant of Kentucky and of a French lady, also of that persuasion. She was born in Paris, and a part of her education seems to have been received in that city; her mother died in Kentucky when Diana was in her fourteenth year, and I infer that subsequently to this event she must have lived with her father, who had considerable property in the immediate vicinity of Louisville. When the Sovereign Rite of Palladism was created by Albert Pike, Vaughan became affiliated therewith, and was one of the founders of the Louisville triangle 11 + 7; he presided at the initiation of his daughter as apprentice, according to the Rite of Adoption, in 1883. She was raised to the grade of Companion, and subsequently to that of Mistress, and at the age of 20 years, says Dr Bataille, she crossed the threshold of the Triangles, as the Palladian lodges are termed.

Three issues were published of "The Free and Regenerated Palladium," but since the conversion of Miss Vaughan, they have been withdrawn from circulation, except among ecclesiastics of the Roman Church, and up to the present I have failed to obtain copies. For the autobiographical portions of this organ, I am indebted to the notices which have appeared in the Revue Mensuelle. They contain an account of two apparitions on the part of the demon Asmodeus, accompanied by phenomena of levitation and fortified by arguments against the theory of hallucination. These early experiences are, however, of minor importance, nor need I again refer to the sensational incidents which accompanied her initiation as Templar-Mistress at the Paris Triangle of Saint-Jacques; but it appears from her memoirs that the intervention of Albert Pike was not in virtue of the supremacy of his personal authority, and that the ordeal of sacrilege was spared her by the clemency of Lucifer himself, who is supposed to appear in person at the Sanctum Regnum of Charleston and to instruct his chiefs, *Deo volente* or otherwise, every Friday, the supreme dogmatic director, who had made his home in Washington, having the gift of "instantaneous transportation," whensoever he thought fit to be present in the "divine" board-room.

On the 5th of April 1889, the "good God" assembled his Ancients and Emerites for a friendly conversation upon the "case" of Diana Vaughan, and ended by requesting an introduction in three days' time. After the best manner of the grimoires, Miss Vaughan began her preparations by a triduum, taking one meal daily of black bread, fritters of high-spiced blood, a salad of milky herbs, and the drink of rare old Rabelais. The preparations in detail are scarcely worth recording as they merely vary the directions in the popular chapbooks of magic which abound in foolish France. At the appointed time she passed through the iron doors of the Sanctum Regnum. "Fear not!" said Albert Pike, and she advanced *remplie d'une ardente allegresse,* was greeted by the eleven prime chiefs, who presently retired, possibly for prayer or refreshments, possibly for operations in wire-pulling. Diana Vaughan remained alone, in the presence of the Palladium, namely, our poor old friend Baphomet, whom his admirers persist in representing with a goat's head, whereas he is the archetype of the ass.

The Sanctum Regnum is described as triangular in shape; there was no torch, no lamp, no fire; the floor and the ceiling were therefore not unnaturally dark, but an inexplicable veil of strange phosphorescent light was diffused over the three walls, the source of which proved on examination to be innumerable particles of greenish flames each no larger than a pin's head. Seated in front of the Baphomet, Miss Vaughan apostrophised Lucifer sympathetically on the subject of the unpleasing form in which he was represented by his worshippers, and as she did so the little flames intensified, while floor and ceiling caught fire after the same ghostly incandescent fashion; a great dry heat filled the vast apartment, and, still spreading, the flames covered her chair, her garments, her entire person. At this point the inevitable thunder began to roll; three and one and two great thunders, after which came five breathings upon her face, and after those breathings five radiant spirits appeared, the first act closing impressively with a final salvo of artillery.

The unhappy Baphomet, dismayed by these extreme proceedings, vanished entirely, and, no expense being spared through the whole of the costly tableaux, Lucifer manifested on a throne of diamonds, but whether the gems were furnished from the treasury of Avernus or from the pockets of bamboozled Freemasons through the wide world, *les renseignments* do not state. Need I say that Miss Vaughan's first impulse was to fall in worship at his feet? But the sordid apparition, instead of accepting the homage with the grace which is native to empire, had recourse to the method of the novelist, and stayed her intention by a gesture. Even at this date, and with the millstone of her conversion placed in the opposite scale, Miss Vaughan's description of her quondam deity would tempt sentimental young women to forgive all his devildom to a being so "superb "in "masculine beauty." I will refrain from spoiling the picture by much of her own minuteness, or by the exclamatory parentheses of her fury against the magnificent gentleman who deceived her. I should like also to omit all reference to the conversation which ensued between them, but for the sake of true art I am constrained to state that Lucifer descended to commonplace. M. Renan tells us that since he left Saint Sulpice he did nothing but degenerate, and the inference is obvious, that he ought to have gone back to Saint Sulpice, despite the literary splendours of the *Vie de Jésus.* Since he last broke a lance with Michael, the devil has debilitated mentally, and the substance of his causerie with Diana reminds one of Robert Montgomery[1] and even worse exemplars. In the unexplored regions of penny periodical romance I have met with many better specimens of supernatural dialogue. As to the sum of his observations, it goes without saying that Diana was chosen out of thousands, and this is what justifies my opinion that his proceedings on this occasion were more fatuous than any of his undertakings since he tried conclusions with divinity.

Very silently during the course of this interview the eleven prime chiefs had returned like conspirators as they

1. Robert Montgomery (1807–1856), English cleric and prolific author of turgin religious poetry, including *Satan, or Intellect without God* (1830).

were, of course in the nick of time, to hear that Miss Vaughan was appointed as the grand-priestess of Lucifer, at which moment there was a fresh burst of circumambient flame and the young lady was transported by her divinity to take part in a grand spectacular drama, divided into two acts.—I. Appearance of Asmodeus with fourteen legions. Exchange of endearing expressions between this personage and Diana. Manifestation of the signature of Baal-Zeboub, generalissimo of the armies of Lucifer, written in fire upon the void. Spiritualisation of the sweetheart of Asmodeus. Diana hungers for the fray. Great pitched battle between the genii of Lucifer and the genii of Adonaï, termed Maleakhs, without the gates of Eden. The Terrestrial Paradise carried by storm after severe fighting. Grand panorama of Paradise. Explanatory dialogue between Diana and her future husband. Appearance of a snow white gigantic eagle on which Diana is to be transported to Oolis, "a solar world unknown to the profane, wherein Lucifer reigns and is adored." II. Miss Vaughan having been transported on another occasion to this mystic planet in the arms of Lucifer himself, the episodes of the second act are held over. She was, however, ultimately returned, safe and sound, to the Sanctum Regnum at Charleston, on the back of the white eagle.

Such is Miss Vaughan's statement, and once more she proceeds to give reasons why she could not have been hypnotised or hallucinated. As in the case of Doctor Bataille I propose to postpone criticism until other witnesses have filed their depositions. At the moment it is sufficient to recognise that, apart from the supernatural element which admits of a simple explanation, if Miss Vaughan be a credible witness, then the central fact of the New and Reformed Palladium must be admitted with all it involves.

CHAPTER IX

How Lucifer Is Unmasked

M. le Docteur Bataille is a mighty hunter before the face of the Lord in the land of Masonry, and through the whole country of Hiram; great also is Diana of the Palladians. After their monumental revelations and confessions, those of all other seceders and penitents who have come out of the mystery of iniquity, "are as moonlight unto sunlight, and as water unto wine." My readers in the two previous chapters have drunk raw spirit, and must now qualify it after the Scotch fashion. The aqueous intellectuality and quiet stream of unpretending deposition peculiar to M. Jean Kostka, will be well adapted to modify undue exaltations and restore order to a universe which has been intoxicated by sorcerers. He will show us how Lucifer is unmasked in an undemonstrative and gentlemanly fashion by a late Gnostic and initiate of the 33rd degree. He writes, as he frankly tells us, in a spirit of reparation and gratitude, having commerced freely with devils during a long series of unholy years. "Blessed be the omnipotent Lord, and blessed the loving kindness which drew me out of the abyss.... To glorify these I unmask the fallen angel." The delicacy of the motive and its setting of chivalrous sentiment will be appreciated even by the victim, and the tenderness of the treatment will prompt Lucifer to pardon his reviler, who has been already pardoned by M. Papus for betraying the order of the Martinists. And to do justice towards an amiable writer, who has scarcely the requisite qualities for seriously damaging or advancing any cause, it may be kind to add that he has considerably exaggerated his own case. After a careful examination of his statement, which is exceedingly naïve, I am tempted to conclude that he has never been near an abyss; he is innocent of either height or depth, and so far from having ever plunged into the infernal void, he has scarcely so much as paddled in a purgatorial puddle. His guilty transcendental experiences are in reality the most infantile afternoon occultism, and his drawing-room diablerie might be appropriately symbolized by the paper speaking-tube of our old friend John King;[1] there is nothing in it when the voice is not speaking, and there is nothing in it when it is.

Since his conversion, M. Jean Kostka has exhibited much harmless devotion towards Joan of Arc, an enthusiasm which originated among occultists, and he has pious memories of St

1. The alleged spirit 'control' of Mme Blawatsky and of other Spiritualist mediums.

Stanislaus Kostka, for which dispositions I trust that all my readers will have the complaisance to commend him. He writes, furthermore, "in the decline of maturity, on the threshold of age, in the late autumn of life," which is his dropsical method of saying that he is past sixty, and he veils a "futile name" under the patronymic of his favourite saint. Jean Kostka is not Jean Kostka, but it is without intent to deceive that he evades any possible responsibility in connection with his concealed identity; it is a kind of pious self-effacement. I hope everyone will believe what he says, and give him all credit for having "turned towards the outraged Church." In matters of evidence, pseudonymous statements are, however, objectionable, and I therefore identify our witness as Jules Doinel, who was chiefly concerned in the restoration of the Gnosis and the establishment of a "Gnostic church" in Paris about the year 1890, and is moreover not unknown as a Masonic orator, and in the world of belles-lettres. M. Papus, with the generosity of a mystic, can only speak well of the pious enthusiast who has betrayed his cause and scandalised the school he represents; he explains that Jules Doinel is a marvellous poet deficient in the scientific culture which might have enabled him to explain in a peaceable fashion the phenomena squandered upon him by the world invisible, so that there were only two courses open for him—renunciation of the transcendental path, or madness. "Let us bless heaven that the patriarch of the Gnosis has selected the former." It is possibly showing gratitude for small mercies, because our friend has saved his reason, but is blood-guilty in the matter of common sense. Meanwhile, the widowed Gnosis illuminates its Ichabod in the cryptic *quartiers* of Paris, Lyons, and so forth.

Every one may agree with M. Papus that Jean Kostka is a very pretty writer in a quiet and shallow way, but, with possibly one exception, he must have withheld the flower of his phenomena in the order of the spirit, for his book is full of sentimental and vapid experiences of the school-miss order, while over the light and spongy soil he has now set the ponderous paving-stones of his new explanation, and toils forward on the road of unreason.

This apart, Jean Kostka, was evidently for many years familiar with the centres and workings of all the cross lights of esoteric thought which meet and interlace in the night of French common thought. He has dwelt among Gnostics, Martinists, Modern Albigenses, and Spiritualists; he appears to have been identified with all, and though he does not accuse himself of the capital offence of conscious Satanism, he has been quite well acquainted with Satanism, and, next best to seeing the devil one's self, he has known many who have. In those days, he tells us, that Lucifer could be visited *chez lui* in an earthly tabernacle, situated in an unfrequented street, from whence the *lointain bruissement du Paris nocturne* might be heard by the pensive traveller if he were not too intent on diabolising. Now, he has found out that Lucifer was *chez lui* everywhere. *Je vise Satan et ses dogmes.* All his psychic faculties have concentrated into a transcendental apparatus for scenting devildom, and he mournfully comes forward to tell us, with a variation of Fludd's utterance; *Diabolus, in quam, diabolus ubique repertus est, et omnia diabolus et diabolus.* "Let it suffice to say that the demonologists have invented nothing and have exaggerated nothing." To the spiritualists Lucifer is John King and Allan Kardec;[1] to the Gnostics, he is the Gnosis, Simon Magus, Helen Ennoia, and anything that comes handy from the Nile valley in the fourth century; to the Martinists, he is the *philosophe inconnu;* to the Albigenses, if there are Parisian Albigenses, he is whatever Albigenses invoke, if they invoke anything; to Madame X., he is Mary Stuart; to his own adepts, within sound of the *lointain bruissement,* he is a *jeune homme blond aux yeux bleus,* whom I understand to have worn a dalmatic, and to have been curiously indebted to the author of *Aut Diabolus aut Nihil;* for the Theosophists, he is that "illustrious demoniac," Madame Blawatsky—his innate delicacy leads him to the permutation of the Typhon V.; and then Freemasonry—it goes without saying that the little horn of Lucifer has displaced all other horns in all the grades and lodges, that the fraternity is his throne and his footstool, and the city of the great king.

If we button-hole Jean Kostka, and ask him to tell us confidentially and upon honour what it is that has changed his views, making him discover the leer of Baal-Zeboub where he once saw the smile of the spiritual Eos, he turns Trappist at once, and goes into retreat with M. Huysman[s]; there is not a syllable of information in all his *beau volume* as to any intellectual process through which he passed on the way, and I suspect that his conversion partook of the nature

1. 'Allan Kardac' was the pseudonym of H. L. Denizard Rivail (1804–1869), the father of French spiritualism.

of a "penetration," to speak his own language, and was not an intellectual operation, but a sudden *volte face*. Jean Kostka has changed his *pinces-nez,* and that is the whole secret:—

> "The reason why I cannot tell,
> But now I hold it comes from hell."

Here is the proof positive; he has nothing in the shape of an accusation; he gets his Lucifer-interpretation out of everything with which he has cut off correspondence by a very simple and civil process of instillation. "I sense it"; *je vise Lucifer.* Thus, the Order of the Knights of Perfect Silence invite their initiates to become architects of the Holy City. Jean Kostka, in possession of the latest tip, says, "read Hell." The Martinists are concerned with the creation of Adam Kadmon, the ideal humanity. Jean Kostka tells you that they are concerned with nothing of the sort, and that Satan is the only person who can really put us up to the secret, which is curious because he immediately advises us himself that the exercise of the three cardinal virtues to the profit of Lucifer is the sum of the whole mystery and the real *sous-entendu* of Martinism. The Masonic grades from Apprentice, Companion, Master, through Knight Rose-Cross to Knight Kadosch, and so forward, are exploited after the same manner by the baldest of processes, that of inverting everything. For example, the sacred word of the 33rd degree in the French Rite, namely, Sovereign Grand Inspector General, is *Deus meumque Jus.* That signifies, says Jean Kostka, that "Lucifer is the sole God and that the material, like the spiritual, world of right belongs to him." If you inquire the process of extraction by which he gets that result, he answers: "I must admit that I have had only a general intuition, but I assure you that it is immense," and he will immediately cite you a password, invite you to take every letter individually, and fit to it just that word which, by another intuition, he perceives belongs to it, when you will see for yourself. Thus, the Kadosch term *Nekam,* which signifies vengeance, having been duly anatomised, will come out as follows:—N (ex) E (xterminatio) K (risti) A (dversarii) M (agni), to wit: "Death, Extermination of Christ, the Great Enemy." Wicked and wily Jean Kostka to outrage the decencies of orthography and against all reason write the name of the Liberator with a K, thereby concealing the true meaning, which revealed for the first time is as follows:—N (equaquam) E (ritis) K (ostka) A (rtium) M (agister), which being interpreted still further, signifies that there was never such a clumsy device!

Now, it goes without saying that a writer with these methods is not to be taken seriously, but it is worth while to appreciate the quality of intelligence which is received with acclamation by the Catholic Church in France as soon as it comes over from the enemy. "Lucifer Unmasked" appeared originally in the pages of the newspaper *La Vérité.* It was immediately reproduced in Spanish by the *Union Catolica;* the clerical press boomed full-mouthed salvos in its honour, and his Eminence Cardinal Parocchi has blessed book or author, or both, and believes that it will make a great impression, "undoubtedly contributing to enlighten minds and lead them back to God."

Jean Kostka, as already indicated, is a spiritual sentimentalist; he has passed by a rapid transition common to such natures from the Gnostic transcendental initiate to the pious Catholic devotee, and he will make an excellent Lourdes pilgrim. As there will be no need to recur to him again, it will be permissible to justify my criticism by some account of his personal experiences. M. Papus speaks of him as the founder and patriarch of the Gnostic Church. Of this same patriarch and primate Jean Kostka also speaks as of another person, recites the facts of his conversion, and hopes he will do better work for the Church of God than he has done for Lucifer. Which is Dr Jekyll and which Mr Hyde in this duadic personality is not of serious consequence, as they have both got into a better way of thinking and acting. Now, since his demission from these high functions, Jean Kostka has found that the chief piece of Gnostic devilry is in denying that the lost angels are eternally damned. On this point he has attained what is rare in him, a touch of personal animosity. To supply the antipodes of heaven, let us say, with a lethal chamber, as a meaner order than that of theological charity does here, in the interests of homeless and snappy dogs, would, in his present state of grace, seem a very wicked proposition. Well, in 1890 Jean Kostka was invited, as I understand, by the chief of the Gnostic Church, that is, by himself, to a chapel in the palace of a lady who figures frequently in his pages under the name of Madame X.; the author takes great credit for concealing her real titles, but he has failed to conceal her identity, and there can be no harm in saying that the reference is to Lady Caithness. He was present upon serious business, in fact, nothing short of assisting at a séance. A medium had been secured, the proceedings began, rappings became audible, an intelligence desired to communicate, and, finally, there was a message, with a name given. It was Luciabel, "whom you know as Lucifer." To this day Jean Kostka does not seem conscious of any element of idiocy in the variation of the old-fashioned name. In the revelation which followed, the intelligence, who seemed amiably disposed despite his sinister connections, informed the circle that, like Jesus, he was engendered eternally from God, that he was exiled from the pleroma, and that he was the Sophia-Achamoth of Valentine, the Helena-Ennoia of Simon Magus, the thought of God which had become anathema, and that he was now in search of love and consolation, both of which might take shape in a Gnostic church and would be highly acceptable. There is, so to speak, a commercial element in the overtures which dries up the feeling of pity, or one might be exceedingly sorry for this lost chord of eternal thought, hoping charitably that we should still somehow hear it in heaven.

Since his conversion the unpretentious marvel of this séance has been a dire trouble to Jean Kostka, partly on account of its eschatology, but still more because the sitters were conscious at its close of a breath passing over their faces, while he himself felt the presence of lips against his own. Poor Jean Kostka! They were all abased on their knees, which happens occasionally, even at séances, to pious people in Paris, and he concludes that he was kissed by Helena-Ennoia, *alias* Lucifer, *alias* Luciabel, who is also described on the charge-sheet of orthodox theology by other and more objectionable titles. The shameful memory causes him to exclaim fervently:—"May he who purged the lips of Isaiah with a burning coal deign to purify mine by the sacred kiss of penitence and pardon: *in osculo sancto.*" There is a touch of sublimity in that, and the *basia* of Baal-Zeboub may well enough be more demoralising than those of Secundus. At the time, however, he founded the Gnostic Church.

We become acquainted with ghosts after various manners, according to our psychic condition. There is the spontaneous and accidental ghost who is seldom caught in the act; there is the able-bodied materialised ghost whom we catch in the act occasionally, and preserve our mental balance by clinging to his watch-chain and seals; they may be distinguished as the timeless ghost and the ghost who occasionally does time. Over and above these two generic specimens there is the ghost that throws, who is separable from the ghost that *hurls,* as our French friends put it. To hurl is to utter objectionable and unreasonable yells, preferably in the dead of night and in lonely places. This ghost is much sought after by specialists.

It would be tedious to name all the varieties, but I can guarantee the unequipped that all known specimens have been carefully labelled, except possibly the odorous ghost, the ghost, that is to say, who manifests exclusively to the olfactory organ. This is an exceedingly withdrawn inappreciable kind, but it is familiar to Jean Kostka, who is a connoisseur in the smell supernatural, and has a trained psychic nose. He can distinguish between the spiritual perfume which characterises, let us say, St Stanislaus and the *odorem suavitatis* of Lucifer. He also an authority on conditions, and gives a ravishing description of the voluptuous enervation diffused over all his limbs when he had a private memorandum from Isis by means of raps during the reception of a master in a blue lodge. On this occasion he tells us that he was inspired to pronounce one of his most wicked and dangerous Masonic discourses. Dear M. Kostka! Dynamite would lose its destroying power in his harmless hands.

At another function—but this was in a red lodge—he was overwhelmed by the presence of Lucifer, who elected and commissioned him to fight in his cause. It was a moment of unwonted intelligence—these are his own words—and he agreed, so incompetence chose its minister, and Frater Diabolus again showed himself a short-sighted rogue, because has not his emissary converted and passed over to the makers of pilgrimages? M. Kostka also at this time was so wicked as to be guilty of a pact, but he reserved two points, "the person of Christ and His mother." The reservation of these sacraments is not specialised as to its kind, but, *mon Dieu,* how distraught was Lucifer to be so palpably tricked by a *trente troisième!* Both these matters were, however, personal to the seer, and the lodges, whether red or blue, seem to have been quite unconscious that they had been entertaining divinity and demon unawares. M. Kostka has, in fact, been distinguished from the common herd of Masons by many favours of Lucifer, and he has naturally been ungrateful, for which I admire M. Kostka.

In succeeding chapters he details at considerable length a variety of hallucinations which experienced on the subject of Helena-Ennoia, and he has also had visions of Jansen, of a false Francis Xavier, a false Christ, &c., but his most important experience was that which he terms Penetration, commonly experienced in autumn seasons and during the mists and mildness of October nights. On these occasions he was conscious of a curious extension of personality by which he seemed to enter into all Nature, and all Nature took voice and interpreted herself intelligibly to him. After music came verbal communications, and then the apparition of forms, chiefly of classical mythology. Most people would have termed this poetic rapture passing into lucidity, but our friend avers that it is the Enemy.

Such have been the experiences and adventures of Jean Kostka in the psychic world, and they are of precisely the same calibre as his critical method. I may say, in conclusion, that, if spared, he will do better in his next book, for he promises another, which is to exhibit in a convincing manner how Lucifer has been vanquished by Joan of Arc. In the meantime we may part from him with due recognition of his absolute good faith and extreme amiability; we may congratulate him on his conversion, and still more upon the very pleasant reading he provides; he does not appear to have unmasked Lucifer, but he has let us into the secret of the best that can be done in that way.

Lastly, the point to be marked in connection with the memoirs and revelations of Jean Kostka is this, that neither in Paris nor elsewhere, neither in Masonry nor in other secret associations, concerning which he has had every opportunity to judge, has he come personally into contact with a cultus of Satan or Lucifer; that he chooses to term certain mystical opinions and practices diabolical, because they are condemned by the Latin Church, is a matter which is perfectly indifferent and exhibits only the forlorn position of a case which resorts to the expedient. But it is highly significant that a man who has mixed among mystics of all grades for probably thirty years, who is affiliated to innumerable orders, and in his present mood would be glad to expose everything, has nothing to tell us of the Palladium, though he dwelt at its gates, and the circles he frequented were at a stone's cast from the alleged Mother-Lodge Lotus of Paris.

CHAPTER X

The Vendetta of Signor Margiotta

To Signor Domenico Margiotta we owe the most explicit account of the great compact between Mazzini and Albert Pike which produced the New and Reformed Palladium. With this institution he does not attempt to connect the anterior order founded in 1730; for him the possession of the Templar Baphomet explains the name which it received, and the passage of that idol from its original custodians he leaves in the same uncertainty as Dr Bataille. This difficulty apart, in Signor Margiotta the question of Lucifer has received a most important witness; he is the most recent, the most illustrious, and masonically the most decorated of all. If I add that he is in one respect to be included among the most virulent, I do not necessarily detract from his value. So far as one can possibly be aware, he is a man of unimpeachable integrity, who gives us every opportunity to identify him, heraldically by his arms and emblazonments, historically by an account of his family, personally by extracts from the *Dizionario Biografico,* masonically by a full enumeration of all his dignities, including photographs of his most brilliant diplomas and printed correspondence from Grand Masters and other exalted potentates of the great Fraternity. It would be difficult, however, in the last respect, to discover many more exalted than himself, for before his demission he was Secretary of the Lodge Savonarola of Florence; Venerable of the Lodge Giordano Bruno of Palmi; Sovereign Grand Inspector General, 33rd degree, of the Ancient and Accepted Scotch Rite; Sovereign Prince of the Order (33rd∴ 90th∴ 95th∴) of the Rite of Memphis and Misraïm; Acting Member of the Sovereign Sanctuary of the Oriental Order of Memphis and Misraïm of Naples; Inspector of the Misraïm Lodges of the Calabrias and of Sicily; Honorary Member of the National Grand Orient of Haiti; Acting Member of the Supreme Federal Council of Naples; Inspector-General of all the Masonic Lodges of the three Calabrias; Grand Master, *ad vitam,* of the Oriental Masonic Order of Misraïm or Egypt (90th degree) of Paris; Commander of the Order of Knights-Defenders of Universal Masonry; Honorary Member, *ad vitam,* of the Supreme General Council of the Italian Federation of Palermo; Permanent Inspector and Sovereign Delegate of the Grand Central Directory of Naples for Europe (Universal High-grade Masonry), and, according to his latest portrait, Member of the New Reformed Palladium. That such a luminary could withdraw from the firmament of the Fraternity and not take after him the third part of the stars of heaven, above all that the Italian Grand Master could have the effrontery to affirm that he had never heard of him and had only discovered who he was after some investigation, are matters for astonishment to the simple.

Professor Margiotta returned to the church of his childhood in the autumn of 1894, and the news of his conversion is said to have so overwhelmed the head-quarters of Italian Freemasonry at Rome that the annual rejoicings upon the 20th of September, when Rome became the Capital of United Italy and when Universal Freemasonry was instituted in 1870, were incontinently suspended. My readers will not attach a high degree of accuracy to this statement, for there does not appear in reality to have been any convulsion of the Order; there was indeed more rejoicing in Jerusalem than lamentation in the tents of Kedron. Signor Margiotta was the recipient of flattering congratulations from eminent prelates; the bishop of Grenoble salutes him as "my dear friend"; the patriarch of Jerusalem invites him to take courage, for he is doing high service to humanity, labouring under the scourge of the Masonic plague; the bishop of Montauban expresses his lively sentiment and entire devotion; the archbishop of Aix regards the revelations as of great importance to the Church; the bishop of Limoges praises and blesses the books of M. Margiotta; the bishop of Mende does likewise, his enthusiasm taking shape in superlatives; the Cardinal-Archbishop of Bordeaux applauds the intention and the effort; the bishops of Tarentaise, of Oran, of Pamiers, of Annecy, take up the chant in turn, and his Holiness the Pope himself sends his Apostolic Benediction over the seal of Peter.

Why did Signor Margiotta abandon Palladism and Masonry? It was not because these institutions were devoted to the cultus of Lucifer, for I do not gather that he was scandalised by that fact at the time when it appears to have become known to him. It was not because sacrilege and public indecency characterised the rituals of initiation in the case of the Palladian Order, for he does not zealously press this charge. It was not, so far as can be traced, because he trembled for the safety of his soul; he does not provide us with a sickly and suspicious narrative of the sentiments which led to his conversion or the interior raptures which followed it; he does not mention that he was the recipient of a special grace or a sudden illustration; he ceased to believe in Lucifer as the good God because that being had permitted his favoured Freemasonry to pass under the "supreme direction of a despised personage who is the last of rogues." In other words, Signor Domenico Margiotta has a strong loathing for Signor Adriano Lemmi; he has long and earnestly desired that Freemasonry should "vomit him" from her breast, but as this has not come to pass, Signor Margiotta decided to vomit himself. Now, when a man embraces religion, he is supposed to forgive his enemies, to do good to them that hate him, to avoid the propagation of scandals, and when he cannot speak well to say nothing; but this is not the special quality of grace which attaches to the second *trente-troisième,* who has come out of Freemasonry to expose and revile the order.

The two narratives which comprise the exposure in question are respectively "Adriano Lemmi: Supreme Chief of Freemasonry," and" Palladism, the Cultus of Satan-Lucifer." Both these books contain a violent impeachment of the

Italian Grand Master which, if it concerned us, would not convince us. Its main points go to show that in the days of his boyhood, Lemmi was guilty of an embezzlement at Marseilles, for which he is said to have suffered at the hands of justice; that he led the life of a Guzman d'Alfarache, in itself sufficiently romantic to condone an offence which should have been effaced with its penalty, supposing the allegation to be true; that he subsequently found himself at Constantinople, where he was thrown among Jews, and is there charged by his accuser with the commission of a still more terrible crime; he, in fact, became a proselyte of the gate, and suffered the rite of circumcision. Later on he is depicted as a political conspirator, an agent and friend of Mazzini, Kossuth, and the patriots of the Revolution, in connection with whom he is made responsible for innumerable villainies which connect him with the apostleship of dynamite. We may pass lightly over these matters, nor need we delay to inquire after what manner Adriano Lemmi may have amassed the wealth which he possesses, nor what questions on the subject of a monopoly in tobacco may have been raised or dropped in the Italian Parliament. All these points, including Signor Lemmi himself, are as little known as they are of little moment in England, and they are wholly outside our subject, except in so far as they exhibit the methods of his accuser, which, indeed, are so objectionable in their nature as to go far towards exonerating their object. Signor Margiotta, at any rate, puts himself so clearly in the wrong, and is altogether so virulent, as to place the inference of personal animosity almost in the region of certitude; one is therefore tempted to accept the explanation offered by the victim, that the Marseilles scandal turns upon a mistaken identity, and his explicit denial that he ever underwent the rite of Jewish initiation. Furthermore, I believe that I shall represent the opinion of tolerant Englishmen when I say that to insult and abuse a man for adopting another faith, however opposed to our own, and even ridiculous in itself, is an odious method in controversy, and for myself I see little to choose between a proselyte of the gate, a renegade Mason, and a demitted Roman Catholic.

The true secret of the Margiotta-cum-Lemmi embroilment does not, I think, transpire in the narratives with which we are concerned; I mean to say that there is an eluding element which must, however, be assumed, if we are to account reasonably for the display of such extreme rancour. An honourable man may object to the jurisdiction of a person whom he regards as a convicted thief, but he does not usually pursue him with the violence of personal hatred. Now, in 1888 Signor Margiotta became a candidate for the Italian Parliament, and he attributes his failure to the hostility of Lemmi, who, prompted by Gallophobe tendencies, brought his influence to bear against a person who was friendly to the French nation. I submit that this assists us to understand the animus of the converted Mason and the lengths to which it has taken him. In all other respects Signor Margiotta displays the most perfect frankness, and does his best upon every occasion to substantiate his statements by formidable documentary evidence. I repeat therefore, that, much as we may regret his acrimony, he remains a most important witness to the existence of Universal Masonry, the existence of the Reformed Palladium, the transfer of the Masonic Supremacy at the death of Albert Pike to the Italian Grand Master, and the split in the camp which followed. He claims also that he is personally acquainted with Miss Diana Vaughan; he extols her innumerable virtues in pages of eloquent writing; he even goes so far as to photograph the envelope of a registered letter which he posted at Palmi, in Calabria, addressed to that lady in London. He indirectly substantiates the narrative of Carbuccia by a long account of his personal dealings with Giambattista Pessina, descending into the most curious particulars; he publishes the secret alphabet of the Palladium, specimens of litanies addressed to the good god Lucifer, and hymns of equivocal tendency attributed to Albert Pike. Finally, he fully admits the Satanic character of perfect Masonic initiation, and contributes a long chapter to swell our recent knowledge upon the subject of "Apparitions of Satan."

As regards Universal Masonry, when announcing his demission and conversion to an officer of the Lodge, Giordano Bruno, at Palmi, Signor Margiotta reveals to him that he and his brethren are ruled, without knowing it, by a supreme rite, and that he, Margiotta himself, Venerable of the Lodge referred to, being a true elect and perfect initiate, constituted the link of connection between the ordinary Masonry of Palmi and this central and unsuspected power. On the same occasion he addressed a long communication to Miss Vaughan, in which he claims that he has ever acted as an honest Mason, faithful to the orthodoxy thereof, and having the cause of Charleston at heart. Now, the circumstances which occasioned these statements, and the good faith which seems to characterise them, are presumptive testimony to their truth; in the absence of any evidence, and merely on *à priori* considerations, it would be intolerable to suggest that their author, while advertising his changed views upon a solemn subject, was guilty of wilful deception.

The centralisation of Universal Masonry in an order known as the New and Reformed Palladium, with Albert Pike at its head, is supported by the citation of a document dated the 12th of September 1874, and being an authority from Charleston for the constitution of a secret federation of Jewish Freemasons, with a centre at Hamburg, under the title of Sovereign Patriarchal Council. It is not the only document emanating from the "Dogmatic Directory" which is printed by Signor Margiotta, but the others are not entirely new, having some of them previously appeared in the memoirs of Dr Bataille. The Luciferian opinions of Albert Pike are exhibited plainly in a letter addressed by him to Signor Rapisardi, famous in all Italy for his poem of "Lucifer," which Signor Margiotta affirms to have been written at the suggestion of the American Grand Master.

But possibly the strongest evidence is less of a documentary kind; the minute account of the warfare waged by Signor Margiotta and other Italian Masons, in which they were helped by Miss Vaughan, to prevent the accession of Lemmi to the sovereign pontificate upon the death of Albert Pike and the transfer of the centre to Rome, seems to bear upon its surface every reasonable sign that it cannot be an invented narrative. Indeed, the first impulse upon reading the testimony of this witness leaps irresistibly to conclude that the denial of the main allegations is no longer possible. A searching analysis does, however, reveal sufficient grounds to warrant a different judgment. In the first place, whereas

Signor Margiotta proclaims the supreme power of the Reformed Palladium, the documents which he cites in his support are, for the most part, documents of the Ancient and Accepted Scotch Rite, about the immense jurisdiction of which there is no question. In the second place, the authority of Albert Pike, as it is seen in most of the documents, is in virtue, not of the Palladium, but of his position as Supreme Chief of the Supreme Mother-Council of the Ancient and Accepted Scotch Rite. What Signor Margiotta terms Universal Freemasonry is not the Palladium at all, but simply the Scotch Rite; one of his own diplomas, reproduced at page 120 of "Adriano Lemmi," is proof positive of this; and in view of the universal diffusion of this rite, no one would deny it the name. In the third place, the documents of Signor Margiotta as regards the Palladium are not to be trusted, because in one instance a gross imposition has been practised provably upon him, and he may have been deceived in others. Hence, although he may be a member of a society termed the New and Reformed Palladium, it may not possess the jurisdiction or the history to which it pretends. In the fourth place I deny that the Grand Central Directories of which I have given particulars, derived from Signor Margiotta, in my second chapter, are in any sense Palladian directories. That of Naples for Europe is said to have twenty-seven triangular provinces, one of which is Manchester, and Mr John Yarker is said to be Provincial Grand Master. Now, I have Mr Yarker's own written testimony that he never heard of the Palladium until the report of it came over from France. Mr Yarker is a member of the 33rd degree of the Ancient and Accepted Scotch Rite, and he is also the Grand Master of the only legitimate body of the Supreme Oriental Rite of Memphis and Misraïm in England, Scotland, and Ireland. Moreover, in most Masonic countries of the world he is either Honorary Grand Master, or Honorary Member in the 95° of Memphis, 90° of Misraïm, and 33° Scottish Rite, the last honorary membership including bodies under the Pike *régime* as well as its opponents. He is perfectly well acquainted with the claim of the Charleston Supreme Council to supreme power in Masonry, and that it is a usurpation founded on a forgery. In a letter which he had occasion to address some time since to a Catholic priest on this very subject, he remarks:—"The late Albert Pike of Charleston, as an able mason, was undoubtedly a Masonic Pope, who kept in leading strings all the Supreme Grand Councils of the world, including the Supreme Grand Councils of England, Ireland, and Scotland, the first of which includes the Prince of Wales, Lord Lathom, and other peers, who were in alliance with him, and in actual submission. Its introduction into America arose from a temporary schism in France in 1762, when Lacorne, a disreputable panderer to the Prince of Clermont, issued a patent to a Jew named Stephen Morin. Some time after 1802, a pretended Constitution was forged and attributed to Frederick the Great of Prussia. This constitution gives power to members of the 33rd degree to *elect themselves* to rule all Masonry, and this custom is followed. . . . The good feeling of Masonry has been perpetually destroyed in every country where the Ancient and Accepted Rite exists, and it must be so in the very nature of its claims and its laws." Mr Yarker has no connection with a supreme dogmatic directorate in any other form than this disputed but perfectly well-known assumption of the Charleston Supreme Council. The term "Supreme Dogmatic Directorate" was not used by Pike, and the confidence enjoyed by the American was never extended to Lemmi, though he may have desired it. Instead, therefore, of all Masonry being ruled by a central authority unknown to the majority of Masons, we have simply a bogus claim which has no effect outside the Scottish Rite, and of which all Masons may know if they will be at the pains to ascertain. When Signor Margiotta informed the officer of the Giordano Bruno Lodge that he secretly represented a central and unknown authority, it is in this sense that we must understand him—that is to say, he represented the interests of the Charleston Supreme Council. Hence the revelations concerning "Universal Masonry" are an exaggeration founded upon a fact, and the Palladian Order, of which Signor Margiotta tells us that he is a member, is at any rate not what it pretends. It has doubtless imposed on him by means of forged documents, as also upon Leo Taxil, and M. Adolphe Ricoux. The writings which it fathers upon Albert Pike, and quoted by Signor Margiotta, as in other cases, are stolen from Éliphas Lévi, the so-called alphabet of the Palladium included. The documentary *pièce de résistance* upon which our author relies as evidence for the existence of an international masonic organisation is a certain *voûte de Protestation,* on the part of a so-called Mother-Lodge Lotus of England, secret Temple of Oxford Street, against the transfer of the Dogmatic Directory from Charleston to Rome, the "Standing Committee of Protestation" being Alexander Graveson, Provincial Delegate of Philadelphia, U.S.A., V. F. Palacios, Provincial Delegate of

Mexico, and Diana Vaughan, Provincial Delegate of New York and Brooklyn. Signor Domenico Margiotta has been grossly deceived over this document. What he prints as the English original in guarantee of good faith, side by side with a French translation, is a clumsy and ridiculous specimen of "English as she is wrote," and the French is really the original. I append some choice specimens:—"To the Most Illustrious, Most Puissant, Most *Lightened* Brothers . . . composing, by right of *Ancient and Members for life,* the Most Serene Grand College of *Emerited Masons."* Here the underlined passages are a Frenchman's method of interpreting into English *Très Eclairés Frères, à titre d'Anciens et de membres à vie,* and *Maçons Emérites.* Again "The protesters numbered six-and-twenty, including twenty-five *sovereign* delegates present at the deed, and one sovereign delegate, who could not *stand by (ne peut être présent),* but the substitute of which wisely and prudently abstained from the vote *at the first turn (au premier scrutin)* and threw a blank ticket at the second, *expound* (verb governed by *protesters*) the *acts and situation thence disastrously resulting* for our holy cause."

Once more: "The present protesting vault *aims at the two ballots (vise les deux scrutins),* and *requests to be proceeded* urgently to their annulment." Again: *"The Charleston's Brothers* . . . have not acted in such a manner as to forfeit *the whole Masonry's esteem* . . . The direction . . . has *not discontinued to prove foresight* . . . It was *injust* to transfer," &c., and so on for sixteen printed pages which certainly deserve to rank among the curiosities of literature. This is the precious document which appears over the signatures of Alexander Graveson and Diana Vaughan, after which I submit to my readers that Signor

Domenico Margiotta may be dismissed with all his file of papers, not as himself deceiving, but as singularly liable to deception, of which he has otherwise given us several signal instances. For example he believes himself to have enjoyed the high privilege of beholding the Prince of Darkness upon two separate occasions. The first was in 1885 at Castelnuovo-Garfagnana in a beautiful old walled garden, belonging to a high-grade Mason named Orestes Cecchi, a fast friend of Margiotta. The time was the forenoon, and the two Masons were smoking under the shade of green trees surrounded by floral delights. Margiotta was a spiritualist and a follower of Allan Kardec; Cecchi had a turn for the Vedas and the occultism of the Eastern world; they were chatting upon the possibility of transmigration; the one doubted, the other affirmed; Cecchi, to convince his companion, informed him that he possessed a familiar who invariably appeared to him under the form of a goat, but he had a look in his eye which proved positively that he was the Grand Architect of the Universe! That there might be no doubt about the matter Cecchi called his familiar, who appeared suddenly, and joyfully caressed his master, at whose command he subsequently licked the hand of the overwhelmed Signor Margiotta, and it became red and painful. Cecchi playfully chided the apparition for not assuming human form, and hinted at the propriety of doing so, but the animal knowingly nodded and incontinently scurried away. Now, I put it to my readers, that Cecchi was exploiting his friend, that a domesticated animal appeared at the summons of his owner in a wooded garden, and that Signor Margiotta is fooling when he pretends to believe that it was the devil.

The second experience was at Naples under the roof of Pessina, about half-past ten in the evening, after a Lodge meeting of the Misraïm rite. Then and there, as a matter of cordial good fellowship, the accommodating Imperial Grand Master evoked a devil to give evidence of his actuality to Margiotta, who, in spite of the episode of the goat, still posed as a doubting Thomas. It was managed by means of a whisky-bottle, out of which, after certain invocations and magical ceremonies, a vapour rose mysteriously, and resolved itself into a human figure, wearing a golden crown, with a brilliant star in the middle. According to the picture which accompanies this delicious narrative, the apparition had the wings of a bat and a tail of the bovine class. It was Beffabuc, the familiar of the magician, who begged him to enlighten the sceptic, but the latter, according to the apparition, was protected by a higher power and would never be persuaded to believe in him. Signor Margiotta gives the names of all who were present at the evocation—twelve members of the 33rd degree, to say nothing of Misraïm dignities. I submit, however, that the episode of the bottle would split the rock of Peter, that the absence of Signor Pessina for twenty minutes previous to the performance, eked out with a little ventriloquism, and some Pepper accessories would explain much, and that there is also another hypothesis which I will leave to the discernment of my readers, and to which I lean personally.

Our witness, in any case, would not be a *persona grata* to the Society for Psychical Research. As he is violent in his enmities, so is he gullible in marvels. His impeachment of Adriano Lemmi must be ruled completely out of court; his thaumaturgic experiences are paltry trickeries; his account of Albert Pike is largely borrowed matter; the magical practices which he attributes to Pessina are derived from the Little Albert and other well known grimoires; the most that follows from his narrative is that certain Italian Masons, probably atheists at heart, pose as partisans of Satan simply to accentuate their derisions of all religious ideas, much after the manner of Voltaire in some of his cynical correspondence. It is a continental form of pleasantry, and an artistic experiment in blasphemy which is taken seriously by the unwise.

I need hardly add that the story of *Aut Diabolus aut Nihil,* which is accepted literally by Doctor Bataille, is also the subject of reverential belief on the part of Signor Margiotta, and as an illustration of his classifying talent, he terms Adriano Lemmi a Mormon because, having obtained a divorce, he, in the course of time, contracted another marriage. Furthermore, the very strong testimony which Signor Margiotta gives to Dr Bataille, directly by eulogium and indirectly by citation, as also the intimate relations which he maintained with Diana Vaughan, make his value as a witness of Lucifer dependent, to a large extent, upon the credibility of these persons, with consequences which will shortly appear. Lastly, his own personal credibility seems seriously at stake when he talks of "triangular provinces." He, and those connected with him, can alone explain what that means; they have never existed in Masonry. Mr Yarker, who, he says, is Grand Master of such a province, has never heard the expression. Mr R. S. Brown, Grand Secretary of the Supreme Grand Royal Arch Chapter of Scotland, also denies all knowledge of the one which, according to Signor Margiotta, is located at Edinburgh.

CHAPTER XI

Female Freemasonry

LAST ON THE LIST of our recent witnesses who have had a hand in creating the Question of Lucifer—not actually last in the order of time but the least in importance to our purpose—is M. A. C. de la Rive, author of "Child and Woman in Universal Freemasonry." He very fairly fulfils the presumption which is warranted by his name; he does not pretend to have come forth from the turbid torrent of Satanism and Masonry which is carrying multitudes into the abyss and effacing temples and thrones in its furious course. He has been content, like a sensible person, to stand on bank or brink and watch the rage and flow. He does not tell us anywhere in his narrative that he is himself a Mason; he has no personal acquaintance with Satan; he has not been guilty of magic, nor has he assisted at a Black Mass. He belongs to a wholly different order of witnesses, and he has produced what is in its way a genuine book, which does not pretend to be more than a careful compilation from rare but published sources, while we can all of us defer to the erudition of a Frenchman who has actually spent on collecting his materials the almost unheard-of space of twelve months. The result is correctly described as "grand in octavo, 746 pages," and is really an inflated piece of Masonic chronology, exceedingly ill-balanced, but, at the same time, undeniably useful. Beginning with the year 1730 it is brought down to 1894, and it is designed to demonstrate the existence at the present day of "adoptive lodges" wherein French gallantry once provided an inexpensive substitute for Masonry in which ladies had the privilege of participating. One of the most learned and illustrious of French Masonic writers, Jean-Marie Ragon, describes such androgyne or female lodges as "amiable institutions" invented by an unknown person some time previously to the year 1730, under the name of "mysterious amusements," which appears to describe them exactly, and one cannot be otherwise than astonished at the extraordinary gravity of nervous and well-intentioned persons who ascribe them such tremendous importance. Whereas they are the fringe of Freemasonry, writers like M. de la Rive persist in regarding them as its heart and centre, while it is also in such institutions that he and others of his calibre expect to discover Satanism. A celibate religion ever suspects the serpent in the neighbourhood of the woman. He discovers Satanism accordingly by reading it into handy passages and bracketing interpretations of his own when the text cannot otherwise be worked. Thus he gets oracles everywhere, and to compel Satan he finds the parenthesis quite as useful as the circle of black magic; it is a juggler's method, but among French anti-Masons it passes with high credit. The question of Female Freemasonry, apart from the Palladian Order, is quite outside our subject; its existence in Spain is a matter of public knowledge, and I have Mr Yarker's authority for stating that in certain countries, one of which is South America, the Rite of Memphis and Misraïm and the Ancient and Accepted Scotch Rite have both initiated women, the latter up to and including the 33rd degree. No adoptive lodges exist or would be tolerated in England within the jurisdiction of the Grand Lodge, and if it can be shown that the Palladian order initiates English women into Masonic secrets, that is performed surreptitiously and in defiance of our Masonic constitutions. As to the schismatic Grand Orient of France, whatever may be done in secret or devised in public upon this point, is of no importance here, but I should add that little credit, and deservedly, is attached in England to any of the so-called revelations which from time to time come over from Paris.

As regards M. de la Rive, apart from this subject, we are unable to extract from his pages anything that is fresh or informing on the subject of our inquiry. Despite the sensational picture which emblazons the title-page, where a full-length Baphomet is directing a *décolletée* Templar-Mistress through the pillars Jakin and Bohaz, there is not a single page in the whole vast compilation which shows any connection between Satanism and Masonry until towards the close, when an adroit tax is levied on the still vaster storehouse of Doctor Bataille. The author tells us clearly enough how adoptive Masonry arose, what rites were instituted, what rituals published, what is contained in these, and it is all solid and instructive. His facts, as already indicated, are borrowed facts, but they come from a variety of sources, and original research was scarcely to be expected from a writer against whom the avenues of knowledge are sealed by his lack of initiation. He concludes, however, that Adoptive Masonry is Satanic by intention, and that even the orphanages of the Fraternity are part of a profound and infamous design to ruin the children of humanity and to perfect proselytes for perdition.

The appearance of "Child and Woman in Universal Freemasonry" was hailed with acclamation in the columns of the *Revue Mensuelle;* it reviewed it by dreary instalments, and when reviewing was no longer possible, had recourse to tremendous citations; as a last effort, it supplied an exhaustive index to the whole work—a charitable and necessary action, for the twelve months' toil of the author had expired without the accomplishment of this serviceable means of reference. And still, as occasion offers, it gives it bold advertisement.

The quaint methods of previous witnesses are amplified by M. de la Rive. Like Dr Bataille, he tells us that the Order of Oddfellows, though quite distinct from Palladism, is "essentially Luciferian," but he does not say why or how—instance of demonstrative method. He regards the Jews with holy hatred as chief ministers of Anti Christ, and characterises them as that nation of which Judas was "one of the most celebrated personages"—specimen recipe for the production of cheap odium in large quantities; but what about Jesus the Christ, whom men called King of the Jews? Fie, M. de la Rive! He informs us that Miss Alice Booth, daughter of General Booth, the founder of the Salvation Army, is one of the foremost Palladists of England—instance of absurd slander which refutes itself.

M. de la Rive must therefore on all counts of his evidence be ruled out of court as a witness. No one denies the existence of Adoptive Lodges in a few countries and under special circumstances, and no sensible person attributes them any importance. Freemasonry as an institution is not suited to women any more than is cricket as a sport, but they have occasionally wished to play at it as they have wished to play at cricket; the opportunity has been offered them, but, except as the vogue of a moment, it has come to nothing. It is, moreover, of no importance to our inquiry if it can be proved that the true head of the Grand Lodge in England is the Princess of Wales and not her royal husband; while concerning the existence of Devil-Worship M. de la Rive has nothing new to tell us, and nothing at first-hand. I therefore ask leave to dismiss him, hoping that he will devote another laborious year to the reissue of Masonic rituals, authentic or not, at the extremely moderate price which he asks for his first volume; originals are scarce and costly, and invention is a pleasant faculty. The interpretation which he chooses to put on them is an interpretation of no consequence, and can never have misled any one who is in any sense worth misleading.

CHAPTER XII

THE PASSING OF DOCTOR BATAILLE

THE MOST OBVIOUS line of criticism in connection with the memoirs entitled *Le Diable au XIXe Siècle* would be the preposterous and impossible nature of its supernatural narratives. To attribute a historical veracity to the adventures of Baron Munchausen might scarcely appear more unserious than to accept this *récit d'un témoin* as evidence for transcendental phenomena. I need scarcely say that I regard this reasoning as so altogether sound and applicable that it is almost unnecessary to develop it. The personal adventures of Doctor Bataille as regards their supernatural element are so transparently fabulous that it would be intolerable to regard them from any other point of view. That an ape should speak Tamil is beyond the bounds of possibility; it is impossible also that a female fakir or pythoness, aged 152 years, should allow herself to be consumed in a leisurely manner by fire; it is impossible that any ascetics could have maintained life in their organisms under the loathsome conditions prevailing within the alleged temple at Pondicherry; it is impossible that any person could have survived the ordeal which Dr Bataille pretends to have suffered at Calcutta,—to have relished and even prolonged; it is impossible that tables and organs should be found suspended from a ceiling at the close of a spiritual séance; it is impossible that the serpent of Sophia Walder should have been elongated in the manner described. When I say that these things are impossible I am speaking with due regard to the claims of transcendental phenomena, and it is from the transcendental standpoint that I judge them. Genuine transcendental phenomena may extend the accepted limits of probability, but when alleged transcendental phenomena do violence to all probability, that is the unfailing test of hallucination or untruth on the part of those who depose to them. These things could not have occurred as they are narrated, and Dr Bataille is exploiting the ignorance of that class of readers to whom his mode of publication appealed. As products of imagination his marvels are crude and illiterate; in other words, they belong to precisely that type which is characteristic of romances published in penny numbers, and when he pledges his rectitude regarding them he does not enlist our confidence but indicates the slight value which he sets on his stake.

At the same time, two reasons debar me from laying further stress upon this line of argument. In the first place we must remember that his unlettered readers have been taught by their religious instructors to believe in the unlimited power of the devil, and they have probably found in the outrageous nature of the narratives a real incentive to accept them. In the second place my own position as a transcendentalist connects me less or more with the acknowledgment of transcendental phenomena, and to distinguish the limits of possibility in these matters would involve a technical discussion for which there is no opportunity here. It is understood, however, that in the interests of transcendental science I reject the miraculous element in Dr Bataille's memoirs.

Another line of criticism also open and leading to convincing results would dwell upon the glaring improbability of the entire story outside that miraculous element. There is no colourable pretence of likelihood, for example, in the connection instituted between fakirs and Freemasons, or between secret societies in China and a sect of Luciferians in Charleston. But the partisans of Dr Bataille are prepared to believe anything of Masonry, and to dismiss likelihood as they would dismiss impossibility. Some arguments are unassailable on account of their stupidity, and of such shelter I intend to deprive my witness. I shall therefore merely register my recognition that this criticism does obtain completely. For much the same reason I shall only refer in passing to another matter which in itself is sufficient to remove these memoirs from the region of actuality; they bristle with the kind of coincidences which are the common convenience of bad novelists to create or escape situations, and are rejected even by legitimate fiction, because they are untrue to life. At the present time the device of coincidence is left to its true monopolists, the Society for Psychical Research and the manufacturers of the penny dreadful. Unreasonable demands are, however, made upon it by Dr Bataille; never in an awkward predicament does the coincidence fail to help him; wheresoever he goes it times his arrival rightly to witness some occasional and rare event, and it places him at once in communication with the indispensable person whose presence was antecedently unlikely. The very existence of his memoirs would have been jeopardised had the Anadyr reached Point-de-Galle immediately before instead of immediately after the catastrophe which converted Carbuccia. At the beginning of his mission against Masonry, coincidence arranged the last illness of the Cingalese pythoness to the exigencies of his date of arrival; it brought John Campbell to Pondicherry and Phileas Walder to Calcutta; at Singapore it fixed a Palladic institution in the grade of Templar-Mistress to correspond with his flying visit on the road to Shanghai. Now, all these coincidences are of the class which come off in fiction and miss in the combinations of real life, but to insist on this point would not disillusionise the believers in Dr Bataille, who will say that he was assisted by Providence. We must show that he has deceived them in matters which admit of verification, over certain points of ordinary fact, which can be placed beyond the region of dispute, and by which the truth of his narrative may be held to stand or fall. I shall confine myself for this purpose to what he states at first hand in his capacity as an eyewitness, and to two salient cases which may be taken to represent the whole. Among the rest some are in course of investigation, and so far as they have gone are promising similar results; the locality of others has been so chosen as to baffle inquiry; and in one or two instances I have failed to obtain results. It is obviously impossible to prove that there is not a native hut in "a thick and impassable forest" at an unindicated distance from Point-de-Galle, or that this hut does not possess a vast subterranean chamber. When we cannot check our witness we must regard what he tells us in the light of those instances which it is possible to fix firmly. Among negative results I may mention an inquiry into the alleged death of a person named George Shekleton in a Masonic lodge at Calcutta. Sir John Lambert, K.C.S.I.E., the commissioner of police at that place, very courteously made investigations at my suggestion, first at the coroner's court, but the records for the year 1880 are not now in existence, and, secondly, among the oldest police officers, but also without result. I applied thereupon to Mr Robert William Shekleton, Q.C., J.P., inquiring whether any relative of his family had died under curious circumstances at Calcutta about the year 1880. His answer is this:—"I never heard anything about the death of a George Shekleton in Calcutta. My elder and younger brother were both living in Calcutta, and if any person of the same name had been living there I should have heard it from them. My younger brother Alexander Shekleton died at Madras on his way home with his wife and children of confluent small-pox; my eldest brother Joseph is still alive." The presumption, therefore, is that Carbuccia's story of the strange fatality which occurred in his presence at a Masonic lodge is without any foundation in fact, but I regard the result as negative because it falls short of demonstration. I am now setting other channels in operation, but as it is not a test case, and not an event which Dr Bataille claims to have witnessed himself, it is unnecessary to await the issue.

If the reader will now glance at the several sections of the sixth chapter, he will find that one of the most important is that entitled "The Seven Temples and a Sabbath in Sheol," where Dr Bataille tells us that he witnessed unheard of operations in black magic on the part of Palladian Masons and diabolising fakirs. The locality was a plain called Dappah, two hours drive from Calcutta. The particulars which are given concerning the edifices on the mountain of granite, but more especially concerning an open charnel where the dead bodies of innumerable human beings, mixed indiscriminately with those of animals and with the town refuse, are left to rot under the eye of heaven, will not impress any one, however unacquainted with India, and with the vicinity of the English capital and seat of government, as wearing many of the features of probability. The facts are as follows:—A place called Dhappamanpour, and for brevity Dhappa, does exist in the neighbourhood of Calcutta, and thereto the town refuse is actually carried by a special line of railway; there is no granite mountain and there are no temples, while so far from it being a charnel into which human bodies are flung, or a place where the adepts of the Palladium could celebrate a black Sabbath and form a magic chain with putrid corpses, it is a great lake covering an area of thirty square miles, and is known by Anglo-Indians as the Saltwater Lake. In the year 1886 it was in course of reclamation, but all that Dr Bataille tells us is specifically untrue, and he could never have witnessed there the things which he describes as taking place in the year 1880. The *récit d'un témoin* is in this matter an invented history.

As a consequence of this bogus experience in Calcutta, Dr Bataille pretends to have been admitted within the charmed circle of the New and Reformed Palladium, and was therefore qualified to be present at the initiation of a Templar-Mistress which took place not long after at Singapore. His account of this initiation turns upon two or three points which do not appear in the synopsis of the sixth chapter. One of these is the existence of a Kadosch Areopagite of the Ancient and Accepted Scotch Rite. But at least, at the period in question, there was no such Areopagite, and the Scotch Rite did not exist at Singapore. The sole Masonic institution was a District Grand Lodge of Ancient Free and Accepted Masons of England in the Eastern Archipelago, working under the warrant of the English Grand Lodge, holding half-yearly communications, and special meetings when the District Grand Master deemed necessary. Its patent dates from March 3, 1878, and the District Grand Master at the time was the Hon. William H. Macleod Read. Three lodges worked under its jurisdiction, two of which were at Singapore and one at Penang, and to one of the former a Royal Arch Chapter was attached. It is needless to say that our author's Misraïm diploma would have obtained his admission to none, and there is no person here in England who would have the effrontery to affirm that he might have fared better by reason of his Palladian degree. It is sufficient, however, to state that there was no Lodge of the Ancient and Accepted Scotch Rite in Singapore at the time of his visit. But the imposition does not end here; Dr Bataille does not merely describe what took place at a lodge which was not in existence—he gives particulars of an address delivered by a certain Dr Murray at a meeting attended by himself. Now, at the date in question, there was no such person either in the town, in its vicinity, or in Penang. There is fortunately an institution among us which is termed the British Museum, and it enables us to verify questions of this kind. Furthermore, when describing the Palladian meeting at the Presbyterian chapel—there was such a chapel by the way—he tells us that the Grand Master was named Spencer, and that he was a *négociant* of Singapore, but there was again no such person in the town or its vicinity at the time, and so his entire narrative, with its ritual reproduced from Leo Taxil, is demolished completely. I submit that these two instances are sufficient to indicate the kind of man with whom we are dealing. It may be a matter of astonishment to my readers that a work even of imposition should be performed so clumsily as to betray itself at once to a little easy research, but it must be remembered that the class of French readers to whom Dr Bataille made appeal are so ignorant of all which concerns the English that skill is not required to exploit them; it is enough that the English are abused. Of our author's qualifications in this respect I have already given some specimens, but they convey no idea of his actual resources in the matter of abuse and calumny. A direct quotation will not be beside the purpose in this place:—" Wheresoever religious influence can make itself felt, there the wife and maid are the purest, the most ingenuous expression of the creation and the divinely touching idea synthetised by the immaculate Mother of Christ, the Virgin Mary; but, on the contrary, in England, and still more especially in the English colonies, under the pernicious influence of the Protestant heresy engendered by revolts of truly diabolical inspiration, the wife and maid are in some sort the opprobrium of humanity. The example, moreover, comes from an exalted place, as is known. The whole world is acquainted with that which John Bull does not himself confess, namely, the private history of her whom Indians term 'the old lady of London,' given over to vice and drunkenness from her youth—Her Majesty Wisky the 1st." I have made this quotation, because it gives the opportunity to dispense with the civility of discussion which is exercised by one gentleman towards another, but would be out of place on the part of a gentleman who is giving a deserved castigation to a disgusting and foul-mouthed rascal. This is the nameless refuse which flings itself to bespatter Masonry. Down, unclean dog, and back, scavenger, to your offal! The scullion in the Queen's kitchen would, I think, disdain to whip you.

Setting aside these scandalous slanders, and returning to the subject in hand, it is clear that when a writer who comes forward with a budget of surprising revelations is shown to have invented his materials in certain signal instances, it becomes superfluous to subject his entire testimony to a laborious sifting, and there is really no excuse to delay much longer over the memoirs of Dr Bataille. It will be needless to state that my researches have failed to discover any such dismantled temple as that described at Pondicherry, and affirmed to be on the English soil adjacent to the French town. It is equally unnecessary to say that the story of the caves of Gibraltar is a gross and absurd imposture, for, in fact, it betrays itself. Parisian literature of the byways has its own methods, and its purveyors are shrewd enough to know what will be tolerated and what enjoyed by their peculiar class of patrons; transcendental toxicology and an industry in idols worked by criminals intercommunicating by means of Volapuk may be left to them.

Nor is it needful to do more than touch lightly upon a pleasant process in piracy by which Dr Bataille lightens the toils of authorship. He has done better than any other among the witnesses of Lucifer in his gleanings from Éliphas Lévi. On p. 32 of his first volume there is a brazen theft concerning the chemistry of black magic, and there is another, little less daring, on p. 67, being a description of a Baphometic idol. It goes without saying that the Conjuration of the Four is imported, as others have imported it, from the *Rituel de la Haute Magie.* The vesture of the master of ceremonies who officiated in the Sanctuary of the Phœnix, one of the mythical temples of Dhappa, is a property derived from the same quarter. So in like manner is part of a magical adjuration in the account of a Sabbath in Sheol. Finally, a method of divination described in a later place (vol. i., pp. 343, 344) will be found in Christian's *Histoire de la Magie.*

The artist who has illustrated the memoirs has acted after the same manner. The two Baphometic figures (vol. i., pp. 9 and 89), are reproductions from Lévi's plates. The Sabbatic figure (Ib., p. 153) is a modification from Christian. The original idea of the shadow-demon on p. 201 will be found in Lévi's sacerdotal hand making the sign of esotericism. The four figures of the Palladian urn on p. 313 are plagiarised in a similar way. The illustration on p. 337, which purports to be a gnostic symbol of the dual divinity, is actually the frontispiece to Lévi's *Dogme de la Haute Magie.* The magical urn on p. 409 is the facsimile of a similar object in another of Lévi's drawings; and if it were worth while to continue, the material for a further enumeration is not wanting. But these matters, after all, are of inferior moment, and to complete the exposure of this witness, I pass to the final points of my criticism.

Dr Bataille publishes an alleged Table of High-grade Masonry as it existed on March 1, 1891, and this document, which is similar in many respects to another of a slightly anterior date, produced by Signor Margiotta, is said to have been prepared by Albert Pike himself; it includes a long list of the persons then in correspondence with the Supreme Dogmatic Directory as Inspectors General "in permanent mission." It is a bizarre medley which includes the Orders of the Druids, Mopses, Oddfellows, and Mormon Moabites in the same connection as the Ancient and Accepted Scotch Rite, the Rites of Memphis and Misraïm, and the San-Ho-Hei. As such, it would be, in any case, a large tax upon the gullibility of readers outside the back streets of Paris. But I determined to make some inquiries among the English names mentioned. For example, Mr R. W. Shekleton, to whom I have already referred, is said, at the period in question, to have been in official correspondence with the Dogmatic Directory, representing the special relations of Ireland, and, having drawn his attention to the point, he has furnished me with the following contradiction:—"The statement in your letter, taken from the book you refer to, that I was in the year '91 in direct correspondence with the Supreme Dogmatic Directory of Charleston is utterly false. I never even heard of any such Body as the Supreme Directory, or of what is called the New and Reformed Palladium. The only communication I ever had with General Albert Pike (whom I had never seen) was in reference to a question of Masonic procedure in America. So far as I am aware the existence of either of the Bodies you refer to is unknown to any of the Masonic Body in Ireland, and I can, with almost certainty, make the same statement in reference to the English and Scotch Masons. Having been for nearly twenty-seven years the Acting Head of the Order in Ireland, I can speak with authority, and you are at liberty in my name to give the most emphatic contradiction to the statements quoted from the book. So far as I am aware, General Pike was never anything more than Sovereign Grand Commander of the Supreme Council of the 33rd Southern Jurisdiction of America."

The case of Mr John Yarker, Grand Master of the Memphis Rite in England, I have already had occasion to mention, and have cited his explicit denial of any acquaintance with the New and Reformed Palladium, but he is included by Dr Bataille in his wonderful enumeration. Upon the general question, Mr Yarker observes: (*a*) that the Scottish or Ancient and Accepted Rite has nothing occult about it, but the Memphis and Misraïm Rites are wholly occultism. (*b*) That Pike has, however, in his lectures added occult matters from these occult Rites. (*c*) That Pike, as a very able man, ruled the whole of the Supreme Grand Councils of the 33° (Ancient and Accepted), which almost all originated from Charleston. (*d*) That this is the only form in which there can be said to have been a Dogmatic Directorate.

In like manner, Mr William Officer of Edinburgh, an initiate of the Scotch Rite, Inspector-General of the Supreme Council of the French Grand Orient, and Hon. Member of its Grand College of Rites, denies his alleged connection with any Central Directory, and has heard nothing of such an institution.

I do not conceive that there is any call to fill space by the multiplication of these denials, and I need therefore only add that I have others equally explicit in my possession. The obvious conclusion is that the alleged Table of High-Grade Masonry is a bogus document founded on some official lists of the Ancient and Accepted Scotch Rite.

Lastly, there are certain statements made by Dr Bataille which warrant the presumption that he could have had little, if any, active acquaintance with the Memphis Rite. That he may have purchased a diploma from Pessina is probable enough; what I learn of the Grand Master of the Neapolitan Sovereign Sanctuary, through sources not tainted like those of the witnesses of Lucifer, does not place him wholly above financial considerations, but Pessina was, and is, totally unrecognised by any Masonic power in the world of Craft Masonry. So far, therefore, from such a diploma acting as an *Open Sesame,* it would have sealed all doors against its owner, and this statement is true not only for ordinary Craft Masonry, but for the great majority of lodges under the Misraïm obedience. Dr Bataille would not, therefore, have much opportunity for participating in that Rite to which he had purchased entrance, and, as a fact, he is wholly ignorant concerning it. For example, he seems to represent the Memphis and Misraïm Rites as enjoying recognition from the Scotch Rite, and the latter as consciously subordinate and inferior, whereas the position is this. Memphis recognises the 33° of the Ancient and Accepted as its first steps, and places 62 degrees upon them, which are not recognised in return. Misraïm also includes the 33° of the Scotch Rite, but in a more irregular arrangement, other degrees being interspersed among them. Pessina's Misraïm Rite has been reduced by him from 90° to 33°, which are virtually those of the Ancient and Accepted Rite approximated to Misraïm teaching. So also he states that General Garibaldi was in 1860, and had been so for many previous years, the Grand Master and Grand Hierophant of the Rite of Memphis for all countries of the globe. This is completely untrue, for, as a matter of fact, Garibaldi succeeded Jacques Etienne Marconis of Paris, becoming president of a confederation of the Rites which was brought about by Mr John Yarker in the year 1881. Before this period he was simply an Hon. Grand Master of Pessina's body. The articles of this treaty, with a true copy of all the signatures attached to it, and with the seals of the Sovereign Sanctuaries against them, is before me as I write. I may state, in conclusion, that Dr Bataille also falsely represents himself to have met with Mr Yarker, who told him that he had personally aspired to the succession at the death of Garibaldi, which Mr Yarker characterizes as "an infamous concoction."

I am in possession of ample materials for illustrating more fully the marvellous inventions produced by this witness of Lucifer, but the instalment here given is sufficient for the present purpose.

CHAPTER XIII

DIANA UNVEILED

THE DISCOVERY OF Leo Taxil and of M. Ricoux has one remaining witness in the person of Miss Diana Vaughan. She also, as we have seen, is a writer of memoirs, and in giving some account of her narrative I have already indicated in substance certain lines of criticism which might be applied with success thereto. We must obviously know more about this lady, and have some opportunity of verifying the particulars of her past life before we can accept her statement that she has written while fresh from "conversion," and is speaking for the first time the language of a Christian and a Catholic. The supernatural element of her memoirs it is not worth while to discuss. Were she otherwise worthy of credit, we might exonerate her personal veracity by assuming that she was tricked over the apparition and hallucinated in the vision that followed it, but I propose submitting to my readers sufficient evidence to justify a conclusion that she does not deserve our credit, and though out of deference to her sex it is desirable, so far as may be possible, to speak with moderation, I must establish most firmly that the motive she betrays in her memoirs is not in many respects preferable to that of the previous witness.

It will be advisable, however, to distinguish that part of the narrative for which Miss Vaughan is admittedly and personally responsible from that which she claims to be derived from her family history. I must distinguish between them, not that I am prepared to admit as a legitimate consequence of her statement that there is any real difference or that I unquestionably regard Miss Vaughan as having created a strong presumption that she is in possession of the documents which she claims to have. I am simply recognising the classification which she may herself be held to make. If in this respect it can be shown that I have mistaken the actual position, I will make such reparation as may be due from a man of letters, whose reasonable indignation in the midst of much imposture will, in such case, have misled him. But there is only one course which is open to Miss Vaughan in the matter, and that is to produce the original documents on which she has based her narrative for the opinion of competent English investigators, in which case Miss Vaughan may be held to have established not the truth of her family history, which is essentially beyond establishment, but her *bona fides* in connection with its relation. After this the portion for which she is personally responsible, and from which there is no escape, will still fasten the charge of falsehood ineffaceably upon her narrative.

In addition, then, to her personal history, Miss Vaughan's memoirs contain:—I. A mendacious biography of the English mystic, Thomas Vaughan. II. A secret history of the English Rosicrucian Fraternity, and of its connection with Masonry, which is also an impudent fraud. The two constitute one of the most curious literary forgeries which are to be met with in the whole range of Hermetic literature; and Hermetic literature, it is known, has been enriched by many triumphs of invention. I shall deal with the narratives plainly on the provisional assumption that Miss Vaughan has been herself deceived in regard to them. They are based upon family papers said to be now in possession of the Charleston Dogmatic Directory. The central facts which are sought to be established by means of these papers have been mentioned already in my eighth chapter, namely, that Miss Vaughan is one of the two last descendants of the alchemist Thomas Vaughan; that this personage made a compact with Satan in the year 1645, that under the name of Eirenæus Philalethes, he wrote the well-known alchemical work entitled "An Open Entrance to the Closed Palace of the King," and that he consummated a mystical marriage with Venus-Astarte, of which the Palladian Templar-Mistress is the last development. For the purposes of these narratives the birth of Thomas Vaughan is placed in the year 1612, and his death, or rather translation, in the year 1678. At the age of twenty-four years, that is to say, in 1636, he proceeded to London, and there connected himself with the mystic Robert Fludd, by whom he was initiated into a lower grade of the Rosicrucian Fraternity, and received a letter of introduction to the Grand Master, Johann Valentin Andreæ, which he took over to Stuttgart and presented. In 1637, having returned to London, he was present at the death of Robert Fludd, which occurred in that year. In 1638 he made his first voyage to America, where he was hospitably entertained by a Protestant minister, named John Cotton, but his visit was not characterised by any remarkable occurrence. At this period the alchemist is represented by his descendant as a Puritan impregnated with the secret doctrine of Robert Fludd. In 1639 Vaughan returned to England, but was immediately attracted to Denmark by the discovery of a golden horn adorned with mysterious figures, which he and his colleagues in alchemy supposed to typify the search for the philosophical stone. At the age of twenty-eight, Vaughan made further progress in the Rosicrucian Fraternity, being advanced to the grade of *Adeptus Minor* by Amos Komenski, in which year also Elias Ashmole entered the order. Accompanied by Komenski, Vaughan proceeded to Hamburg, thence by himself to Sweden, and subsequently to the Hague, where he initiated Martin de Vriès. A year later he visited Italy, and made acquaintance with Berigard de Pisa. This was a pious pilgrimage which testified his devotion to Faustus Socinus, for Miss Vaughan, on the authority of her documents, regards the Italian heretic, not only as a conscious Satanist, but as the founder of the Rosicrucian Society, and the initiator of Johann Valentin Andreæ, whom he also won over to Lucifer. On his return Thomas Vaughan tarried a short time in France, where he conceived the project of organising Freemasonry as it exists at the present day, and there also it occurred to him that the guilds of the Compagnage might serve him for raw material. When, however, he returned to England, he concluded that the honorary or Accepted Masons, received by the Masonic guilds of England, were better suited to his purpose. Some of these were already Rosicrucians, and among them he set to work. In the year 1644 he presided over a Rosicrucian assembly at which Ashmole was present. At this time also Oliver Cromwell is said to have been an accepted Mason, and it was by his intervention that, a year later, Thomas Vaughan was substituted for the headsman at the execution of Archbishop Laud, for the object already described. It was after his compact with Lucifer that the alchemist wrote the "Open Entrance." His activity in the Rosicrucian cause then became prodigious, and the followers of Socinus, apparently all implicated in the Satanism of their master, began to swell the ranks of the Accepted Masons. At this time also he began his collaborations with Ashmole for the composition of the Apprentice, Companion, and Master grades, that is to say, for the institution of symbolical Masonry. In 1646 he again visited America, and consummated his mystic marriage, as narrated in the eighth chapter. In 1648 he returned to England, and one year later completed the Master grade, that of Companion having been produced during his absence, but following the indications he had given, by Elias Ashmole. In 1650 he began to issue his Rosicrucian and alchemical writings, namely, *Anthroposophia Theomagica* and *Anima Magica Abscondita,* followed by *Lumen de Lumine* and *Aula Lucis* in

1651. The Rosicrucian Grand Master Andreæ died in 1654, and was succeeded by Thomas Vaughan, whose next step was the publication of his work, entitled "Euphrates, or the Waters of the East." In 1656 he is said to have published the complete works of Socinus, two folio volumes in the collection, entitled *Bibliotheca Fratrum Polonorum*. Three years later appeared his "Fraternity of R.C.," and in 1664 the *Medulla Alchymiœ*. In 1667 he decided to publish the "Open Entrance," the MS. of which was returned to him by the editor Langius after printing, and was subsequently annotated in the way I have previously mentioned. During the early days of the same year Vaughan converted Helvetius, the celebrated physician of the Hague, who in his turn became Grand Master of the Rosicrucian Fraternity. In 1668 he published his "Experiments with Sophic Mercury" and *Tractatus Tres,* while ten years later, or in 1678, the year of his infernal translation, he produced his edition of "Ripley Revived" and the *Enarratio Trium Gebri*.

From beginning to end, generally and particularly, the narrative I have summarised above is a gross and planned imposture, nor would any epithets be so severe as to be undeserved by the person who has concocted it, because it does outrage to the sacred dead, in particular to the greatest of the English spiritual mystics, Thomas Vaughan, and to the greatest of the English physical mystics, Eirenæus Philalethes. For the mendacious history confuses two entirely distinct persons—Eugenius and Eirenæus Philalethes. It is true that this confusion has been made frequently, and it is true also that at the beginning of my researches into the archælogy of Hermetic literature I was one of its victims, for which I was sharply brought to book by those who knew better. But a young and unassisted investigator, imperfectly equipped, has an excuse which will exonerate him at least from a malicious intention. It is otherwise with a pretended family history. When documents of this kind reproduce blunders which are pardonable to ignorance alone, and upon a subject about which two opinions are no longer possible, it is certain that such documents are not what they claim; in other words, they have been fabricated, and the fabrication of historical papers is essentially a work of malice. Furthermore, when such forgeries impeach persons long since passed to their account, on the score of unheard of crimes, they are the work of diabolical malice, and this is a moderately worded judgment on the case now in hand. Thomas Vaughan, otherwise Eugenius Philalethes, was born in the year 1621 at Newton, in Brecknockshire. The accepted and perfectly correct authority for this statement is the *Athenæ Oxonienses* of Anthony Wood, but he is not the only authority, and if he be not good enough for Miss Vaughan, she can take in his place the exhaustive researches of the Rev. A. B. Grosart, whose edition of the works of the Silurist Henry Vaughan have probably been neither seen nor heard of by this unwise woman, in the same way that she is ignorant of most essential elements in the matters which she presumes to treat. The authority of a laborious scholar like Dr Grosart will probably be of greater weight than the foul narrative of a Palladian memoir-maker, who has not produced her documents. From this date it follows that in the year 1636 Thomas Vaughan was still in the schoolboy period, not even of sufficient age to begin a college career. He could not, as alleged, have visited Fludd, the illustrious Kentish mystic, in London, nor would he have been ripe for initiation, supposing that Fludd could have dispensed it. In like manner, Andreæ, assuming that he was Grand Master of the Rosicrucians, would not have welcomed a youngster of fifteen years, supposing that in those days he was likely to travel from London to Stuttgart, but would have recommended him to return to his lesson-books. The first voyage to America and all the earlier incidents of the narrative are untrue for the same reason. In place of wandering through Denmark, the Hague, and Sweden, initiating and being initiated, he was drumming through a course at Oxford; in place of pious pilgrimages to the shrine of Socinus, he was preparing to take orders in the English Church, and the narrative which is untrue to his early is untrue also to his later life. After receiving Holy Orders he returned to his native village and took over the care of its souls. He was never a Puritan; he was never a friend of Cromwell; he was a high-churchman and a Royalist, and he was ejected from his living because he was accused by political enemies of carrying arms for the king. He never travelled; on the contrary, he married, at what period is unknown, but his tender devotion to his wife is commemorated on the reverse pages of an autograph alchemical MS. now in the British Museum, which belies furthermore, in every line and word, the Luciferian imposture of the Paris-cum-Yankee documents, by its passionate religious aspiration and its adoring love of Christ.

When Vaughan came up to London, it was as a man who was somewhat out of joint with English, in spite of his Oxford career, because he was a Welsh-speaking man, and when he took to writing books, he apologises for his awkward diction. He accentuates also his youth, which would be warrantable at the age of twenty-eight, but would be absurd in a writer approaching forty years. This point may be verified by any one who will refer to my edition of Vaughan's *Anthroposophia Theomagica.* The works of Thomas Vaughan, besides *Anthroposophia Theomagica,* are *Anima Magica Abscondita,* published in 1650; *Magia Adamica* 1650, apparently forgotten by the "authentic documents" of Miss Vaughan, as are also "The Man-Mouse" and "The Second Wash, or the Moore scoured once More"—satires on Henry More, written in reply to that Platonist, who had attacked the previous books. These belong to the year 1651, as also does *Lumen de Lumine;* "The Fame and Confession of the Fraternity R.C." appeared in 1652, not 1659, as the "family history" affirms; *Aula Lucis,* 1652 (not 1651); and "Euphrates," 1655. What is obvious everywhere in these priceless little books is the devotion of a true mystic to Jesus Christ, and to gift them with the sordid interpretation of a French-born cultus of Lucifer is about as possible as to attribute a Christian intention to the calumnies of Miss Vaughan's documents.

In the year 1665, at the house of the rector of Albury, a chemical experiment with mercury cost the Welsh alchemist his life, and he was buried in the churchyard of that village in Oxfordshire.

It is clear, therefore, that the wonderful archives in the possession of Miss Vaughan give a bogus history of Eugenius Philalethes, but they are also untrue of Eirenæus. It is untrue that this mysterious adept, whose identity has never been disclosed, was born in 1612; he was born some ten years later.

The source of both dates is "The Open Entrance to the Closed Palace of the King"; but that which Miss Vaughan champions is based upon a corrupt reading in a bad version, and she has evidently never seen the original and best of the Latin impressions, that of Langius, though she has the presumption to cite it. That edition establishes that he wrote the treatise in the year 1645, he being then in the twenty-third year of his age—whence it follows that the date of his birth was most probably 1622, and the history with which he is invested by Miss Vaughan is again a misfit; it is putting man's garments on a boy. Furthermore, there is not one item in her statements concerning the "Open Entrance" which is not directly and provably false. It was not printed, as she indicates, under the supervision of the author; it was not printed from the original MS., nor was that MS. returned to Philalethes after it had passed through the press. It is shameful for any person, male or female, however little they may consider their own fair fame, to so far violate the canons of literary honour as to make dogmatic statements concerning a work which they cannot have seen. The preface prefixed to this edition by Langius completely refutes Miss Vaughan. Here is a passage in point:—"Truly who or what kind of person was author of this sweet, must-like work, I know no more than he who is most ignorant, nor, since he himself would conceal his name, do I think fit to enquire so far, lest I get his displeasure." Again— "To pick out the roses from the most thorny bushes of writings, and to make the elixir of philosophers by his own industry, without any tutor, and at twenty-three years of age, this perchance hath been granted to none, or to most few hitherto." Langius, moreover, laments explicitly the fact that he did not print from an original MS. He printed from a Latin translation, the work of an unknown hand, which had come into his possession, as he tells us, from a man who was learned in such matters. Miss Vaughan's pretended autograph, with its despicable marginal readings, is obviously a Latin copy, whatever be its history otherwise. The original was in English, and when Langius was regretting its loss, "a transcript, probably written from the author's copy, or very little corrupted," was in possession of the bookseller William Cooper, of Little Saint Bartholomews, near Little Britain, in the city of London, who published it in the year 1669, to correct the imperfections in the edition of Amsterdam. This transcript also establishes that the "Open Entrance" was penned when the author was in his twenty-third year.

As a matter of fact, Philalethes does not appear to have superintended the publication of any of his writings, and here Miss Vaughan again exhibits her unpardonable ignorance concerning the works with which she is dealing. To prove that her reputed ancestor was alive after the accepted date of Thomas Vaughan's death, she triumphantly observes that in the year 1668 he published his experiments on the preparation of Sophic Mercury and *Tractatus Tres.* But the latter volume was a piracy, for in his preface to "Ripley Revived" the author expressly laments that two of its three treatises had passed out of his hands, and he feared lest they should get into print, because they were imperfect works preceding the period of solid knowledge which produced the "Open Entrance." Again, so little was he consulted over the appearance of the "Sophic Mercury" that the printer represents it as the work of an American philosopher, whence it has been fathered upon George Starkey.

Eirenæus Philalethes was undoubtedly a great traveller and he visited America, but there is no ground for supposing that he was ever in Italy, and that either he or Thomas Vaughan edited the works of Socinus is an ignorant fiction, for which even Miss Vaughan can find no better warrant than the evasive place of publication which figures on the title-page of the *Bibliotheca Fratrum Polonorum,* namely, Eirenæopolis. In like manner she erroneously credits him with the authorship of the *Medulla Alchemiœ,* which is the work of Eirenæus Philoponos Philalethes, otherwise George Starkey.

These facts fully establish the fraudulent nature of Miss Vaughan's family history, by whomsoever it has been devised, and seeing that where it is possible to check it, it breaks down at every point, we need have no hesitation in rejecting the information which it provides in those cases where it cannot be brought to book. The connection of Faustus Socinus with the Rosicrucian Fraternity, as founder, is one instance; this is merely an extension of the imposture of Abbé Lefranc in his "Veil Raised for the Curious," and it rests, like its original, on no evidence which can be traced. Another is the Rosicrucian Imperatorship of Andreæ, and yet another the initiation of Robert Fludd. Again, the connection of Philalethes with John Frederick Helvetius is based on speculation only, and that of Ashmole with the institution of symbolical Masonry has never been more than hypothesis, and not very deserving at that. I regret to add that, on the authority of her bogus documents, Miss Vaughan has given currency to a rumour that the founder of the Ashmolean Museum poisoned his first wife. She deserves the most severe reprobation for having failed to test her materials before she made public this foul slander. Furthermore, in that portion of her materials which is concerned with her family history, she is not above tampering with the sense of printed books. The worshippers of Lucifer are represented as invariably terming their divinity the "good God"—*Dieu bon,*—or our God—*notre Dieu*—to distinguish him from the God of the Adonaïtes, and the references made to the Deity by Philalethes in the "Open Entrance" she falsely translates by these Luciferian equivalents, thus creating an impression in the minds of the ignorant that he is not speaking of the true Divinity. After this it will hardly surprise my readers that a pretended translation from a MS. of Gillermet de Beauregard, which she states to be preserved in the archives of the Sovereign Patriarchal Council of Hamburg, is simply stolen from an *Instruction à la France sur la vérité de l'Histoire des Frères de la Roze-Croix,* by Gabriel Naudé, who ridiculed and reviled the Order. I submit in conclusion that, in view of the facts already elicited, it is not worth while to inquire into the value of the episode concerned with the judicial murder of Archbishop Laud, and to elaborately argue that Oliver Cromwell was the last person in England to be implicated in such a transaction, he, at the period in question, being briskly employed in checkmating his King, who was at Oxford in winter quarters, and having neither the power nor opportunity to meddle with the details of an execution. The incident, in a word, is worth as much and as little as the abominable story of the subsequent pact with Lucifer or the foolery of the mystic marriage.

The critical investigation of Miss Vaughan's alleged documents having led to these results, it remains to be seen how far the other portions of her narrative will bear analysis. So long as she confined the more responsible part of her memoirs to personal experiences in the science of conversion and to the relation of her Eucharistic raptures, the lovers of ardent reading in this order of sensation were the only persons who could lay a complaint against her if she failed to fulfil their requirements. So long also as she fixed the scene of her history in a comparatively remote place, and among men now dead, she was partially protected from exposure, but when she transfers her revelations to England she is treading on dangerous ground, and she has in fact fallen into the pit. She has had the temerity to meddle with the modern history of Rosicrucian societies, and has undertaken to inform her readers after what manner she has come into possession of the rituals of the revived Rosicrucian Order, and her account is specifically untrue. She is undoubtedly acquainted with the grades of the order, but she could have obtained these from more than one published source—as, for example, the late Kenneth McKenzie's "Cyclopædia of Freemasonry",[1] or from my own "Real History of the Rosicrucians." But even if she possess the rituals, she has not come by them in the manner she describes. Her account is as follows:—"The Fraternity of the Rose-Cross comprises nine degrees of initiation—1. Zelator; 2. Theoricus; 3. Practicus (Miss Vaughan writes *Praticus,* which would be the error of a French person who does not read Latin and not the error of an English or American person as she claims to be); 4. Philosophus; 5. Adeptus Minor, according to the variants of Valentin Andreæ, or Adeptus Junior, according to the variants of Nick Stone (those were the variants of Nick Stone which were ostensibly burned in 1720 by the Grand Master Theophilus Desaguliers, but were not in reality destroyed; transmitted to trusty English brethren, after the death of Desaguliers, they passed from reliable hands to others also reliable, until the reconstitution of the Rose-Cross; for the reconstituted association exists actually in England, Scotland, the United States, and Canada, and those variants of the grades which were made by Nick Stone, are at the present day deposited with Doctor W. W. W., living at Cambden (*sic*) Road, London, Supreme Magus of the Rose-Cross for England, AT WHOSE HOUSE I HAVE TRANSCRIBED THEM); 6. Adeptus Major; 7. Adeptus Exemptus; 8. Magister Templi; 9. Magus."

Miss Vaughan's literary methods are not exactly captivating, and the enormous parenthesis is hers, but the capitals

1. The correct title is *The Royal Masonic Cyclopædia* (1877).

which close it are mine. The English doctor mentioned is well known to transcendentalists, and he is actually a high-grade Mason; he is also personally well-known to myself. To the best of his recollection he has never at any time met any person terming herself Diana Vaughan. More especially, no such individual has ever called at his house, much less copied any rituals of which he may be in possession. There is therefore only one term by which it is possible to qualify Miss Vaughan in her account of this matter, and if I refrain from applying it, it is more out of literary grace than from considerations of gallantry, for when persons of the opposite sex elect to make themselves odious by gross imposition, they cannot expect to escape the legitimate consequences at the hands of criticism any more than another class of female malefactors will escape on the plea of their sex at the hand of justice.

The subject of Luciferian Freemasonry has been under discussion in the columns of *Light* long before the appearance of this volume, and a number of transcendentalists, including one of great eminence—Mr Charles Carleton Massey—a few high-grade Masons, and myself, have exposed the pretensions of the French conspiracy. In most cases, and by more than one person, copies of the various issues were sent to Miss Vaughan through her publisher, and if she be not, as I hinted in that journal, the Mrs Harris of Freemasonry, there is little doubt that they reached her like other friendly offerings which she acknowledges in odd corners of her memoirs. It is probably in consequence of the exposures made in *Light* in connection with others said to have been made recently in Canada that in the eighth number of her memoirs she threatens to turn somewhat desperately on her critics. I understand that the Australian boomerang is a weapon that comes back to its caster, and the vindictive feeling which has prompted Miss Vaughan to a fresh burst of revelation has returned upon herself in a very overwhelming manner. "I am driven, and I will do it," is her position. "I will reveal the English Palladists such as they actually and personally are." And she does so to her own destruction as follows:—"The actual chief of the English Luciferians is Doctor William Wynn Westcott, living at 396 Cambden Road, London, whom on a previous occasion I mentioned only by his initials. It is he who is the actual custodian of the diabolical rituals of Nick Stone; it is he who is the Supreme Magus of the Socinian Rose-Cross for England." She proceeds to give the names of the Senior and Junior Sub-Magi, the members of the Grand Council, the chiefs of what she terms the Third Luciferian Order, and the Masters of the Temple, otherwise the Metropolitan College. Similar particulars follow concerning the York College, the College of Newcastle-on-Tyne, and that of Edinburgh.

Now, Dr Wynn Westcott is a high-grade Mason, as I have said, and he occupies a professional position of influence and importance; it is clear that a gratuitous attempt to fasten upon him charges of an odious character is an exceedingly evil proceeding and places the person who does so outside all limits of tender consideration. When Miss Vaughan states that Dr Westcott is a Palladist, a diabolist, a worshipper of Lucifer, or however she may elect to distinguish it, I reply that she is guilty of a gross libel, which is at the same time an abominable and cruel falsehood. When she says that she has been received at his house, I reply that she has not been received there, and that Dr Westcott is likely to require better credentials from female visitors than are supplied by the infamous inventions in the "Memoirs of an Ex-Palladist." When Miss Vaughan affirms that she has transcribed Dr Westcott's rituals at the house of Dr Westcott, I reply that this would be an untrue statement if the lady who made it were an intimate friend, and it is doubly untrue when affirmed by a perfect stranger. When Miss Vaughan states that Dr Westcott is the head of a Society which worships Lucifer, I reply that she is speaking falsely of a body concerning which she is in complete ignorance, and when an ignorant person thus attributes evil she or he does not only act foolishly but with exceeding malice. Miss Vaughan is henceforth upon all accounts outside that category of literary honour which makes it possible for criticism to be concerned with her and still preserve its dignity. Lastly, Miss Vaughan alleges that the official appointments made by Dr Westcott as Supreme Magus of the Society in question for the year 1896 were submitted to Adriano Lemmi and approved by him. This allegation is false *in toto.* Neither in a general nor a special sense is Dr Westcott responsible to Lemmi or to any Italian Freemason; what is more, no personal or written communication has at any time passed between them, and save as a past Grand Master Dr Westcott has never heard of the person to whose commands he is thus supposed to be subject. It will be seen that the baseless nature of this absurd statement involves all others of its kind, and there is no reason to attach the slightest credibility to anything which has been advanced concerning the supreme position of Adriano Lemmi, who, further, himself denies it, and, whatever his past history, is as much entitled to belief as accusers who betray their true character in this unenviable manner.

The Society which has thus been attacked in the person of its Supreme Magus is of singularly unpretending nature, simple as regards its history, and making no claim either to Masonic or Mystical importance. It does not claim or possess a connection with the original Rosicrucian Fraternity. It does not attribute antiquity to the rituals which it uses. It was founded by Robert Wentworth Little, who died in 1878, and has been in existence somewhat less than forty years. Its sole connection with Masonry is that it only initiates Masons. It neither enjoys nor expects recognition from the Grand Lodge of England. It is literary and antiquarian in its object, and came into existence chiefly for the study of the history of Freemasonry and of other secret societies. Its members are required to believe in the fundamental principles of Christian doctrine. The Metropolitan College has only four convocations and one banquet annually; the number of Fratres upon the Roll of Subscribers is fifty-four. It has attracted Masons interested in the antiquities of their craft and has no other sphere of influence. It publishes occasional transactions, the dimensions of which are regulated by an exceedingly modest income. I mention many of these particulars merely to place a check upon exaggerated notions. Some of the provincial Colleges have a larger membership, but they are of precisely the same character. It is not a society of occultists, though, like innumerable other bodies, it counts occultists among its brethren. Finally, no religious cultus of any kind is performed at its meetings, and no woman has ever passed its threshold.

The Societas Rosicruciana in Anglia is Rosicrucian only in its name, as it is Masonic only in its name, and its members are not Miss Vaughan's *ex-Frères d'Angleterre.*

It is certainly and in all respects necessary that something effectual should be done to curb a slanderous and evil tongue which has the audacity to impress the most sacred feelings of religion into the service of wilful lying. Dr Westcott is not the only English Mason who has suffered the undeserved indignity of gross aspersion from this unclean pen. Another victim is Mr Robert S. Brown, Grand Secretary of the Supreme Grand Royal Arch Chapter of Scotland, who is also a member of the Ancient and Accepted Rite, and of nearly all Masonic Orders, the Societas Rosicruciana in Anglia included. This honourable gentleman is especially recommended by Miss Vaughan to the attention of Catholics in Edinburgh, being the city in which he resides. She describes him as a dangerous sectarian, a veritable sorcerer, and the evil genius of one of her own relatives. She states further that he is an Elect Magus of the Palladium, that he protects Sophia Walder when she visits Scotland, and that he was a great admirer of Phileas Walder, at whose instance he consecrated himself to the demon anti-Christ. In each and all these statements this malicious woman has lied foully. I communicated with Mr Brown on the subject, and hold his written denials, which are at the service of any person who desires to see them. Mr Brown says:—"I am not an Elect Magus of the Palladium. I never to my knowledge saw Miss Walder, and never knew Miss

Vaughan, or anyone of the name, man, woman, or child. I never heard Miss Walder named till I received your letter, and never knew of the existence of the Palladian Order, if it does exist, till I saw it mentioned in articles in 'Light' and the 'Freemason's Chronicle'(London).... With reference to the particular statements in this copy of the *Mémoires,* no doubt the writer has succeeded in getting hold of the facts in most cases as to the official positions of the parties named, which of course are easily obtained; the little details regarding some of us would indicate the presence of an agent in our midst or near at hand. The 'inventions' and most slanderous statements regarding most of us are, however, outrageously false and wicked. My house has never had the honour (!!!) of entertaining Miss Walder or any other lady of like character; it is not a chemical laboratory, and I have never exercised myself in these *mysterious experiences* either there or elsewhere. I am a humble member of the Episcopal Church of Scotland, and, I trust, a sincere follower of the Master.... I count nearly all the gentlemen named in this vile proclamation among my friends, they are all good men and true, and I hope to associate with them for many years to come. I most emphatically deny the vile aspersions cast on their characters and my own, and you have my full authority to do so as far as the same may serve your purpose." My readers will agree that the clear and temperate statement of Mr R. S. Brown brands Diana Vaughan with indelible disgrace in the eyes of the civilised world.

There is a limit to the necessity of exposure, but should Miss Vaughan manifest any desire to have further instances of her mis-statements I will undertake to supply them. I will only add here in conclusion my personal opinion that Miss Vaughan has not been for any length of time a resident in an English-speaking country, much less can she have received, as it is alleged by some of her friends, an American education. The proof is that she makes characteristic French blunders over English names. Thus, we have *Cambden* on each occasion for Camden, *Wescott* for Westcott; we have *baronnet* for baronet, *Cantorbéry* for Canterbury, *Kirkud-Bright* for Kirkcudbright; we have hybrid combinations like *Georges Dickson,* impossibilities like *Tiers-Ordre Luciferien d'Honoris Causa,* and numerous similar instances.

To behold "Diana unveiled" was equivalent in alchemical terminology to attaining the *magnum opus.* The reputed author of the "New Light of Alchemy" testifies that some persons had in his own day and to his certain knowledge attained this supreme privilege. It is not of my own seeking if in another sense I have made public the same spectacle, and thus broken with the traditions of secret science. It would have been preferable from one point of view to have discovered Lucifer behind the mask of Masonry than to have found the conspiracy against it another *Tableau des Inconstances des Démons* in which the *infidelité et mécréance* connected with the old false witness, abound after a manner undreamed of by Bodin and Wierus, for it is distinctly disconcerting to think that a great church is so little honoured by her combatants and converts.

It only remains to state, and I do so with extreme reluctance, that the evidence of Signor Domenico Margiotta, which seems so strong in itself, can only be accepted, as we have seen, in connection with the credibility of Miss Vaughan, and as this has completely broken down, we cannot do otherwise than regard that part of his evidence which is concerned with Palladism as the narrative of a person who has been very seriously misled. And I think he has otherwise shown us that he is not a judicious critic of the materials which have come into his hands. He should never, for example, have printed his list of Palladian Lotus Lodges—so far as regards Great Britain, it is undeniably a false list. Take that of Edinburgh as a typical instance. Mr Brown, who has every opportunity of knowing, tells me there is absolutely no truth in the statement that there is in Edinburgh a Mother, or any, Lodge of the Palladian Order. "Neither is there a Triangular Province—whatever that may mean—such as is described. All is absolutely false."

CHAPTER XIV

The Radix of Modern Diabolism

We have finished with the witnesses of Lucifer, and I think that the search-light of a drastic criticism has left them in considerable disarray. We approach the limit of the present inquiry, but before summing up and presenting such a general statement or conclusion as may be warranted by the facts, there is one point, left over hereunto, and designed for final consideration, because it appeals more exclusively to professed transcendentalists, which it will be necessary to treat briefly. I have already indicated that sporadic revivals of black magic have occasionally been heard of by mystics here in England, and from time to time we have also heard vaguely of obscure assemblies of Luciferians. Quite recently an interview with Papus, the French occultist, published in *Light,* mentions a society which was devoted to the cultus of Lucifer, star of the morning, quite distinct from Masonry, quite unimportant, and since very naturally dead. Now, a large proportion of mystics here in England are High-Grade Masons, and if a society of the Palladium had extended to anything remotely approaching the proportions alleged, they could not have failed to know of it. I will go further and affirm that our non-Masonic transcendental associations have abundant opportunities to become acquainted with institutions similar to their own, and it is preposterous to suppose that there could be several Palladian triangles working their degrees in this country without our being aware of the fact. But we have not been aware of it, and our only informations concerning Palladism have come to us from France. We do not accept these informations; we know that the persons here in England who are alleged by French false witnesses to be connected with the Palladium are not so connected, and are now learning of it for the first time. The statements concerning Mr John Yarker are categorically untrue; the gross calumny published by the "converted" Diana Vaughan about Dr Wynn Westcott, who happens to be a High-Grade Mason, she will never dare to come forth from her "retreat" and reaffirm within the jurisdiction of these islands, because she knows well that a British jury would make a large demand upon her reputed American dollars. Let us, however, put aside for the moment the mendacities and forgeries which complicate the question of Lucifer, and let us approach Palladism from an altogether different side. I believe that I may speak with a certain accent of authority upon any question which connects with the French magus Éliphas Lévi. I am an old student of his works, and of the aspects of occult science and magical history which arise out of them; in the year 1886 I published a digest of his writings which has been the only attempt to present them to English readers until the present year when I have undertaken a translation *in extenso* of the *Dogme et Rituel de la Haute Magie,* which is actually in the hands of the printer. Now, it has not been alleged in so many words that the radix of Modern Diabolism and the Masonic cultus of Lucifer is to be found in Éliphas Lévi, but that is the substance of the charge. Most, or all, of the witnesses agree in representing him as an atrocious Satanist, an invoker of Lucifer, a celebrater of black masses, and an adept in the practical blasphemies of Eucharistic sacrilege; all of them father either upon the Palladium or upon Pike a variety of documents containing gross thefts from Lévi; some of them, directly and upon their own responsibility, cite passages from his works, always with conspicuous bad faith. Finally, they agree in connecting him with the foundation of the New and Reformed Palladium through his alleged disciple Phileas Walder; and one of them goes so far as to say that Palladism was a further development or restoration of a Satanic society directed by Éliphas Lévi and operating his theurgic system, which he in turn, if I rightly understand the mixed hypothesis of M. de la Rive, may have derived from the Palladic rite of 1730. If we accept for the moment this origin of the reformed order, it will follow that if the occult doctrines of Éliphas Lévi have been seriously misunderstood or grossly defamed by the witnesses, the diabolical or Luciferian connection of Palladism does not wear the complexion which has been ascribed to it. It is represented as: (*a*) outwardly Masonic, and (*b*) actually theurgic.

(*c*) It is Manichæan in doctrine. (*d*) It regards Lucifer as an eternal principle co-existent, but in a hostile sense, with Adonaï. (*e*) It holds that the beneficent deity is Lucifer, while Adonaï is malevolent; (*f*) Certain sections of Palladists, however, recognise that Lucifer is identical with Satan, and is the evil principle. (*g*) This section adores the evil principle as such. Now, in each and all these matters the Palladian system conflicts with that of Lévi.

To give a colourable aspect to their hypothesis, the witnesses affirm that Lévi was a high-grade Mason. He was nothing of the kind; he affirms most distinctly in his "History of Magic," that for any knowledge which he possessed about the mysteries of the fraternity, he owed his initiation only to God and to his individual studies. Secondly, the practice of ceremonial magic, which is what the witnesses understand by theurgy, is a practice condemned by Lévi, except as an isolated experiment to fortify intellectual conviction as to the truth of magical theorems. He attempted it for this purpose in the spring of the year 1854, and having satisfied himself as to the fact, he did not renew it. Thirdly, the philosophy of Éliphas Lévi is in direct contrast to Manichæan doctrine; it cannot be explained by dualism, but must be explained by its opposite, namely, triplicity in unity. He shows that "the unintelligent disciples of Zoroaster have divided the duad without referring it to unity, thus separating the pillars of the temple, and seeking to halve God" (*Dogme,* p. 129, 2nd edition). Is that a Manichæan doctrine? Again: "If you conceive the Absolute as two, you must immediately conceive it as three to recover the unity principle" (*Ibid.*). Once more: "Divinity, one in its essence, has two fundamental conditions of being—necessity and liberty" (*Ibid.*, p. 127). And yet again: "If God were one only, He would never be Creator nor Father. If He were two, there would be antagonism or division in the infinite, and this would be severance or death for every possible existence; He is therefore three for the creation by Himself, and in His image of the infinite multitude of beings and numbers. Thus He is really one in Himself and triple in our conception, by which we also behold Him triple in Himself and one in our intelligence and in our love. This is a mystery for the faithful and a logical necessity for the initiate of the absolute and true sciences" (*Ibid.*, p. 138). And the witnesses of Lucifer have the effrontery to represent Lévi as a dualist! I will not discredit their understanding by supposing that they could misread so plain a principle, nor dissemble my full conviction that they acted with intentional bad faith. Fourthly, Éliphas Lévi regarded Lucifer as a conception of transcendental mythology, and the devil as an impossible fiction, or an inverted and blasphemous conception of God—divinity *à rebours*. He describes the Ophite heresy which offered adoration to the serpent and the Caïnite heresy which justified the revolt of the first angel and the first murderer as errors fit for classification with the monstrous idols of the anarchic symbolism of India (*Rituel,* pp. 13, 14). Is that diabolism? Is that the cultus of Lucifer? True, Lévi did not believe in the personal existence of a father of lies, and if it be Satanism not to do so, let us be content to diabolise with Lévi while the false witnesses illustrate the methods of their father.

It is unnecessary to multiply quotations, but here is one more: "The author of this book is a Christian like you; his faith is that of a Catholic deeply and strongly convinced; therefore his mission is not to deny dogmas, but to combat impiety under one of its most dangerous forms, that of erroneous belief and superstition. . . . Away with the idol which hides our Saviour! Down with the tyrant of falsehood! Down with the black god of the Manichæans! Down with the Ahriman of the old idolaters! Live God alone and His incarnate Logos, Jesus the Christ, Saviour of the world, who beheld Satan precipitated from heaven!" Go to, M. le Docteur Bataille! *À bas*, Signor Margiotta! Phi, diabolus and Leo Taxil!

Seeing then that Éliphas Lévi has been calumniously represented, and that he was not a Satanist, he could not have founded a Satanic society, nor could a Manichæan order have been developed out of his doctrines. Hence if a Palladian Society do exist at Charleston, it either owes nothing to Lévi, or its cultus has been falsely described. In other words, from whatever point we approach the witnesses of Lucifer, they are subjected to a rough unveiling. In the words of the motto on my title, the first in this plot was Lucifer—*videlicet,* the Father of Lies!

CHAPTER XV

Conclusion

It remains for us now to appreciate the exact position in which the existence of the Palladian Order is left after all suspicious information has been subtracted. We have examined in succession the testimony of every witness to the discovery of Leo Taxil and M. Adolphe Ricoux, and it has been made entirely evident that they are of a most unsatisfactory kind. I make no pretence to pass a precise judgment upon Leo Taxil, for I am not in a position to prove that the Palladian rituals which appear in "Are there Women in Freemasonry?" can be characterised as invented matter. Granting his personal good faith, there are still many obvious questions, one of which is the connection between the Palladians and Masonry. As regards the so-called Paris triangle, from which the information was obtained, as regards the ritual itself, there is obviously no such connection, except the fantastic and arbitrary rule that initiation is imparted exclusively to persons possessed of Masonic degrees. It is patent that such an institution is not Masonic, though it possesses some secrets of Masonry. The Societas Rosicruciana in Anglia, as we have seen, is an association based upon precisely the same regulation, but it has no official position. Should a circle of Catholic priests conspire for the formation of a society dedicated to black magic and the celebration of the Satanic mass, that would not be the Church diabolising. No institution, and no society, is responsible for the unauthorised acts of individual members. At the same time, if it should be advanced by hostile criticism that the invention of rituals is easy, and that the literary antecedents of Leo Taxil are not precisely of that kind which would lead any cautious person to place blind confidence in his unchecked statements, I am compelled to say that I should find considerable difficulty in challenging such a position.

Mgr. Meurin, the next witness, deserves, by his position and ability, our very sincere respect; compared with the octogenarian sentimentalism of Jean Kostka, the violence of Signor Margiotta, and the paste-pot of M. de la Rive, one breathes *à pleine poitrine* in the altitudes of ecclesiastical erudition, artificial as their eminence turns out; the art sacerdotal does not concern itself with preposterous narratives, so that it disputes nothing with the art of Bataille; it has never stood in need of conversion, and hence is exempt from the hysterical ardours and languors of Diana Vaughan. But the archbishop's interpretation of Masonry is based upon another interpretation of Kabbalistic literature, which can be accepted by no person who is acquainted therewith, and would have scarcely been attempted by himself if he had known it at first hand. In the matter of Palladian Masonry, he can tell us only what he has learned from Ricoux.

It is agreed upon all sides that we dismiss Dr Bataille. He does not disclose the name and nation which he adopted during his Masonic career, and hence the persons whom he states that he met are, with one exception, not in a position to contradict him, because they are not in a position to identify him. The personality of the one exception is not particularised, but may be guessed without the exercise of much skill in divination, and here I must leave the point, not because I am disinclined to speak plainly and thus risk the possibility of being mistaken, but because Dr Bataille informs us that this one confidant is in his power, and that he could procure for him or her a term of penal servitude. Lastly, he is not in a position to exhibit his Palladian diplomas, which were demanded by the dispensing authorities when he first fell under their suspicion and have not been returned to him. While we are therefore prevented from checking his affirmations in what most concerns our inquiry, we see that at all points where it is possible to control him he has completely broken down; the miraculous element of his narrative transcends credit, and his statements upon a multitude of ordinary matters of fact are beneath it. When we connect these points with the mode of publication he has seen fit to adopt, and remember the kind of motive which usually attaches to that mode, we have no other course but to set him entirely outside consideration. His book is evidentially valuable only to close the question. He may have visited Charleston; he may have made the personal acquaintance of Albert Pike,

Gallatin Mackey, Phileas Walder, and his daughter Sophia; three of these persons are dead and cannot testify; the fourth acknowledges that he attended her medically at Naples; she protests against his betrayal, but she does not betray in return his Masonic identity, though I need scarcely add that she does not substantiate his statements. On these points my readers may be reasonably left to form their own judgments.

Miss Diana Vaughan is a lady who, in spite of much notoriety, is not in evidence; with one exception no credible person has ever said that he has seen her; that exception is Signor Margiotta. It would not, however, be the strongest line of criticism to dispute her existence; we may accept very gladly all that her Italian friend is good enough to say in regard to her personal characteristics, but we know that she has tried to deceive us, with conspicuous ill-success it is true, yet in a gross and most wicked manner. As to Signor Margiotta himself, with all his imperfections, he is the strongest witness to the discovery of Leo Taxil. I have admitted the great apparent force which belongs to his enormous array of documentary evidence, and I have established the nature of the complications which make that evidence extremely difficult to accept.

Lastly, Jean Kostka and M. A. C. de la Rive, though they came within the scope of our inquiry, are not Palladian witnesses. It would appear, therefore, that Leo Taxil and M. Adolphe Ricoux are, for the most part, neither honoured in their witnesses nor in a position to stand alone. The evidence which has grown out of their discovery is in an exceedingly corrupt state, and in summing the Question of Lucifer, as an impartial critic, I shall therefore simply propose to my readers the following general statement:—In the year 1891, Leo

Taxil and M. Adolphe Ricoux state that they have discovered certain documents which show the existence of a Palladian Society, claimed to be at the head of Masonry, and in the year 1895 Signor Domenico Margiotta states that he belonged to that society and gives further particulars concerning it. A number of other witnesses have also come forward whose evidence must, for various reasons, be completely rejected. It is in all respects much to be deplored that Signor Margiotta has largely and approvingly cited the testimony of two of these witnesses who are most open to condemnation, and that he has himself exercised an imperfect and uncritical censorship over papers which have come into his hands. From first to last all documents are open to strong suspicion.

Such is the slender residue which results from this sifting of Lucifer; if I have made my final statement thus indeterminate in its character, it is because I wish my readers to form their own conclusions as to Leo Taxil and Domenico Margiotta, and because I believe that, before long, further evidence will be forthcoming. I have little personal doubt as to the ultimate nature of the verdict, but at the present stage of the inquiry, with all the exposures which I have had the satisfaction of making fresh and clear in my mind, I would dissuade any one from saying that there is "nothing in" the Question of Lucifer; it is at least obvious that there is no end to its impostures, in which respect I do not claim to have done more than trim the fringes of the question. It is not therefore closed, and, if I may so venture to affirm, it assumes a fresh interest with the appearance of this book. It deserves to rank among the most extraordinary literary swindles of the present, perhaps of any, century. The field which it covers is enormous, and there is room, and more than room, for a score of other investigators who will none fail of their reward. Within the limits of a moderate volume, it is impossible to take into account the whole of the issues involved, while the importance which is to be attributed to the subject should not be lightly regarded, seeing that in France, at the time of writing, it provides an apparently remunerative circulation to two monthly reviews, and that its literature is otherwise still growing. At the present moment, and for the purposes of this criticism, a few concluding statements alone remain to be made; they concern the position of Italy in connection with the so-called Universal Masonry, some aspects of the history of the Scotch Rite in connection with the recent revelations, and the interference of the Catholic Church, wisely or not, in the question.

The one Mason whose rank corresponds in Italy to that of Albert Pike in America is not Adriano Lemmi, but Signor Timoteo Riboli, Sovereign Grand Commander of the 33rd and last degree of the Ancient and Accepted Scotch Rite. Adriano Lemmi is, or was, Grand Master of the Craft Section of Italy and Deputy Grand Commander only of the Supreme Council of Italy of the 33°. The pretended Grand Central Directory of Naples, which governs all Europe in the interests of Charleston, with Giovanni Bovio for Sovereign Director, is a Masonic myth—*pace* Signor Margiotta. Signor Bovio is a Member of the Grand Master's Council and a 33° at Rome. There is a Neapolitan Section of the Ancient and Accepted Rite, but it has powers only up to the 30°, and as such has no authority in general government, nor does Bovio appear to be a member of the Neapolitan section, though as a member of Lemmi's Council, and a 33°, he no doubt has his share in the government of the Neapolitans.

The history of the Ancient and Accepted Rite as given by Signor Margiotta and sketched in my second chapter is an incorrect history. The facts are as follows:—A person named Isaac Long was engaged in propagating the French Rite of Perfection of 25° in America before 1796; in that year he gave the degrees to one de Grasse and also to de la Hogue, who established a Consistory of the 25° at Charleston. In 1802 this Consistory had blossomed into a Supreme Grand Council, 33° and at a little later period they forged the name of Voltaire's friend, Frederick the Great of Prussia, to what Mr Yarker terms "one of the most stupidly concocted documents ever palmed upon an ignorant public." However this may be, Long does not seem to have been at any time a member of this body. This is how the "Mother Council of the World" is said to have come into existence, and Charleston has established Supreme Councils 33°, between 1811 and 1846, in France, Ireland, Scotland, England, and elsewhere.

There is no foundation for the legend of the Charleston Templar relics, namely, the skull of Jacques de Molay and the Baphomet, beyond the fact that one of the grades, the 23° of the old Rite of Perfection and the 30° of the modern Rite, uses a representation of the Papal tiara in its ceremonies and also of the crown of France, in allusion to Pope Clement V. and Philip le Bel.

I can find no Mason, of what grade or rite soever, who has ever heard of Pike's Sepher d'Hebarim, his book called Apadno, or lectures in which he imparted extracts unacknowledged from Éliphas Lévi; they may rank with triangular provinces, Lucifer *chez lui,* the skull of Molay, and the Palladium; in other words, they are lying myths. Nothing which Pike has or is known to have written has any Luciferian complexion. He has collected into his lectures a mass of mystical material from rites like Memphis and Misraïm, but it is alchemical, theosophical, or dealing with ancient symbolism, the mysteries, pre-christian theology, &c. As to Pike himself, a Mason of high authority observes in a private letter:—"He was one of the greatest men who ever adorned our Order. He was a giant among men, his learning was most profound, his eloquence great, and his wisdom comprehensive; he was a scholar in many languages, and a most voluminous writer. He was an ornament to the profession to which he belonged, namely, Law; he fought the cause of the red man against the American government many years ago, and prevailed in a large degree. I believe he was a true and humble servant of the One True and Living God, and a lover of humanity."

Having regard to all these facts, it is much to be regretted that the Catholic Church should have warmly approved and welcomed the extremely unsatisfactory testimony which connects Masonry with Diabolism. When the report of Diabolism first reached the ears of English mystics, and it was understood that the Church had concerned herself very seriously in the matter, I must confess that a hidden motive was immediately suspected. A recrudescence of mediæval Black Magic was in no sense likely to attain such proportions as to warrant the august interference; it seemed much as if Her Majesty's government should think it worth while to suppress the League of the White Rose. But when it transpired that the Question of Lucifer was a new aspect of the old question of Catholic hostility to Masonry, the astonishment evaporated; it was at once seen that Modern Diabolism had acquired an extrinsic importance because it was alleged to be connected with that Fraternity which the Church has long regarded as her implacable enemy. I must be permitted to register clearly the general conviction that if black magic, sorcery, and the Sabbath up to date had been merely revived demonomania, had been merely concerned with the black paternoster, the black mass, or even with transcendental sensualism and the ordeal of the pastos, the Roman hierarchy would not have taken action as it has, nor would the witnesses concerning these things have been welcomed with open arms; as a fact, no interest whatsoever is manifested in the doings of diabolists who operate apart from Masonry. Now, the hostility of Continental Masons towards Catholicism, in so far as it provably exists, has been largely or exclusively created by the hostility of the Church, and we know that he hates most who hates the first. In so far, therefore, as the Church has concerned herself by encouragement, which has something of the aspect of incitement, in the recent revelations, we shall have to bear in mind her attitude, while the history of forged decretals and bogus apostolic epistles will reveal to us that she does not invariably exercise a searching criticism upon documents which serve her purpose.

The sorcery of the nineteenth century is under no circumstances likely to justify the faggots of the fifteenth; it might be easier to justify the sorcery. As much by mystics as by the Church Catholic, modern black magic may be left to perish of its own corruption. But an attempt on the part of the Church to fasten the charge of diabolism on the Masonic Fraternity has credibly another motive than that of political hostility, which seems held to justify almost any weapon that comes to hand. At the bottom of her hatred of Masonry there is also her dread of the mystic. Transcendental science claims to have the key of her doctrines, and there is evidence that she fears that claim. Black magic, which, by the hypothesis, is the use of the most evil forces for the most evil purposes, she does not fear, for it wears its condemnation on its forehead; but mysticism, which accepts her own dogmas and interprets them in a sense which is not her own, which claims a certitude in matters of religion that transcends the certitude of faith, seems to hint that at one point it is possible to undermine her foundations. Hence she has ever suspected the mystic, and a part of her suspicion of Masonry has been by reason of its connection with the mystic; she has intuitively divined that connection, which by Masons themselves, for the most part, is not dreamed at this day, and when suggested is generally somewhat lightly cast aside. It would be quite out of place at the close of the present inquiry, which, from a wholly independent standpoint, has sought to justify a great fraternity from a singularly foul aspersion, to attempt enforcing upon Masons a special view of their institution, but it is desirable, at the same time, to be just towards the Catholic Church, and to affirm that we, as mystics, are on this point substantially in agreement with her. The connection in question was for a time visible, and remains in historical remembrance; from the beginning of its public appearance till the close of the eighteenth century, the history of Masonry is part of transcendental history. That connection has now ceased to manifest, but there is another which is integral and permanent, and is a matter of common principles and common objects. Let it be remembered, however, that connection is not identity; it is not intended to say that the threshold of Masonry is a gate of Mysticism, but that there is a community of purpose, of symbolism, of history, and indirectly of origin, between the two systems.

All true religion, all true morality, all true mysticism have but one object, and that is to act on humanity, collective and individual, in such a manner that it shall correspond efficiently with the great law of development, and co-operate consciously therewith to achieve the end of development. Under all the mysteries of its symbolism, behind the impressive parables of its ritual, and as equally, but if possible more effectually concealed, beneath the commonplace insistences of its moral maxims, this end is also proposed by the occult initiations of Masonry; and if it be defined more explicitly as the perfection of man both here and hereafter, and his union with what is highest in the universe, we shall see more clearly not only that it is the sole fundamental principle of all religion, its very essence, divested of creed and dogma, but also inherent in the nature of symbolical Masonry, and "inwrought in the whole system of Masonic ceremonies."

As mystics, however, we consider that the ethical standard of Masonry will produce good citizens to society and good brethren to the Fraternity, but it will not produce saints to Christ. There is an excellence which is other than the moral, and stands to morality in precisely the same relation that genius bears to talent. The moral virtues are not the *summum bonum,* nor the totality of all forces at work in the development of man, nor actually the perfect way, though they are the gate of the way of perfection. Now, the mystic claims to be in possession of the higher law which transcends the ethical, from which the ethical derives, and to which it must be referred for its reason. That the lost secret of Freemasonry is concerned with special applications of this higher law which connect with mysticism, we, as mystics, do hold and can make evident in its proper time and place. Here, and personally, I am concerned only with a comprehensive statement. In addition to its body of moral law, which is founded in the general conscience, or in the light of nature, Masonry has a body of symbolism, of which the source is not generally known, and by which it is identified with movements and modes of thought, and with evolutionary processes, having reference to regions already described as transcending the ethical world and concerned with the spiritual man. From every Masonic candidate, ignoring the schismatic and excommunicated sections, there is required a distinct attitude of mind towards the world without and the world within. He is required to believe in the existence of a Supreme Intelligence, with which his essential nature corresponds in the possession of an indestructible principle of conscious or understanding life. Beyond these doctrines, Masonry is wholly unsectarian ; it recognises no other dogmas; it accredits no form of faith. Now, Mysticism is a body of spiritual methods and processes, based, like the Masonic body of ethical methods and processes, on these same doctrines. Every man who believes in God and immortality is the raw material of a mystic; every man who believes that there is a discoverable way to God is on the path of conscious mysticism. As this path has been pursued in all ages and nations by persons of widely divergent creeds, it is clear that however much mysticism has been identified with special spheres of religious thought and activity, it is independent of all.

But while Masonry would appear to regard the evolution of our physical, intellectual, and moral nature as the best preparation for that larger existence which is included in its central doctrine, and would thus work inward from without, mysticism deems that the evolution of the spiritual man and the production of a human spirit at one with the divine constitute the missing condition requisite for the reconstruction of humanity, and would thus work outward from within. Neither Mason nor Mystic, however, can ignore either method. The one supplements the other; and seeing that the processes of mysticism are distinct from what is still a subject of derision under the name of transcendental phenomena, as they are wholly philosophical and interior, not to be appreciated by the senses, a secret experience within the depths and heights of our spiritual being, an institution which believes in God and immortality, and by the fact of immortality in the subsistence of an intimate relation between the spirit and God, will not look suspiciously on mysticism when it comes to understand it better.

I have spoken of Masonic symbolism, and the method of instruction in Masonry is identical with that of mysticism; both systems are "veiled in allegory and illustrated by symbolism." The significance of this correspondence would not be measurably weakened were there no similarity in the typology, no trace of mystic influence in Masonic rite and legend. But there is a resemblance, and the types are often identical, though the accredited interpretation varies. Masonry, as a fact, interprets the types which belong to our own science according to the criterion of ethics, and thus provides a prolegomena to Mysticism, as ethics are a necessary introduction to the inner science of the soul. There is naturally a minor body of conventional typology which is tolerably exclusive to the craft, but the grand and universal emblems, characteristic of symbolical Masonry as distinct from the operative art—these are our own emblems. The All-Seeing Eye, the Burning Star, the Rough and Perfect Ashlar, the Point within a Circle, the Pentalpha, the Seal of Solomon, the Cubic Stone—all these belong to the most lofty and arcane order of occult symbolism, but in mystic science they illumine more exalted zones of the heaven of mind. The rites, legends, and mysteries of the great Fraternity are also full of mystical allusions, and admit of mystical interpretation in the same manner, but their evidential force is weaker, because ceremonial and legend in the hands of a skilful commentator can be made to take any shape and any complexion; it is otherwise with the symbols of the Brotherhood which were possessed by us before the historical appearance of Masonry. So also the Masonic reverence for certain numbers which are apparently arbitrary in themselves is in reality connected with a most recondite and curious system of mystic methodical philosophy, while in the high titles of Masonic dignity there is frequently a direct reference to Mysticism.

If we turn from these considerations and approach the historical connection through those still undetermined problems which concern the origin of Masonry, we shall discern not unfortunately a way clear to their solution, but a significant characteristic pervading every Masonic hypothesis almost without exception—namely, an instinctive desire to refer Masonry in its original form to sources that are provably mystic. In the fanciful and extravagant period, when archæology and comparative mythology were as yet in their childhood, this tendency was not less strong because it was mostly quite unconscious. To pass in review before us the chief institutions of antiquity, with which Masonry was then said to be connected, would be to sweep the whole field of transcendental history, and when we come to a more sober period which recognised the better claim of the building guilds to explain the beginnings of the Fraternity, the link with Mysticism was not even then abandoned, and a splendid variant of the Dionysian dream took back the mediæval architects to the portals of Eleusis and of Thebes.

When the history of Freemasonry becomes possible by the possession of materials, its chief philosophical interest centres in one country of Europe; there is no doubt that it exercised an immense influence upon France during that century of quakings and quickenings which gave birth to the great revolution, transformed civilisation in the West, and inaugurated the modern era. Without being a political society, it was an instrument eminently adaptable to the sub-surface determination of political movements. At a later date it may have contributed to the formation of Germany, as it did certainly to the creation of Italy, but the point and centre of Masonic history is France in the eighteenth century. To that country also is mainly confined the historical connection between Masonry and mystic science, for the revival of

Mysticism which originated in Germany at the close of the eighteenth century, and thence passed over to England, found its final field in France at the period in question. There Rosicrucianism reappeared, there Anton Mesmer recovered the initial process of transcendental practice, there the Marquis de Puységur discovered clairvoyance, there Martines de Pasqually instructed his disciples in the mysteries of ceremonial magic; there the illustrious Saint-Martin, *le philosophe inconnu,* developed a special system of spiritual reconstruction; there alchemy flourished; there spiritual and political princes betook themselves to extravagant researches after an elixir of life; there also, as a consequence, rose up a line of magnificent impostors who posed as initiates of the occult sciences, as possessors of the grand secret and the grand mastery; there, finally, under the influences of transcendental philosophy, emblematic Freemasonry took root and grew and flourished, developing ten thousand splendours of symbolic grades, of romantic legends, of sonorous names and titles. In a word, the Mysticism of Europe concentrated its forces at Paris and Lyons, and all French Mysticism gathered under the shadow of the square and compass. To that, as to a centre, the whole movement gravitated, and thence it worked. There is nothing to show that it endeavoured to revolutionise Masonry in its own interest. The Fraternity naturally attracted all Mystics to its ranks, and the development of the mystic degrees took place as the result of that attraction.

By the year 1825 a variety of circumstances had combined to suspend transcendental activity, and the connection with Masonry ended, but the present revival of mystic thought is rapidly picking up the links of the broken chain; secretly or unobtrusively the spirit of transcendentalism is working within the Fraternity, and the bogus question of Lucifer is simply a hostile and unscrupulous method of recognising that fact. If Masonry and Mysticism could be shown in the historical world to be separated by the great sea, the consanguinity of their intention would remain, which is more important than external affinity, and they are sisters by that bond. But they have not been so separated, and on either side there is no need to be ashamed of the connection. With all brethren of the Fraternity, "we also do believe in the resurrection of Hiram," and we regard the Temple as "an edifice immediately realisable, for we rebuild it in our hearts." We also adore the Grand Architect, and offer our intellectual homage to the divine cipher which is in the centre of the symbolic star; and we believe that some day the Mason will recognise the Mystic. He is the heir of the great names of antiquity, the philosophers and hierarchs, and the spiritual kings of old; he is of the line of Orpheus and Hermes, of the Essenes and the Magi. And all those illustrious systems and all those splendid names with which Masonry has ever claimed kindred belong absolutely to the history of Mysticism.

THE END

Diana Vaughan and the Question of Modern Palladism

A Sequel to *Devil-Worship in France*

Arthur Edward Waite

"Many men both of high and low condition in these last years past, have to my knowledge seen Diana unveiled."
—*A New Light of Alchemy*

"Farewell to all occult adventure; the farce is played."
—Arthur Macthen, *The Three Impostors*

PREFACE

THE CONSPIRACY OF discredited journalists, *soi-disant* ex-Masons, and purveyors of pornographic literature in Paris, to which we are indebted for the invention of Modern Palladism, has run its course, and has exposed its own motives more effectually than any criticism which from the nature of the case is confined chiefly to documentary analysis. It has ceased from plotting against Masonry, and has said its last word upon the connection of diabolism and transcendental phenomena. There is no longer any question of "Lucifer in the Lodges," or of the ingenious lady who for the past three or four years has so fascinated, scandalized, and perplexed the impressionable people of Paris. The various persons of the comedy have taken leave of their masks and the master of the revels has come before the curtain, has declaimed his epilogue, and has bowed his thanks before a numerous and representative company. As a defender of the Catholic Church against the secret societies, Leo Taxil has played his part, and the mummery is now at an end. He has shown us a variety of lucrative, and in themselves not un-amusing, uses to which a papal encyclical can be put which were quite undreamed of by the sovereign pontiff when he published the *Humanum Genus* epistle, and if some additional odium must attach to him, he has had his compensation beforehand in the subscriptions of believers, while it is otherwise of small consequence to the author of the *Bible Amusante.* In conjunction with Mr. C. C. Massey, I was the first writer to draw attention to the true nature of the intrigue, and the disclosures thus initiated, originally in the columns of "Light," and afterwards in my book entitled, "Devil Worship in France," gave an impetus to continental criticism which has at length driven the imposition to unmask itself. Leo Taxil has come forward, and in the presence of the press-representatives of a large number of papers, assembled by invitation in the saloon of the Paris Geographical Society, has avowed that the whole transaction was a deception from beginning to end. He has proclaimed also that he was never a genuine convert to the Catholic faith, and that his life has been devoted to the invention of literary rascalities and hoaxes. As to Diana Vaughan, she is a type-writer in his employment. His speech was the culminating impudence and the crowning cynicism of one of the best planned mystifications of modern times. It is small wonder that it enraged a meeting which was perhaps divided equally between the delegates of his dupes and his exposers, and he had to be protected by the police. Having regard to the fact that the machination which is now apparently stamped out has extended over many years, has imperilled the reputations of many persons both dead and living, and was once at least on the brink of deceiving the legislative centre of the Latin Church; that it did positively, and even for a considerable time, impose upon ecclesiastics of the highest position; it is in every way desirable to show the real motives which have led to the confession of Leo Taxil. He has attempted to pose as a species of Divine Comedian, creating a universal deception, and would now vanish amidst the plaudits of his own enthusiasm at the magnificence of his achievement. It must therefore be pointed out that he is not a splendid impostor but a mercenary adventurer who has been actuated throughout by the basest motive and has made use of the sorriest means. Without going over the ground already traversed in my previous work, to which the reader may be referred for a full presentation of the flagitiousness of the conspiracy, I propose to show briefly how and why the impostor was compelled to unmask, not as the master-stroke of a gorgeous deception but as the last refuge and valedictory audacity of an exposed culprit. An account of the various embroilments and revelations which forced the hand of Leo Taxil, and led up to the final denouement, will also furnish the readers of *Devil-Worship in France* with a kind of historical conclusion to an investigation in which many persons all over the world have taken considerable interest; simultaneously it will afford an opportunity to note some residual questions which may still lead to confusion; and to utter, if I am so far warranted, a word of timely warning to the enemies of Masonry and Mysticism. I have borne in mind the possibility that some persons who may be attracted by the dimensions of this modest volume will not have the leisure or inclination to make acquaintance with the larger work to which it is a sequel, and by the occasional extension of a reference I have placed them in a position to understand the chief points involved.

The literature, largely periodical, which is represented by this brief summary is of enormous dimensions, and naturally includes much which was of consequence at the time because it helped to ensure the end, with which, however, its importance has passed away. It is said that in France alone over four hundred newspapers pronounced against Diana Vaughan, while the books and pamphlets which have appeared in that country, in Germany, and in Italy, would form a considerable contribution to a Masonic bibliography. It is unnecessary to enumerate them formally; if anyone in the time to come should have occasion to refer to this curious and not uninstructive episode in the history of Masonry and Mysticism, he will not, I think, need to go further than the resources of this and its companion volume. The recital finally serves to indicate through what difficulties many creditable persons continued to believe in the monstrous fiction of Palladian Masonry.

I

The Conspiracy in Outline

PRIOR TO THE YEAR 1885 Leo Taxil was a writer of indecorous romances published in serial form, an anti-cleric, and a retailer of discreditable stories concerning ecclesiastics, especially in high places. He became a Mason, but was expelled from the Order. About the date mentioned, the house which published his lucubrations appears to have failed, and Leo Taxil then pretended to awake to the enormity of his literary life. Thereupon he announced his conversion, and, I believe, attributed it to the intercession of Joan of Arc. He had naturally a grudge against the Masons, and he determined to turn it to account. Thus his plot against the Fraternity, which culminated in the unfinished Memoirs of Diana Vaughan, is not altogether a product of the present decade. It began some twelve years ago, when the ex-atheist and pornographer produced his first volume of fraudulent revelations under the title of the "Brethren of the Three Points." Having never passed beyond the initial grade of Apprentice, he was practically in possession of nothing but public knowledge, *plus* the resources of a profligate imagination, and in England at least the percentage of genuine information contained in that work would be well within the possibilities of many who were not Masons. It would also be known in France to the readers of Ragon and other accredited historians and expositors of the Fraternity. There is no reason to suppose that this publication, though it may have circulated to a certain extent, produced any considerable impression, and the same observation applies to the "Cultus of the Grand Architect," which appeared shortly after, and is little more than an unauthorised Masonic directory. It was said of Leo Taxil: *Il a fini de manger du cure; il mange, aujourd'hui, du franc-macon;* but it was imperative that he should provide more inviting fare for his readers, if he would continue to get bread for himself. In a fortunate moment it occurred to him to exploit the history of what is called Adoptive Masonry, and electrify reputable people, especially the wives of Freemasons, by revealing that there were lodges for women in connection with the ordinary lodges, and that the worst construction which could be placed on them would not exceed the truth.

He distributed the imaginary institutions with a lavish hand over the whole country; he invented names for each of them, and pseudonyms for their most prominent members. The effrontery succeeded, it brought money to its purveyor, and there is no need to say that he continued. He reprinted his work on "Sister-Masons" while it was still in circulation, providing a new title and some additional sections. One of these contained the fiction of "Palladian Masonry," or "Luciferian Spiritism," presumably founded on some obscure society for the propagation of Sabbatic Orgies, wholly unconnected with Freemasonry. Its pretended rituals have been traced, I believe, to a source more banal than abominable, and it was his province to colour them. In this manner did the mysterious Order issue ready-made from the brain of Leo Taxil, and has since filled Europe with its rumour. I suppose that the creation must again have served the one purpose of its author, and I infer that his next step was to enter into collusion with another writer much more obscure than himself, namely, Adolphe Ricoux, for the production of a pamphlet, in defence of his bogus revelations, entitled "Are there Lodges for Women?" It contained a pseudo-Instruction of Albert Pike, the most illustrious Mason of his age, Grand Commander of the Supreme Mother Council (Ancient and Accepted Scottish Rite) of the United States Southern Jurisdiction, advocating the worship of Lucifer as the true God, licence in sexual intercourse, and other follies and enormities. Much about the same time he became connected with Dr. Bataille, *alias* Dr. Hacks, and a vast publication was projected in weekly numbers under the title of *Le Diable au XIXe Siѐle*, which had a very wide sale, and extended to nearly 250 issues. The worship of Lucifer in the lodges of Palladian Freemasonry, diabolical manifestations in return, and a general history of pseudo-supernaturalism in the nineteenth century, were among the disclosures made in this work. It is most ingenious, most entertaining, and is likely to be remembered as a curiosity when all interest in the conspiracy which manufactured it shall have passed away. Among other characters introduced in this colossal narrative we hear the first account of the mysterious Paris-American, Miss Diana Vaughan. *Le Diable au XIXe Siècle* having run its course, was replaced by a monthly review which also had a large circulation. The conspiracy was now at its height. Works on Female Freemasonry from other pens, the confessions of Domenico Margiotta, an Italian ex-Mason, and member, as he said, of the Palladium, with a formidable array of documents supplemented the previous evidence, but directly or indirectly they were all the work of Leo Taxil. Presently the Palladian Grand Mistress, Diana Vaughan, was said to have arrived from New York; there was a split in the camp of the Palladists; at the head of the new faction she was about to establish a Luciferian Order of her own, and she actually issued three numbers of a review pretending to be founded in its interest. These also were the work of the conspiracy. At the end of three or four months the conversion of the lady was announced, and was followed by the publication of her memoirs in monthly numbers. It was at this juncture that I began the analysis of all the evidence which afterwards appeared under the title of "Devil-Worship in France."

There was full justification for that criticism. Whatever the absurdity of the charges there is no doubt that they were being largely countenanced by the Catholic Church. No voice had as yet been raised against them in the Catholic Press; the pope had granted an audience to Leo Taxil; Cardinal Parocchi, cardinal-vicar of Rome, had felicitated him for exposing "the turpitude of the androgyne Lodges"; Mgr. Meurin had written a colossal impeachment of Freemasonry based on the documents of Adolphe Riocoux; the bishop of Grenoble had furnished a flattering testimonial on the importance of these heinous revelations; the *Revue Catholique* of Coutances had blindly identified itself with the conspiracy, Margiotta had the papal benediction and a sheaf of episcopal plaudits. When a great Church is on the eve of a considerable folly, it matters little that the deceivers are themselves worthless, and those who describe me as the enemy of Catholicism would perhaps do better to recognise the hand of a friendly critic who had at least the intention to save it from steps that seemed imminent, and would at least imperil its dignity. The opinion which I ventured to express that the Question of Lucifer, in so far as it was known in England, would assume a fresh interest with the publication of *Devil-Worship in France,* was justified by the reception of the work. It was founded upon no undue idea of its intrinsic deserts, for it appeared at a time when it was impossible to close that question, and it bears all the marks of the haste with which it was written. It was designed to draw attention to the egregious nature of the accusations which were pouring forth from the French press, directed on the one hand against the Masonic Fraternity and on the other against modern transcendentalism, and representing, or rather pretending to represent, the interests of the Catholic Church. By manifesting, so far as I was then able, the fraudulent nature of the accusation, it was my hope to put Englishmen on their guard, and to give an occasion to other investigations. The work received precisely the kind of welcome which I could have desired most; it was regarded as an honest and so far successful attempt to get at the truth of the matter. On the

Question of Lucifer itself, it aroused considerable curiosity, and was the means of directing that curiosity into a proper and wholesome channel. The moderate edition which was printed circulated over a very wide area and has, in fact, penetrated into all parts of the English speaking world; I do not think that any Englishman would have been likely after its appearance to be deceived by the Parisian conspiracy, had no further developments and no final *denouement* followed. The press-opinions quoted elsewhere convey no idea of the discussion which directly and indirectly arose out of the work.

At the time of publication I endeavoured to dissuade persons who were not acquainted with the issues from minimising the importance of the question. It was the depreciation of this importance which I had every reason to expect at the hands of the general reader, and especially of the general press. It is difficult to realise in this country the strength and activity of the Anti-Masonic movement abroad, and the fact that in the Question of Lucifer it had gone to preposterous lengths was one of no little moment when regarded rightly. But it was naturally difficult to get it regarded rightly. When Masonry and the Mysticism with which it has been always connected are accused of diabolism, the revival of Black Magic, and so forth, the general reader, knowing little of Masonry and nothing at all of Mysticism, is, of course, prompted to say that the charge is absurd, and that it is the wiser course to treat it with contempt. The accusation against Masonry, in particular, he would say, refutes itself; it is not worth a moment's notice, and should be permitted to die of itself. But it was not an accusation preferred against ordinary lodges; it was the pretended disclosure of a secret directing centre, and the developments which have come to pass since the issue of *Devil-Worship in France* are proof positive that it had to be killed before it would die; since then it has attracted more attention and has been more agressive than ever. At the time also when I undertook my examination, it was doing anything but refute itself; in France and in Italy it was gaining adherents daily, and was certainly a more profitable investment to those who were immediately concerned than are many gold-mines to their shareholders. A question, furthermore, which profoundly impressed our French neighbours could not be wholly nugatory, and, outside ordinary Masonry, the charge of Black Magic is inherently absurd to those only who are in ignorance of the direction in which some occult investigations are likely to lead those who pursue them or of the kind of performances which take place in certain occult associations. The public ignorance is a very bad measure of possibilities in this order.

The event at least has proved that there was every warrant for my warning. In spite of much favourable criticism, I think that the keynote of the press was the significant hint that I might have found a shorter way. "A laborious and too serious investigation of a repulsive folly," said the *Civil and Military Gazette,* quite failing to grasp the fact that we were dealing not with a folly but with a highly profitable and well-planned form of fraud, which at the moment seemed on the point of deceiving the greatest of the Christian Churches and would still be running its course triumphantly if investigators like myself had not taken it seriously in hand. "Hardly worth the serious consideration here afforded it," said the

Scotsman, but it has needed additional consideration, even more serious, before it has been possible to dismiss it, definitely unmasked, as the facts of this narrative will testify. "The accusation that Satanism is a branch of Freemasonry," said the *Daily Telegraph,* "is so wholly foolish, that the bare mention of it is enough to cause laughter," and this represents what I anticipated would be the public verdict. And yet we have to remember that the Latin Church has consistently and throughout stigmatised Freemasonry as a Satanic institution, and it was in the nature of things only a matter of time that it should be accused of actually dealing with the devil. The accusation came at length; it came when there had been recently a great recrudescence of what is called transcendentalism and occultism, when therefore for many people the charge of diabolism was not inherently an absurd charge; it came also supported by a great array of depositions and documents; it was taken seriously, attracting large attention, and although it is well to laugh, it is not idle to have another motive for mirth than that of inherent fatuity. Having said what seems to be called for in defence of the line of action which I and others adopted, it remains only to give some account of the progress and fortunes of the conspiracy during the months which have intervened since the publication of *Devil-Worship in France.*

II

The Railleries of Dr. Bataille

As there is no reason to suppose that Leo Taxil would have unmasked his own imposture unless it had ceased to be profitable or till his position became untenable, so there is no call to accredit him with more ingenuity than is sufficient for the equipment of an accomplished trickster. It would be gratuitous, for example, to assume that he planned quarrels and secessions among his collaborators to lead up to his triumphant exhibition in the face of all Paris, and almost with Europe for his audience. It is highly probable that so far as Taxil was concerned the conspiracy has missed its mark; his supreme ambition was to mislead the entire Catholic Church, and to obtain through the Trent Congress a judgment in favour of his revelations. It was an infeasible ambition, and he understood only the least intelligent section of his intended victims, but in any case secessions from his own camp were certainly destructive to his interests, and we may, I think, take it that they occurred in the ordinary course of the events which lead up commonly to the detection of impostors. Furthermore, in the present case they bear all the marks of spontaneity. There can be no doubt that the *magnum opus* of the conspiracy was the work entitled *Le Diable au XIXe Siècle,* which pretended to be the memoirs of a Catholic spy who had investigated high-grade Masonry in the chief countries of the world for the purpose of unveiling the iniquities practised therein. I was the first to expose the innumerable inventions which entered into this narrative but the subsequent adventures of its author are scarcely less entertaining than his original confessions. About a week after the publication of *Devil-Worship in France,* which took place in the early days of June 1896, an English gentleman residing in Paris, who was interested in the allegations against Masonry, took advantage of his presence on the spot to make a personal investigation in the form of a visit to the author of *Le Diable au XIXe Siècle.* He appears to have been received affably and discovered that Dr. Hacks, alias Dr. Bataille, had cut himself adrift from the conspiracy, had married, and set up as a medical practitioner in a handsome suite of rooms. He explained quite frankly that when he was a bachelor, doing press-work on the *Petit Journal,* he was invited to join a number of other journalists in the production of *Le Diable au XIXe Siècle,* and was glad to accept the unusual remuneration offered. His co-operation was limited, however, to a small part of the first volume. "When he found that it was going beyond an amusing caricature, was being taken seriously by some people, and was dealing with personal questions, he withdrew." At the same time, and actuated apparently by a feeling of professional loyalty, he would say nothing concerning his associates, but "it was evident that he looked with great gusto on the financial success of the publication, and with enjoyment on the credulous folly of mankind." He further affirmed himself to be, and to have been always, an absolute materialist and disbeliever in the supernatural. "His position in this respect is so firm that he announces that he has resigned his membership in the *Société des Sciences Psychiques* because that body admits the possible existence of the supernatural."

A hostile narrative appearing in an English newspaper may not have reached the headquarters of the conspiracy and might not have been noticed if it had. However, a few weeks later the Anti-Masonic Congress of Trent made the question of Diana Vaughan almost of European interest, while there was also, and in consequence, a considerable inquiry abroad as to the identity of Dr. Bataille. Among other organs, the Catholic newspaper *L'Univers*, whose editor is M. Eugene Tavernier, began to demand information, and it was supplied by no one so promptly as the Doctor himself, who offered two statements which were calculated, in his opinion, to preclude the periodical in question from going further astray concerning *Le Diable au XIXe Siècle* and Miss Diana Vaughan-burning questions, he observed "for some thousands of imbeciles." He affirmed, firstly, and as before, that he merely collaborated over a part of the first volume, and, secondly, that he was a complete stranger to the affair of Diana. Later on in a letter to *La Vérité* he denied the authorship of the articles which had appeared over the signature of Dr. Bataille in the columns of the *Revue Mensuelle,* whilst registering his utter indifference to any opinion which might or might not be held concerning him by Catholics. These admissions were followed by others full of racy insolence, addressed to M. Tavernier and to *La Libre Parole,* in one of which he solicits an advertisement of an *à la carte* restaurant, which he had recently opened, as a compensation for an injurious criticism. The medical profession, he acknowledges, was not patronised sufficiently in his person, and he had to look elsewhere for his livelihood. Previously to his experience as a ship's doctor he had been a clown!

But if Dr. Bataille regarded his readers in general as so many "imbeciles" who were fair sport for his impositions, he had no words to express his derision of that inner circle of believers who took the pains to address him personally. Among these there was a certain abbé, who, having approached him by letter, was placed by him in written communication with "Diana Vaughan." She, in her reply, recommended him to have recourse to "the good doctor" for advice as to the best means of establishing a Hospital of the Sacred Heart. When Dr. Bataille washed his hands publicly of the affair of Diana, the ecclesiastic wrote to him, saying that he was stupefied and overwhelmed, upon which the gay physician enclosed the letter to M. Gaston Mèry, editor of *La Libre Parole,* saying:—"Read it; linger over it, tell me, are there not some moments, and is not this one of them, when the literary jester experiences a sweet joy, a delicious hilarity, which more than compensates for his labours and solicitude? What think you of your country after that? . . . And it is three years at least since I went out of the whole business, since I have set foot in the shop of the publishers; and I have not even glanced at the second part of the *Diable au XIXe Siècle;* while for me Diana Vaughan is only a vague name. Yet it is to me this man addresses himself that be may cease from being stupefied!!!?

It is needless to say that Dr. Hacks makes a false statement as to the period when he severed his connection with the obscure publishing house of MM. Delhomme et Briguet, for certainly in October, 1894 he was running a Clinique Saint Sulpice, apparently in the back parlour of their establishment, and it was advertised on the covers of the Memoirs. A month later in the same year the address was changed, but the publishers received correspondence for the institution and its physician, as appears by another advertisement.

The letter last quoted was written at the beginning of Nov. 1896. To complete the confessions of the Doctor it is only necessary to record that M. Villarmich, of the staff of *La Libre Parole,* interviewed him also a little later on. He was found in a comfortable apartment above his restaurant on the Boulevard Montmartre, where, by the pleasantry of its proprietor, the stained glass windows exhibited heads of Lucifer. The doctor, it is stated, affected frankness and good nature, but there is evidence to show that he is by disposition a genial scapegrace. He explained that on the appearance of the *Humanum Genus* Encyclical, he concluded that there was money to be made out of the "known credulity and the unknown idiocy of the Catholics." A Jules Verne was needed, and he became that Jules Verne. *Voilà Tout,* said the doctor. The same idea, he continued, had occurred to Leo Taxil, whereupon he came to an understanding with that personage and some other friends. The result was *Le Diable au XIXe Siècle.* Enumerating the most absurd of his stories, he states that they drew tears of laughter from his collaborators, but the latter thought that he was going too far and would spoil all. He assured them that the stories would pass, and they did. "In a word, it was the most brazen defiance ever offered to human stupidity, and it was accepted." He severed his connection because he grew sick of his collaborators; *il n'y a pas des gens plus embêtants que ces la.* In any case, he observed that he had "made his pile," after which he transferred his versatile pen to *L' Illustration,* then had a turn at photography, and finally, purchased the restaurant, which at the time of the interview was "going very well."

As to Leo Taxil, the doctor hesitated, and then sought to maintain his sincerity. When his complicity in the inventions of his collaborator was objected, the answer was that Taxil's nature was most complex and very difficult to analyse. Concerning Diana Vaughan, that was purely Leo Taxil's matter; "he invariably told me that he was her honorary agent," much after the same manner that Dr. Hacks once signed himself "honorary Catholic."

The statements made at this interview will, of course, bear no examination. If Dr. Hacks conceived the idea of the imposture and suggested it to Taxil, the latter could not have attempted to mystify him over the affair of Diana, which was part of the jugglery. It is also highly improbable that the plot originated in the manner that it is described. The *Humanum Genus* Encylical was promulgated in 1886 and the idea of exploiting the Catholics did not take effect, so far as Dr.

Hacks was concerned, till 1892. In the meantime it had been put to more than one application by Leo Taxil.

How was the conspiracy affected by the *volte-face* of the accredited author of its revelation-in-chief, and by the scandalous details which accompanied it? The impression on a casual review would be that it had received its death-blow, and had it been possible to glance into the obscure lodging of the venal pamphleteer—according to the "Memoirs of an Ex-Palladist," Leo Taxil dwells in one of the poorest quarters of Paris, in a "modest apartment" situated on the fifth floor—or into the shop of his bookseller, we should no doubt have found them all in considerable confusion. But they had a way out of the difficulty. They were catering in the main for foolish people, though not entirely so foolish as might appear; they took the risk and it succeeded.

It was explained quite simply that Dr. Hacks had been bought by the Freemasons, to which that eminently saleable peronage replied: "If I confessed to my readers assembled that I had fooled them, they would not credit me, and it may be presumed that they gave credit to Leo Taxil when he invented the above interpretation." It was not, however, till Oct. 1896, or subsequently to the Trent Congress, that I can trace any words of self-defence on the part of the prime conspirator. It then took the shape of a letter addressed by Leo Taxil to the editor of the Turin *Italia Reale,* and was published in the *Revue Mensuelle.* Therein it is denied that Dr. Hacks was always a convinced materialist, or that a work entitled *Le Geste,* which contains proof positive of his free thinking, really represented his views. It is also sought to establish a distinction in time between the worthless publication in question and *Le Diable au XIXe Siècle* but this seems wholly untrue. The date on the title-page of *Le Geste* is 1893, while the memoirs began their course in the November of the preceeding year, and it is therefore fully evident that the intermediate publication did not represent an antecedent opinion, more especially as the former pretends to have been the result of a mission representing convictions in religion so far back as the year 1880. Leo Taxil forgot this point or he would have sought his explanation elsewhere.

To this account of the extinction of Dr. Bataille, I have only to add that among the ecclesiastical supporters of the revelations, the bishop of Grenoble and Canon Mustel would appear to have entirely adopted the view taken by the conspiracy as to the motives which had actuated its former associate. In a moment of unwonted effrontery, M. Hacks went so far as to suggest that Canon Mustel had a hand in the preparation of *Le Diable au XIXe Siècle.* The credulity of the editor or the *Revue Catholique* of Coutances seems to have been so abysmal that it is possible to save his intelligence only at the expense of his integrity, and some of his evidence conflicts so seriously with that of other persons more highly placed than himself, while the warmth of his defense has so much the accent of a partisan, that the question of his sincerity might be conceivably within the pale of discussion. But I believe there is no real doubt of his honesty, and so also there is most certainly none of his folly.

III

The Margiotta Embroilment

Could anything be more culpable than the motives which originated *Le Diable au XIXe Siècle,* it would be the effrontery of the subsequent admissions, and could these be surpassed by anything it would be by the insolence of the Taxil explanation. It is, however, an indifferent conspiracy which cannot survive one defection. Over that of Dr. Hacks there was mourning in a truly charitable spirit. He was deplored rather then abused; he had yielded to the arts of the enemy; he must be prayed for; there were extenuating circumstances; he had really been a genuine Catholic; he was now probably mad. But Leo Taxil had yet to be confronted by another secession, and to reckon with another quarrel, not less squalid in its details, but more rancorous and bitter, for the patience of the conspiracy was exhausted, and it felt that its time was short. The first public result of the Bataille embroglio appeared in England June 27, 1896, and a few days later the *Revue Mensuelle* found itself forced to take notice of certain startling acts and accusations on the part of a personage only second in importance to the reputed author of *Le Diable au XIXe Siècle.* I refer to Domenico Margiotta, the Italian ex-Mason whose evidence, as first published, was apparently so strong, had so little to do with diabolism, and seemed to be a crux for criticism. He was one of the witnesses of Lucifer whose case I held over for judgment in the light of any later facts which might transpire. It was left in the opinion that further evidence would be shortly forthcoming and without much doubt as to the ultimate nature of the verdict. *Devil-Worship in France.* p. 305. I have no ground to take credit for any particular sagacity in having expressed this view, and the fresh revelations were not of a character which was to be antecedently expected. They were evidently unlooked for by the conspirator-in-chief, or this at least seems the most natural way to account for his violence. Words of the strongest kind were inefficient to express the loathing which he conceived for his quondam associate when the split took place between them. With the comparative attitude I think we should all agree if the interest had not quite passed away. In the first place, Dr. Hacks is a man of considerable literary ability; Margiotta has none. In the second place, once Hacks determined, for reasons of his own, to make a clean breast of his share in the imposture, he did it with little reservation; he gave his reasons and he spared his comrades. But Margiotta throughout showed himself in a pitiful light, his spite was against his associates; they were the impostors, he was still the man of honour, and he also the chief victim; he lied and swindled, but he shifted the responsibility on Leo Taxil. Having the manner of a paid servant, and confessing to a deed of engagement, he had also the peculiar venom and treachery which distinguish a menial who has somehow lost his place, or a minor accomplice who has not had an equal share of the booty.

The first signs of secession on the part of the Italian must have been exhibited shortly before or shortly after the publication of his second book. See *Devil-Worship in France* Ch. X. For myself I am disposed to regard that work as the product of his mutiny, an attempt to elaborate the conspiracy independently on his own account. Unlike "Adriano Lemmi," it was devoid of any documents which could lay claim to originality, and shows plainly that be was separated from the prolific source of all such valuable adjuncts. It evoked no notice whatsoever in the *Revue Mensuelle,* but twelve months passed away before the reason of this silence transpired. The initial source of our information is the tenth number of the "Memoirs of an Ex-Palladist." It then appeared that Domenico Margiotta had been for some time past circulating a scandal which took shape ultimately in the following terms:—"The Diana Vaughan whom I knew in 1889, at Naples, has always remained a Palladist, and there was no exception in her favour as to the rule of the Pastos." [*Devil-Worship in France* pp. 66,67.] The history of her conversion is only a mystification to allure the Catholics. The Diana Vaughan who writes the "Memoirs of an Ex-Palladist" and the "'Eucharistic Novena," etc., is a false Diana. I defy her to come forward, for those who make use of the name of the New York Grand Mistress can exhibit only some adventures whom I will immediately convict of imposture. As to the true Diana Vaughan, the comedy now playing is to her a matter of indifference; she is the first to laugh at it. She diabolises more than ever in the Triangles; she has made her peace with Lemmi."

I may spare my readers an account of Miss Taxil's alleged feelings at this outrage offered to her honour; her sentiments cover many pages of pious ejaculation and exclamatory wrath. Legal proceedings were, of course, her first impulse, but her best friends assured her, as was otherwise sufficiently obvious, that they might not be successful. In view of this uncertainty she permitted the Christian to triumph, and contented herself with exhibiting the motives which prompted Margiotta to adopt this unworthy cause. Some time after the publication of "Adriano Lemmi," Diana Vaughan was suppose to have repaired to Naples. There had just been an earthquake in Calabria, and she says: "I received a letter from M. Margiotta, which recounted among other things, that a palace of his ancestors at Palmi had collapsed, and he begged me to pay for its rebuilding, or at least favour him with the trifle of a hundred thousand francs. I made inquiries and learned that the palace was in reality a small house let to an apothecary and that it had not been seriously injured. In a word, I found the request indiscreet, and gave him to understand as much. Hence this wrath. Our relations ceased at this point."

In the following month the *Revue Mensuelle* reproduced the justification of Diana with a commentary by Leo Taxil explaining why the organ of the conspiracy had so long kept silent in all that regarded Margiotta, and giving further details as to the conduct of the Italian. By these it would appear that Margiotta was already disposed to abandon his distinction between the two Dianas and now suggested that his acquaintance with the mysterious lady was much closer than he had admitted. Taxil adds, on the auricular evidence of a friend, that there was a further accusation emanating from the same quarter, and one of the utmost foulness, constituting the most violent outrage which could be afforded to a woman even of dissolute morals.

Another witness reported Margiotta as saying:—"What would you have? It is the fashion to make a virtue of it. Like others, I have celebrated her purity, but all the high-grade Masons, myself included, know perfectly well that she is *une hysterique insatiable.*"

The article in the *Revue Mensuelle* was republished in pamphlet form with certain additions, impeaching the honesty of Margiotta in several amusing ways. For two months he remained overwhelmed apparently by his enemies. On the 2nd of November, he wired from Grenoble to M. Gaston Mèry, editor of *La Libre Parole,* as follows:—"Reliable information: Madame Taxil is Vaughan. Taxil an accomplice Bataille imposture. Devil-publisher's speculation, with complicity of Taxil-Bataille. Will forward you Taxil autograph copy. Assume responsibility. Margiotta."

I do not observe that this communication was ever followed by the promised document. Signor Margiotta, however, next, and finally, so far as I am aware, addressed himself to *La France Libre* of Lyons, confessing that, so far as he was concerned, the Vaughan revelations were wholly fraudulent. "Despite an apparent duality, Taxil and I were actually one person, speaking, thinking, and writing by the mouth, mind, and pen of the inventor of Diana Vaughan. An agreement bound me to this man, a barbarous agreement which imposed the obligation of accepting without discussion, the materials, deeds, and documents, which entered into the body of the work. It was under such conditions that I came to transcribe the phases of the pretended conversion of his Diana, to affirm that I had seen with my own eyes this beautiful soul now reconciled to God, when, as a fact, I had neither seen nor known her except through the statements of Taxil."

I must confess that the life and the savour has gone out of this wonderful embroilment, thus briefly epitomized. How, it will be asked, was it possible for two sharpers to quarrel over the character of a woman whom they both knew to be a myth unless it was by previous agreement for the good of the comedy? It is not worth debating, but I do not think the device was ever thought of; I infer that Margiotta was kept in the dark by Taxil; that he believed to some extent in the communications he received from her, that he believed in her wealth, that he did try to borrow money from her, and. that his eyes were only opened slowly to the real facts of the case. In any event, there is only one point which is now of some moment; that in spite of these scandalous episodes, in spite of this second secession, "Diana Vaughan" had still a public to appeal to, and independent organs, and Canon Mustel, and the bishop of Grenoble still prenouncing in her favour. But in spite also of the incredible heroism it was increasingly evident that the days of the conspiracy were numbered. Its death-blow, however, had still to come.

IV

The Trent Congress and Diana Vaughan

THE WHOLE WORLD is acquainted more or less with the doings of the Anti-Masonic Congress held last year at Trent. The Report of that Congress was issued in due course, and was based entirely on the books and official acts of the Masonic body itself. It found that the religious doctrines by which Freemasonry has been inspired are those of nature-worship, and that the various beliefs publicly professed by Freemasons under different names may be summed up as Monism, Idealistic Pantheism, Materialism, and Positivism. The connecting link between all is the identification of the universe with God.

There is every indication to show that at its first rumour the conspiracy had hoped much from the Congress. Having a sheaf of most alluring revelations, it believed that the bait would take. They had been thoughtfully planned to supply the one thing wanting to complete the case of the Church against Masonry. There is not the least reason to doubt that the Catholic Church would have given, so to speak, the third part of the triple crown of Peter to find Satanism flourishing in the Lodges. It would not have welcomed the conspiracy as it undoubtedly and lavishly welcomed it if it had not brought fervid good news. A bona fide manifestation of Lucifer at Freemason's Tavern or Washington, would have made the vast halls of the Vatican echo with pious jubilation would have proclaimed itself *urbi et orbi*. But the grey age of the Latin Church is not only within its own limits an astute and experienced age, it is also one of honour and sanctity, and every right-thinking mind, in a land where there is now little real prejudice and practically no Protestantism, is perfectly well aware that she does not stoop to a partnership with liars and imposters. Could the Taxil conspiracy have presented itself unexposed to the Congress, it would have met with a different reception, but the report of my own investigations became known in France concurrently with the secessions of Hacks and Margiotta and the divulgations which accompanied them. The Congress was therefore on its guard, and Leo Taxil must have repaired to its deliberations in the city of great council with substantial assurance before hand that his cause was lost. To drawback was, however, impossible, and, of course, there was a bare possibility that, in the chapter of accidents, a way might be found through the difficulties which now beset him. It was obvious in any case that the literature of the so-called Palladium was not likely to be passed over in silence. As Father Portalié has observed, the proportions to which it had extended would have rendered such an omission both an error and a grave danger.

It was possible, however, to set aside the acknowledged writings of Leo Taxil and also those of Margiotta, while the force of hostile criticism was directed against the pretended "Memoirs of an Ex-Palladist" and the evidences connected therewith. After an animated debate in which Leo Taxil took part, and offered gross insults to those who demanded precise and verified data on the subject of Diana Vaughan, her birth, her conversion, and her baptism, the entire question concerning her was referred to a commission at Rome, which eventually threw up the investigation without arriving at an absolute conclusion. The only judgment which it really pronounced was that "the artifices employed by certain persons during the last few months would provoke rather an unfavourable view of the subjects under consideration." Decisive arguments were, however, wanting to decide (*a*) as to the existence of Diana Vaughan; (*b*) as to her conversion; (*c*) as to the authenticity of her writings. This declaration was pronounced on Jan. 22nd. 1897. It had been for some time foreseen by the conspiracy that a favourable pronunciation was a forlorn hope, and it had taken refuge in affronting the Commission upon every conceivable head. It had been obvious for a long time that the partisans of the supposed ex-Palladist had a very simple task before them in order to establish her existence. They need only produce the certificate of her birth, the name of the priest who baptized her, and of the bishop who authorized her first communion. For obvious reasons they could do none of these things, and issue after issue of the memoirs of the imaginary "Miss" were filled with excuses and explanations as to why the first was impossible and the others were inexpedient. It was affirmed that the laws of registration were exceedingly loose in America, and loose above all in Kentucky. When it was pointed out that by the depositions of her witnesses and by statements of her own she was born in Paris there was, of course, no answer forthcoming. It was advanced also that the name of the priest and the bishop by whom she was reconciled to the Church would, if published, involve the locality of the convent into which she proposed to retire when her mission of revelation was accomplished, and this was to endanger her life. These subterfuges, which ought to have deceived no one, satisfied many, just as the gross insults offered to members of the Catholic hierarchy, to say nothing of the foremost representatives of the Catholic press, seem to have been regarded indulgently not only by lay believers but by priests. It remains simply incredible that any person, above all any ecclesiastic, in France or in England, could have cherished any expectation that there would be a favourable issue to the Question of Diana Vaughan, could be solicitous for her ultimate triumph, and could publicly state that they prayed for her intentions at the altar of God, when offering the sacrifice of the Mass, after reading the shameful pages in which this alias of Leo Taxil offered all injury not merely to priests like Father Gruber in Austria and Father Portalié in Paris, but to prelates who had occasion to deny the patronage which she had unlawfully appropriated. It is scandalous marvels of this kind which will remain among the permanent delights of Leo Taxil when he looks back upon his colossal imposture.

After the publication of *Devil-Worship in France* the

Memoirs continued to run their course, telling mendacious stories, some of which I was at the pains of exploding at the time, but there is now no necessity to publish the results. At length it was announced that Miss Vaughan would come forward and confound her enemies. The date of her appearance was fixed and an itinerary was published of her progress through France, Belgium, England, Scotland, and Italy. At the first meeting, however, the "Conference Diana Vaughan" proved to be the Conference Leo Taxil with the result now known to every one.

The account which has been given in this and the preceding sections has, I think, made it abundantly clear that the author of the conspiracy unmasked to save himself from a more rough unveiling. I believe furthermore that the dénouement was precipitated by facts which have not at present transpired, and the directions in which they should be sought may perhaps be gathered from the indications of the seventh section. There are other residual questions which also require to be considered, and I think the opportunity should be embraced to give publicly for the first time an authoritative summary of the doctrines of Albert Pike which have been the subject of so much distracted reference.

V

The Secret Doctrine of Albert Pike

The Report of the Trent Congress does little more than italicize the salient points of the *Humanum Genus* Encyclical. In answer to that Encyclical the Grand Lodge of England protested that Freemasonry in this country had no opinions political or religious, and herein it did no more than describe an actual fact which is practically of universal knowledge. It will be well, however, to give the views of the Ancient and Accepted Scottish Rite as represented by the Grand Commander of the Southern Jurisdiction of the United States, the late Albert Pike. As regards the political aspect, I shall cite certain passages from his reply to the *Humanum Genus* epistle, while as regards the religious views which he held personally and certainly sought to impress on Masons under the obedience of his Rite, the information will be derived from the secret lectures of which we have heard so much through the medium of the French conspiracy, and chiefly from those which are available only to initiates of the higher degrees. The justification for so doing must be found in the odious calumnies which have been circulated concerning the teachings of this important and learned Mason, which also are likely to remain in the minds of many persons after the other influences of the deception have passed away.

The reply to the Encyclical of Pope Leo was, I believe, publicly available at the time of its appearance, but it is not well known in this country, at least at the present day. The summary of the political position is briefly this, that Freemasonry has at no time conspired against any polity entitled to its obedience or to the esteem of men generally. "Wherever now there is a Constitutional Government which respects the rights of men and of the people and the public opinion of the world, it is the loyal supporter of that Government. It has never taken pay from armed Despotism, or abetted persecution. It has fostered no Borgias; no stranglers or starvers to death of other Popes, like Boniface VII; no poisoners, like Alexander VI and Paul III. It has no roll of beatified Inquisitors and other murderers; and it has never, in any country, been the enemy of the people, the suppressor of scientific truth, the stifler of the God-given right of free inquiry as to the great problems, intellectual and spiritual, presented by the Universe, the extorter of confessions by the rack, the burner of women and of the exhumed bodies of the dead. . . . Its patron Saints have always been St. John the Baptist and St. John the Evangelist, and not Pedro Arbues d' Epila, Principal

Inquisitor of Zaragoza, who, slain in 1485, was beatified by Alexander VII in 1664." The inferences from this statement are, I think, quite clear and simple. It is a declaration that Governments both political and religious may abdicate their right to rule, and that a time may come when men, whether Masons or not, neither can nor should continue to countenance, support, or tolerate such Governments. I have no inclination to defend or to discuss this principle, which exceeds the province of the merely historical student. I should regard the right of superseding corrupt governments as an imprescriptible part of human liberty, but the Catholic Church claims to be a Divine Institution over which there is no Jurisdiction within the sphere of human liberty. The two standpoints cannot be reconciled, and time must decide the issue, if indeed, virtually speaking, it has not already decided it. It is the struggle of Divine Right in one or other of its two aspects against the right of free government and of free intellectual inquiry. On the one side it is not more the struggle of the Catholic Church than it is of political autocracy, on the other it is not more the opposing effort of Freemasonry than it is of any enslaved people demanding a Constitution, or yearning, and even plotting, for the downfall of some tyrannical dynasty. In any case, Albert Pike is careful to point out that Freemasonry does not more condemn the excesses of the Papacy "than it does those of Henry VIII of England, the murderer of Sir Thomas More and that of Servetus, and those of the Quakers put to death by bigotry in New England; than the cruel torturing and slaying of Covenanters and Non-Conformists, the ferocities of Claverhouse and Kirk, and the pitiless slaughtering of Catholic

Priests by the revolutionary fury of France. It well knows and cheerfully acknowledges the services which some of the Roman Pontiffs and a multitude of its clergy have in the past centuries rendered to Humanity. It has always done ample justice to their pure lives, their good deeds, their self-denial, their devotedness, their unostentatious heroism . . . It has always done full justice to the memoirs of the faithful and devoted Missionaries of the Order of Jesus and others, who bore the Cross into every barbarous land under the sun, to make known to savages the truths and errors taught by the Roman Church, and the simple arts of civilisation. It has never been the insensate and unreasoning reviler of that Church. . . ." In particular, "there has never been any opposition on the part of Freemasonry, to Catholicism as a religion" in America. Such is the standpoint of Albert Pike concerning the Church in what I may venture to term its political aspect. Surely it expresses the feeling and opinion of every intelligent person outside the Roman Communion. It is perhaps well to add that the private instructions of the Grand Commander do not differ from his more public utterances. "It is not the mission of Masonry," he observes elsewhere, "to engage in plots and conspiracies against the civil government. It is not the fanatical propagandist of any creed or theory; nor does it proclaim itself the enemy of Kings. It is the apostle of liberty, equality, and fraternity; but it is no more the high-priest of republicanism than of constitutional monarchy." If therefore in certain countries and at certain distracted periods we undoubtedly find that the apparatus of the lodges has been made to serve the purpose of plot and faction, Masonry as an institution is not more responsible for the abuse than is the Catholic Church as a whole for the poisoned sacraments of a Borgia pontiff.

The religious doctrines of Pike, as they are found in his secret lectures, so far as they are developed from the immutable dogmas of Freemasonry, the existence of a God and the immortality of the soul, possess an inferential authority. It is unlawful for any person denying these dogmas to be made a Mason. "The Grand Orient of France has been proclaimed by the Free-Masonry of Great Britain and the United States to be no longer a Masonic Power." And why? Not because it has denied the existence of a God, but because it has ceased to make the belief in that Being an essential condition of initiation. From the standpoint of Albert Pike the personality of the Divine Nature is also an essential dogma, and speaking historically there can be no doubt, I think, as to this, though there can be also no doubt that it has been at all times and everywhere evaded. It is sufficient to point to this dogma for a refutation of the accusation of Pantheism. At the same time the majority of Masons, supposing their best intentions, will probably talk Pantheism, by an intellectual confusion, when discussing the connection between God and the universe, but so also will as large a proportion of persons outside Masonry. Beyond these dogmas, neither Albert Pike nor anyone can say anything which is of authority, either in books or lectures, and this is especially pointed out by the American Grand Commander, in the preface to his "Morals and Dogma," when he observes that "every one is entirely free to reject and dissent from whatsoever herein may seem to him to be untrue or unsound." My object in quoting these lectures, as already indicated, is not so much to provide a reply to the Report of the Trent Congress, which is based on a misapprehension, as to exhibit the private opinions of Albert Pike and to clear his memory of all possible connection with the gallimaufry of Palladian nonsense.

Though certainly most illustrious as a Mason, and the man to whom the present immense prestige and influence of the Scottish Rite must be largely referred, it is not necessary to say that he had his intellectual limitations, and though he began life as a poet with some conspicuous evidence of vocation his literary methods are not altogether successful and at times are not less than intolerable. To state in the preface to a work of almost encyclopaedic proportions that about half of it is borrowed matter by no means renders it superfluous to separate text from citation; to do otherwise leads inevitably to confusion, but in analysing "Morals and Dogma," one is everywhere beset by this difficulty. When I published *Devil-Worship in France* I was substantially convinced, in my own mind that Leo Taxil and his confederates had dressed up distorted passages taken from Éliphas Lévi and had fathered them on Albert Pike. I was wrong altogether. Subsequent to the appearance of that work I became convinced that the conspiracy had access to unpublished documents of the Ancient and Accepted Rite in America which themselves had borrowed those passages. I believe now that other documents, which up to the present I have failed to see, were also in possession of Leo Taxil, and what he did was to produce them with variations adapted to his Palladian purpose. The "Morals and Dogma" swarms with passages taken directly from Lévi without any acknowledgment beyond that already mentioned, and also without any marks of quotation. On this point it is not necessary to dwell further; the work as a whole has the merits and defects which characterise such ingarnerings; it is of course imperfectly digested, and the student must expect discrepancies, even over matters of importance. There is one on the face of the lectures which it is impossible to pass over because it is concerned with the religious aspect of Masonry. The disclaimer issued by the Grand Lodge of England found little acceptance with the Scottish Rite in America. Among the most influential members of that Rite at the present day it appears to be held that "as a system of philosophy Masonry must of necessity have a religious mission and a doctrinal propaganda," but not of a "sectarious kind," because it deals with those "fundamental principles upon which all faiths are founded." Now, in the tenth lecture of Albert Pike, which belongs to the Grade of "Illustrious Elect of the Fifteen," it is laid down that Masonry is not a religion. "He who makes of it a religious belief, falsifies and denaturalizes it." But in a later lecture, belonging to the higher grade of "Grand Master Architect," it is said that "the religious faith taught by Masonry is indispensable to the attainment of the great ends of life." If Masonry be an institution possessing religious faith then it is most certainly to be regarded as a religion, and it follows that Albert Pike did not always choose his words very carefully, seeming in this instance to confuse the conceptions of sect and religion. It is, however, a misuse of terms only, and there is no need to insist on it.

When this initial difficulty has been permitted to disappear, we shall have no trouble to ascertain the precise nature of the religious aspect attributed to Masonry. It will appear at first sight to be merely of the "natural" order. "If we could cut off from any soul all the principles taught by Masonry, the faith in a God, in immortality, in virtue, in essential rectitude, that soul would sink into sin, misery, darkness, and ruin. If we could cut off all sense of these truths, the man would sink at once to the grade of the animal." Here is the full expression of natural religion, the sum of light which the intellect unaided by revelation is supposed to reach. As to revelation itself, a special construction is placed upon the admitted Christian aspects which must tend to its rejection in the sense that revelation is understood by the orthodox Christian Churches. "Believe that there is a God; that He is our father, that He has a paternal interest in our welfare and improvement; that He has given us powers by means of which we may escape from sin and ruin; that He has destined us to a future life of endless progress towards perfection and a knowledge of Himself—believe this, as every Mason should, and you can live calmly, endure patiently, labour resolutely, deny yourself cheerfully, hope steadfastly, and be conquerors in the great struggle of life. Take away any one of these principles, and what remains for us? Say that there is no God; or no way opened for hope and reformation and triumph, no heaven to come, no rest for the weary, no home in the bosom of God for the afflicted and disconsolate soul; or that God is but an ugly blind *Chance* that stabs in the dark; or a *somewhat* that is, when attempted to be defined, a *no-what* emotionless, passionless, the *Supreme Apathy* to which all things, good and evil, are alike indifferent; or a jealous God who revengefully visits the sins of the fathers on the children, and when the fathers have eaten sour grapes, sets the children's teeth on edge; an arbitrary *Supreme Will,* that has made it right to be virtuous and wrong to lie and steal, because *It pleased* to *make* it so rather than otherwise, retaining the power to reverse the law; or a fickle, vacillating, inconstant Deity, or a cruel, blood-thirsty, savage Hebrew or Puritanic one, and we are but the sport of chance and the victims of despair." The system of inverted theology devised by Leo Taxil in the interests of his Palladian romance would appear to certain minds, and might have been to Pike among their number, only a degree more impossible than some parts of the inheritance which Christianity has derived from Israel. But this syllabus of natural religion protesting against the aspects of revelation which are in antagonism with the fatherhood of God and the apparent rights inherent in the everlasting sonship of humanity is not the important part of the "Morals and Dogma." We know the strength and weakness of natural religion; we know also the full force of the objections raised on the subject of the only revelation about which there is any serious debate. No Masonic initiation and no secret lectures are likely to restate these old cases with any special freshness, and if there were nothing more in the doctrine of Albert Pike there would be no need to draw attention to it, except in so far as might be necessary to clear his memory from calumnious accusation. I have stated elsewhere that the transcendental aspect of Masonic teaching has been denied, but from the standpoint of the Ancient and Accepted Rite it does possess such a teaching, and there are some at least of its initiates who regard it as the glory of the Fraternity. But the application of the teaching has been lost, in other words, the transcendental practice is wanting. There are those also who deplore this loss, and the momentous character of Pike's unpublished writings resides wholly in the fact that they are an attempt once more to interlink Masonry with Mysticism. Albert Pike was a disciple of Éliphas Lévi, and Éliphas Lévi was the first writer in modern times who seriously attempted to place the doctrines of esoteric philosophy in a new light before the world. The vast work which the Supreme Council of the Thirty-Third Degree for the Southern Jurisdiction of the United States published "by its authority" under the title of "Morals and Dogma" is in reality a translation in part and a commentary in full, having a special application to Masonry, of and upon the works of Éliphas Lévi, from whom all its inspiration is drawn and to whom all its value must be ultimately referred. Its "natural religion" is modified by the transcendentalism of Lévi, and its Masonry is transfigured in the light of the old sanctuaries of initiation. We find therefore that the most influential and the most coherent school of the Fraternity has, under the auspices of one dominant mind, resolved itself into a school of Mysticism, and the justification for the last chapter of my former work is abundantly displayed. The lecture which is connected with the thirty-second degree of the Rite, or "Sublime Prince of the Royal Secret" is a presentation of the magical doctrine, and this, in other words, constitutes what I have termed the "Secret Doctrine of Albert Pike," which, so far as his influence extended, has become also that of the Ancient and Accepted Scotch Rite. It is not merely a doctrine of amiable but insufficient natural religion or merely a sentimental criticism of revealed religion prompted by a pleasant anthropomorphism which would deny the connection between the Great Father and a God of Shambles and Hecatombs, of human bakeries and holy Inquisitions. It does indeed recognise and revere the implanted instinct of natural religion and it does indeed reject conceptions which blaspheme the Divine Nature, but it believes also that behind the universal testimony of all peoples in all periods to the existence of revelation, there abides the Secret Doctrine, the mystery of all sanctuaries, participation in which was the end of every initiation. Whether Pike or Lévi attained to that doctrine is another question, which cannot be discussed here, but it has been thought that the French adept was in touch with sources of instruction which cannot be referred to more clearly, and there is some evidence in Pike's lectures to indicate that he did not misconceive his teacher. I need only add that the crass doctrine of dualism has no place in such a system. It is replaced by the doctrine of Equilibrium, and Albert Pike explains the "Royal Secret" imparted to the recipient of the 32nd degree in the terms of the transcendental counsel concerning the Kabbalistic "Mystery of the Balance."

"It is the Secret of the Universal Equilibrium:—Of that Equilibrium in the Deity, between the Infinite Divine Wisdom and the Infinite Divine Power, from which result the stability of the Universe, the unchangeableness of the Divine Law, and the Principles of Truth, Justice and Right which are a part of it. . . .— Of that Equilibrium also, between the Infinite Divine Justice and the Infinite Divine Mercy, the result of which is the Infinite Divine Equity, and the Moral Harmony or beauty of the Universe. By it the endurance of created and imperfect natures in the presence of a Perfect Deity is made possible; and for Him also, as for us, to love is better than to hate, and forgiveness is easier than revenge or punishment. . . .—Of that Equilibrium between Necessity and Liberty, between the action of the Divine Omnipotence and the Free-will of man, by which sins and base notions, and ungenerous thoughts and words, are crimes and wrongs justly punished by the law of cause and consequence. . . .—Of that Equilibrium between Good and Evil, and light and darkness in the world, which assures us that all is the work of the Infinite Wisdom and of an Infinite Love; and that THERE IS NO REBELLIOUS DEMON OF EVIL, OR PRINCIPLE OF DARKNESS CO-EXISTENT AND IN ETERNAL CONTROVERSY WITH GOD OR THE PRINCIPLE OF LIGHT AND OF GOOD: by attaining to the knowledge of which Equilibrium we can, through Faith, see that the existence of Evil, Sin, Suffering, and Sorrow in the world, is consistent with the Infinite Goodness as well as with the Infinite Wisdom of the Almighty. . . .—Of that Equilibrium between Authority and Individual Activity which constitutes Free Government, by settling on immutable foundations Liberty with Obedience to Law, Equality with Subjection to Authority, and Fraternity with subordination to the Wisest and, the Best . . .—and, finally, of that Equilibrium, possible in ourselves, which Masonry incessantly labours to accomplish in its Initiates, and demands of its Adepts and Princes . . . between the Spiritual and the Divine and the Material and Human in man. . . . This Equilibrium teaches us, above all, to reverence ourselves as immortal souls, and to have respect and charity for others, who are even such as we are, partakers with us of the Divine Nature, lighted by a ray of the Divine Intelligence, struggling like us towards the light. . . . Such is the TRUE WORD of a Master Mason; such the true ROYAL SECRET, which makes possible, and shall at length make real, the HOLY EMPIRE of true Masonic Brotherhood."

Éliphas Lévi, of whose views the above passage is simply a verbal paraphrase, has said that "all religions have issued from the Kabbalah and all return therein"; understanding the term in the wider sense of the universal traditions of transcendentalism, we may accept the statement, and may rejoice that Freemasonry in its religious aspect has also set its face towards Jerusalem.

VI

Women and Freemasonry

According to an ancient and fundamental law of the Fraternity, which is the subject of reference by Albert Pike, no woman can be made a Mason. The reason is not, however, as impostors like Cassanova have asserted, because of a physical impediment; it is a law of the same kind as that which renders an atheist ineligible. In both cases the law has been occasionally abrogated, and it is within possibility that it may be some day entirely cancelled as regards the initiation of the female sex. To indicate the feeling on the subject which obtains among some Brethren occupying high positions in the Ancient and Accepted Scottish Rite, I cannot do better than quote the following remarks from a private letter in my possession:—

"To the eternal disgrace of Masonry it must be acknowledged that women are not initiated, but such an admission is quite a different thing from humbly begging to be allowed to deny it. Will any man tell me why, if Masonry be a philosophy, a code of morals, or anything else that is good, women should not be permitted to share in it? Have women no souls to save? Are they incapable of comprehending Masonic teachings? Are they less benevolent, generous, or self-sacrificing than men? Was Masonry made for the 'Genus Man' or merely for the sexual animal man? These and a thousand questions of similar import may well be asked of those who defend the exclusion of women from Freemasonry, and they may be defied to answer them.

"How has it come about that women are excluded from Freemasonry? It cannot be denied that our Masonry, as well as our religion, has come to us from the Jews, or that it retains many of the peculiar customs of that people. With them a woman was chattel property, to be bought and sold. She was a slave in her person, and had no soul to save. Her position in the early Christian Church was very little better, nor has it improved much in the Orthodox Churches of to-day. All of them avail themselves of the power which women wield in the home circle to propagate their doctrine and increase their receipts, but when it comes to giving her a voice in church management or in public teaching, that would be sacrilege. Since the days of St. Paul, woman has not been allowed to have an opinion of her own on religious matters. The social condition of woman has followed very much the same line in countries under the domination of the Roman Catholic Church. Spain and her dependencies are good examples; there a woman has but few advantages over her caged sister of Guiana. In France her condition may be better, but it is not until you come to Protestant lands that any effort is made to give woman her equal rights. Indeed it is not so many years ago that in protestant England a man could sell his wife, and beat her with a stick up to the diameter of his thumb. Nor even at this day in all protestant countries, can she hold property in her own right, while in very few does she possess a voice in the elections or hold public positions. Appearing in the light of a slave, unable to control her own time or actions, it was thus that woman came of necessity to be excluded from Masonry.

"The unfortunate fact that the name of the "Genus" is also that of the male animal of the human family, coupled with the ignorance and the dishonesty of many of the so-called teachers of man, resulted in the misconstruction of many passages in the Bible, and this, together with our inherited Jewish peculiarities and prejudices, resulted in placing woman in the very degraded position which she has occupied for so many centuries. Fortunately, this condition is beginning to correct itself in America. There are many androgynous societies flourishing here, such, for example, as the Eastern Star, whose female membership is restricted, I believe, to the female relations of Freemasons; then too the Oddfellows have a degree of Rebecca, to which women are admitted. Than are also the Good Templars, a Temperance Society, which is androgynous, and the Rechabites, which, I believe, is an association of the same character. So you see that androgynous societies are not wanting on this side of the Atlantic, whatever may be thought of them in Europe. Amongst them I do not think that the Rite of Adoption can be numbered as one that has made much headway. About 40 years ago there were lodges of the Good Samaritan having fair membership, and this degree it is my impression was one of the Rite of Adoption."

"I have here draughted a line of defence which, I think, Masonry ought to pursue. It certainly seems to me that advocates of the exclusion of women from the Mysteries have before them a long and difficult task to maintain their position."

VII

Who Is Diana Vaughan?

A conspiracy of the magnitude of that conceived by Leo Taxil must almost inevitably have behind it some questions which the fullest exposure has failed to settle, and even a plenary confession of fraud does not entirely determine. I must presently indicate the existence of the Palladian Order as a point over which Catholic criticism promises to go astray. There is another matter which now fortunately has no consequences attaching to it, but in which some interest may remain. Is there any person existing who really bears the name of Diana Vaughan and claims to have some connection with Freemasonry? Leo Taxil has publicly stated that the Diana Vaughan of the Memoirs was a female clerk employed by himself at a small stipend to conduct the correspondence arising out of that work. From this it has been concluded that she bears the name in question. When we remember, however, that there is full evidence from her existing letters to show that she is a Frenchwoman, this inference becomes improbable. At the same time, curiously enough, there is some reason to think that a person bearing this name is not unknown in America. At the present time it is confined to an interview with Mr. William Oscar Roone, cashier of the National Bank of Ohio, and said to be an old friend of Albert Pike. In the course of the interview it was stated that Diana Vaughan had been long known to him in a mental state which necessitated medical supervision. Her family, composed of honourable protestants of Kentucky, was obliged to incarcerate her in an asylum, some six or seven years ago. At the end of several months she left as she was supposed to have been cured. Her whereabouts at the present time are quite unknown to Mr. Roone, but it is probable enough that she repaired at some period to Paris, and fell into the hands of persons who have been exploiting her delusions. As she is an orphan and of age, her surviving relations in the Union have no power over her; her uncle is the only person who might exercise some authority, but he is very old, she has outwearied him, he asks only to die in peace, and has declined to intervene in any way.

Assuming that this report, the original of which I have not seen, has not been garbled by the conspiracy, the question seems settled so far. It remains however to say that the genuine Miss Vaughan and her family are not persons of any consequence in Kentucky. Among many documents, now somewhat roughly shorn of their importance, recently collected by me for the further exposure of the conspiracy, there is one which seems conclusive on this point. It is the result of an inquiry which I addressed to the American Consul in London, requesting direction as to how I might best proceed to ascertain whether a person named Vaughan was a wealthy owner of real estate and a cattle-breeder in the neighbourhood of Louisville between the years 1870 and 1885; also, and if so, whether he had a daughter named Diana. As they were alleged to be persons of position, there was no doubt, I added, that they could be traced easily. It so happened, I was informed in reply to this inquiry, that there was a gentleman at the Consulate who had been born and bred in Louisville, had lived there all his life up to three months previously, and had always occupied an official position in that City; he could not fail to know every person of any prominence therein, but at the same time he had never heard of Diana Vaughan or of her father. The name in itself, I may add, is by no means uncommon; in the year 1883, one T.W. Vaughn (note orthography, which may, however, be a misprint) appears among the Annual members of the Polytechnic Society of Kentucky.

To these facts must be added one more curious point, derived from the latest issues of the "Memoirs of an Ex-Palladist," but I see no reason so far to doubt its truth. It appears that a lady named Mrs. Phillips, a resident of Chicago, has arrived recently in Paris, indeed on the eve of the *denouement,* to expose the imposture of Taxil, on the ground that she is the only genuine Diana Vaughan who has ever been connected with the Masonry of America. That connection involves, however, no Palladism, no Female Freemasonry of the La Rive kind. Mrs. Phillips is merely a member of that Society of the Eastern Star, mentioned in the previous section, which is composed of the daughters, sisters, and widows of Freemasons. As this may or may not be the lady who is mentioned by Mr. Roone, it is possible that there are two genuine Dianas, a fact which may yet lead to some fantastic results. But how did the report of either reach Leo Taxil, and why did he risk their coming forward? Or hoax and imposture as it was, is it not possible that the "colossal conspiracy," like most first-rate impositions, was connected with and arose out of certain facts, as Palladism, Universal Freemasonry, and the directing centre out of the ambition of the Scottish Rite, so the "Memoirs of an Ex-Palladist" from the vapourings of the crazy Diana, who had come somehow, as Mr. Roone suggests, into connection with the conspirators? On this hypothesis the case of Mrs. Phillips is simply a curious coincidence.

However it may ultimately turn out, two things seem morally certain, (*a*) That no person named Diana Vaughan has ever been heard of at Charleston, and (*b*) That any person bearing that name, whether in Kentucky or Chicago, has no title to a connection with that branch of the Vaughan family in England which is represented by the Earls of Lisburn. As to the first point, I hold the most express testimony of Mr. Nathaniel Levin, 33°, Inspector-General of South Carolina, and that of his deputy, Mr. Samuel S. Buist, with whose deceased Brother, Henry Buist, the late Albert Pike invariably stayed when he had occasion to visit Charleston. As to the second point, the Earl of Lisburn has kindly obtained for me no less express testimony, the result of researches undertaken by a member of his family. All these documents were originally intended for publication but the necessity has now passed away.

VIII

Some Consequences of the Conspiracy

One of the most conspicuous lessons of the late disclosures is to exhibit how completely the Catholic Church, with all its opportunities, misconceives the real issues, hostile or not, of Freemasonry, and how entirely in the dark it remains as to any of the truly mystical fraternities. The fact is stamped upon every line of the papal encyclicals. Freemasonry in its intellectual centres simply represents and mirrors the constant flux of modern opinion upon all speculative subjects. It includes beyond doubt in its ranks the shades of philosophical thought which correspond to the findings of the Trent Congress. It also numbers Spiritualists, Theosophists, and representatives without number of the higher schools of Mysticism. If it were said that there were Mormons among Masons, I do not know that it could be denied. In the days when there was a Protestant England it was in England a Protestant institution, in the sense that the preponderating sentiment of its members was under the obedience of the 39 articles or some other Reformation standard. At the present day there is no preponderating religious sentiment, though there is a tacit agreement to abide informally by certain conventions on condition that they exact nothing outside the terms of the conventions, and thus the Church of England gives Grand Chaplains to Masonry in the same way that the Imperial Power or its delegate gives prelates to the Church. In this as in other matters it is one of the most signal ingenuities of modern arrangement that the old offices and the old orders prevail without any conspicuous challenge on condition that there is no authoritative construction of their importance. As to the ultimate opinions of any person in or out of Masonry, they are under the obedience of individual predilection, if any, and the result is *chaos magnum infirmatum*. There is no doubt that the Italians as a nation are predisposed constitutionally to hold their opinion less peaceably for others and for themselves than we do here in England or than is done commonly in America, and hence the Masonry of Italy embodies more troublesome elements than our own, but that is a peninsular prejudice which judges a universal institution by its special complexion in a peninsula.

The findings of the Trent Congress are, on the whole, extremely meagre and insufficient. The varieties of religious opinion among Masons are indefinitely more complex and manifold. It goes without saying that from the standpoint of the Church it is a heretical institution because it is composed of heretics. It seems scarcely worth while to call congresses to pronounce upon a fact which nobody has ever challenged. To represent it, however, as in the van of intellectual free thought is a view which, speaking generally, the Fraternity does not appear to have earned. The majority of blue lodges might well turn red as their rivals at the complimentary suggestion, but it is not in unwelcome contrast to another imputation with which we are all more familiar, that which represents Masonry as the emblazonment of unmeaning mediocrity, where the *ne plus ultra* of all initiation is the maximum point of good fellowship which it is possible to reach at a banquet.

The charges against Freemasonry are in other respects too numerous for any special point to reside in one of them. It is, however, reassuring, after a crucial examination of conscience, to find that it has not as yet diabolised, and that it has not a directing centre.

In France at least the result of these allegations is a victory and a vindication obtained under the best circumstances, for it has remained passive throughout, permitting the accusations of its enemies to multiply until they strangled one another. In England and in America, the two countries which for obvious reasons were the scenes selected for most of the inventions, the same policy of masterly inactivity has also wisely prevailed, for although I have been described in Paris as the mouthpiece of Masonry, acting under the orders and inspired by the supreme chiefs of the "Luciferian Rose-Cross," I do not need to inform readers in England that I acted on my own initiative and with so little official assistance that on one occasion the Supreme Council of the Scottish Rite in Great Britain saw fit to refuse me information upon a simple point of fact, because, I suppose, it might seem to be arming a defender.

The result to the Catholic Church must be inevitably that which it has anticipated, and has indeed in a sense pointed out by the pen of one of the most able French critics of the conspiracy, Father Eugène Portalié, of the Society of Jesus. It is perfectly true, and cannot be too distinctively indicated to Masons and Transcendentalists, that the Church in its official capacity did not welcome, countenance, or tolerate the scandals which were devised in her name, but did at need unmask them. There is no call to look further than the impartial spirit with which papers like the *Tablet* of London have treated the matter throughout. There has been no hint that the issues were unimportant, or an occasion for jesting, as implied in less instructed quarters. For months subsequent to the publication of the first edition of *Devil-Worship in France,* which was reviewed at great length, the columns of the organ in question have been open to the discussion of the subject, and so far as its attitude may be taken to represent that of the Church itself in England it must be frankly stated that in her crusade against Masonry she has no desire for the assistance of unsavoury confederates, self-constituted allies as they are. It should be observed also that the latest and most trenchant exposures of the Anti-Masonic conspiracy are the work of the Catholic press. The secular journals have for the most part questioned, wondered, and jeered, or occasionally, in a mood of ingenuity, have offered fabrications of their own to explain the fabrications of the conspiracy. At the same time that conspiracy wore the mask of the Church, claimed to be acting in her interests, adopted her language, cited her authority, seemed to be following her lead, and she, on the other hand, was admittedly not unprepared for evidence of the kind which has been manufactured, while a few of her foremost ecclesiastics have believed in it up to the last, and it is barely possible, in some modified sense, may go on giving credit to it. In France, Mgr. Fava, long after the true position of affairs was, owing to Catholic criticism, transparent, one would have thought, to every reasonable being, gave the weight of his episcopal position to the express statement that there was a Diana Vaughan, that it was she who was writing, that she had made her first communion, and that Findel and other Freemasons were attempting to mystify the Catholics. The feelings of this excellent prelate at the present moment deserve the lively sympathy, and will certainly not be the scorn, of any generous Mason. In England there is one ecclesiastic and one only, so far as I am aware, who in spite of the opprobrium heaped by "Diana Vaughan" upon every member of the hierarchy who dared to discredit her revelations, has continued to expect that she would ultimately justify herself, and is said, no doubt untruly, to have placed his presbytery at her disposal on the occasion of her promised visit to London. He occupies a respected but not important position, and he too will command our good feeling. But the influence which has been exercised in this manner cannot fail to take its effect, and so also must the benedictions and congratulations obtained from Cardinal Vicars, Papal Secretaries, and, it is said, even the Pope himself, at a period when the truth was not known. They may have been explained afterwards, and their formal character exhibited; those who transmitted them may now see, and may not be backward to acknowledge, as indeed has been done, that they were entrapped by a colossal mystification, but their patronage could be quoted at the moment, it was quoted far and wide, and it has performed its work, which is mischievous to the cause of the Church, whose case against Freemasonry is peculiarly difficult to sustain before the tribunal of universal opinion, because it is grounded on considerations with which public opinion disagrees, and the worst thing which could befall it is a connection, however transient, with ridiculous accusations and proved imposture. The manifest duty of those who have been falsely accused by that imposture is not also to make themselves ridiculous by mistaking their accusers, who are neither enemies to Freemasonry nor friends to the Church, nor otherwise friends of the Fraternity seeking by underhand measures to discredit an institution which offers battle to it, but simply rogues, having nothing at heart but their own advantage. Were it otherwise, as yet may be said, the Fraternity is as much above their assistance as the Church which for the moment seems almost to have joined with us in denouncing and unmasking them. It remains only to say that the credulity of certain Catholics, some of them highly placed, has been taught a wholesome lesson and there is no need for Masons or Mystics to enforce its application.

There is one point, however, upon which it may be well

to utter a word of timely warning. Indications are not wanting in certain ecclesiastical quarters where the exposure of the late conspiracy has been most active and most successful, which cannot therefore be regarded as wanting in discernment, that there will be an attempt to save the question of Palladism from the general wreck. Father Portalié observes in his admirable pamphlet: "The Catholic press has been accused of denying all intervention of Satan in the Lodges, and the *Revue Catholique* of Coutances has named me as one of those hypercritical persons who deny everything. This is an attempt to create a diversion, but the press has not been entrapped. Like the Roman Commission, the majority of the journals have discussed only the lying nature of the Bataille *cum* Vaughan collection. The question of Palladism is otherwise vast, and several members of the Commission have shown, by their example, that the imposture of Diana may be repudiated but at the same time the Satanism of the Lodges may be admitted on the ground of anterior documents. . . . The last word has not been spoken on this point, and we congratulate the *Rivista Antimassonica* that it is undertaking the revision in question." Now, the original Order of the Palladium, constituted in 1737, made no mark whatsoever, and bears no more traces of Satanism than do the knights and dames of the Primrose League. There can be no doubt that it died of inanition, but it was so obscure that it scarcely possesses a history. Its alleged reconstitution in 1870 and its alleged diabolical rituals are inventions of Leo Taxil, and they collapse with him. The *Rivista Antimassonica* will therefore do well to be very careful in its revision of the documents which are supposed to give evidence of this Order. When those furnished from the literary bordello of Leo Taxil have been set aside, I doubt very much whether there will be any documents left to work upon. It must be taken for what it is worth, but after supplementing my own ordinary sources of knowledge, which are not inconsiderable, by the most careful inquiry, I can learn nothing concerning such an institution, either connected or not connected with Masonry. I can give my honourable assurance that it is extremely unlikely the existence of such an Order would have escaped me had it possessed a thousandth part of the diffusion which is attributed to it. The absurdity of its alleged position in Freemasonry has, of course, long been transparent, but that was a part of the Taxil imposture, and that also ceases with his extinction. In this connection I may quote the observations which were made upon certain points by a gentleman who possesses the highest degree of the Scottish Rite, was a personal friend of the late Albert Pike, and actively engaged in his Masonic propaganda. "It has always seemed to me," he said, referring to a passage on p. 28 of my previous work, "that the weak point in the organisation of Masonry has been the want of a directing centre, and in this it shows a most remarkable departure from its teachings. Efforts tending in part towards that result have been made from time to time, but have always failed, as, for example, the movement to form a General Grand Lodge for the United States, and a General Grand Priory with the Prince of Wales at its head. The power of the Roman Church is its organization, which can be, and is, enforced by its teachings. Masonry has no such weapon of defence, and as a consequence there is a constant tendency to disintegration and the minimizing of the governing power. I think therefore that instead of denying the existence of a central authority, the Fraternity should be found rather deeply regretting its absence."

IX

Conclusion

The collapse of the French conspiracy has been the signal on the part of those who have so nobly defended the Church from the imputation of a connection therewith to recall the faithful to the true field of battle. There is to be neither peace nor armistice; the polemics of the immediate past are simply to clear the issues. "Forget Diana Vaughan and return to the combat, guided, not by the revelations of adventurers, but by the encyclicals of the Popes, such are the wise counsels of the Roman Commission." This is the exhortation of Father Portalié, and he adds a special reference to the letters of Leo XIII which "denounce the antichristian and antireligious plans of Masonry, all converging to establish the reign of naturalism upon the ruins of the Church." The spirit of those letters is fully expressed in a pontifical address to the bishops of Italy on Dec. 8, 1892.

"It is insufficient to be on guard against the ambushes of the infamous sect; it is necessary to take the offensive, using the same arms, furnished by faith, which have already served conspicuously against paganism." Since therefore war is inevitable, it remains to say that the Fraternity has no reason to be afraid, and we may perhaps look before long for some change in its own policy. "The defenders of Freemasonry," says one of my correspondents, who is a member of the 33rd. degree of the Scottish Rite, under the obedience of the Southern Jurisdiction of the United States, "have resolved themselves into apologists, and when anything has been asserted against Masonry by the Roman Church as a matter to be condemned by it, the apologists, like timid creatures, have hastened to deny its existence, until, were we to believe them, Freemasonry exists no longer, even in thought. In my judgment, this system of defence is utterly a mistake. Since Masonry has become a semi-public institution, it should boldly proclaim its object, and not endeavour to seem a nonentity. When struck, let it strike back, as Pike did in his reply to the *Humanum Genus* Encyclical, and not let it acknowledge itself a criminal simply because the Church of Rome says it is."

I may be permitted to refer in concluding to the suggestion of one or two of my reviewers that I should follow this exposure of Modern Diabolism in its alleged connection with Masonry by an account of the other varieties of Satanism which are peculiar to the associations instituted for the express purpose of offering divine worship to the devil. There is evidence to show that such associations exist, and there was one at Naples in the year 1885, of which I have had a full account from a person who was initiated therein, and appears to have taken part in its orgies. I have no reason whatever to distrust the statements which were confided me, more especially as they included matters which reflected little credit upon my informant. The outlines correspond broadly to those which have been depicted by Huysman[s] but they were more abominable even than those. It remains only to say that the Society in question was not Masonic, it had no political complexion, and no supernatural manifestations, real or alleged, in connection with its rites. It celebrated the *missa spermatica* followed by a frenetic debauch. It has now dissolved or migrated; at least my informant went in search of it on a recent visit to Naples and could find no trace of its existence. The history of Modern Satanism like that of the Black Sabbath is that of *la hysterie insatiable,* and something more. If the materials for writing it existed it would scarcely serve a purpose—unless it was that of Leo Taxil, to whom, I think, on all accounts it may be most advantageously left. The revenues of the recent conspiracy may, of course, have been more than sufficient to support him in what would be regarded as opulence among the literati of the boulevards, but if not he has already exhibited a fund of information and sagacity concerning *La Corruption Fin de Siècle,* and I can imagine no person better suited at the moment by the nature of his researches to extend our store of knowledge as to the mysteries of the *Venus mascula.* It is a satisfaction to be able to add that the reception of my book among Masons has not at all justified the common accusation of languid interest shown by the rank and file of the brethren towards all that concerns the Craft. It is sometimes said that the Fraternity in England possesses no literature because Masons fail to support any enterprise of the kind. Possibly the average brother is not a more serious personage than the average man anywhere, and I must admit that it is frequently the members of the higher and so-called spurious grades who take a literary interest in the Order, but personally I have no cause to complain of what has resulted from my first attempt to interest and vindicate the Institution.

APPENDIX

Some Opinions of the Press

The *Tablet* says: "The clever but not convincing book of an honourable opponent. Struck, as all honourable minds must be, with the enormity of the charges recently laid against Palladian Masonry attached to the cultus of Satan, and having, we take it, no absolute proof upon which to join direct issue with them, Mr Waite puts the witnesses to the charges through rigorous tests as to their credibility. And we are not sorry he does so. . . . The net result of his book upon our mind is that we should receive all evidence as to Palladian Masonry with caution, and suspend a final judgment until we have exacted evidence as irrefragable as the nature of the case admits. . . . For those who wish to examine the whole question of Satanism and Palladian Masonry, we commend the book as a temperate and conscientious endeavour to clear it from a hideous stigma, by one who, himself a Mystic or Transcendentalist, has evidently much 'first-hand information' of the higher grades of Masonry."

The *Echo* says: "We have to thank Mr Waite for definitely tackling "the question of Lucifer" in the scholarly and lucid volume that now lies before us. . . . We trust, now that Mr Waite has brilliantly vindicated Freemasonry another student as careful and exhaustive will tackle that other question of Satanism which has been ignored in this volume, but has provided glorious material for sensational journalism this many a long day."

Mr. William Le Queux, writing in the *Literary World,* says: "Occultists will welcome Mr Waite's lucid and timely work dealing with the much-discussed Question of Lucifer and the existence of Palladian Masonry. . . . In the present revival of mystic thought this book comes opportunely, for it is a very careful and honest examination of all the available authorities. While it confirms the rumour of the existence of a *cultus diabolicus* in our midst, it shows at the same time how utterly unreliable are all the so-called disclosures which during the past couple of years have been used as newspaper 'padding,' and afforded constant food for sensation-mongers. The genuine exposure of devil-worship has yet to be written, and we hope Mr Waite's further investigation will enable him to write it."

The *Freemason* says: "Mr Waite's well-written book is as interesting as a romance. . . . The Order has fallen into good hands, and owes him some gratitude; the book is critical, scholarly, and dispassionate."

Mr. John Yarker, English Grand Master *ad vitam* of the Ancient and Primitive Rite of Masonry, writing in the *Freemason's Chronicle,* says: "My knowledge . . . is obtained from A. E. Waite's *Devil-Worship in France,* a most interesting book. . . , the end of which is that Mr Waite pronounces the charges to be 'lying myths.'"

Mr. P. Legge, writing in the *Contemporary Review,* says: Mr Waite's *Devil-Worship in France,* though written 'by a transcendentalist for transcendentalists' is a clear, condensed, and, on the whole, fair account of the controversy."

The *Daily Telegraph* says: "Mr Waite's laudable intention in compiling his book is to show that no association prevails between Satanism and true Mysticism. . . . For those who have time to fathom the depths of mental imbecility to which men, and women too, are capable of falling, and the heights of credulity they are able to reach, portions of Mr. Waite' s book dealing with the revelations of Dr. Bataille and 'Diana Vaughan'—a sort of Luciferised Madame Blavatsky—cannot fail to possess considerable attractions."

Light says: "As an indispensable historical account of the question up to the date of publication, its value cannot be impaired. . . . Mr. Waite is entitled to say that the Question of Lucifer 'assumes a fresh interest with the appearance of this book.' All must accord to the author the praise of diligence in an intricate inquiry, beset with prejudice, and agree that he has approached it in a generally judicial spirit, and has put it into an attractive literary form. The result is that Mr. Waite' s book will certainly be the starting point of information for English readers interested in the subject, even if it is not the last word of criticism."

The *Two Worlds* says: "The present volume is the last, though apparently not the final, outcome of the Luciferian Question, and as the work of a gentleman who is one of the foremost specialists in the domain of occult science, and a distinguished authority upon all matters relating to mysticism, particularly of the archaic order, it is worthy of our respectful consideration. . . . Mr. Waite's knowledge of the history and literature of masonry is evidently both wide and deep, and this, conjoined with his long experience in what is loosely called occult manifestations, fits him in a peculiar degree for the laborious task of sifting the evidence for the allegations made. He appears also to have a remarkable acquaintance with the various mystical confraternities which flourish in our midst to-day, of the existence of which little is known beyond the circles of membership. . . . He has contrived to make his book not only convincing and explanatory, but extremely entertaining, in virtue of the rich vein of humour running through it. . . . It is this element which will go far to give the book something more than an ephemeral interest."

Mr. W. T. Stead, writing in *Borderland*, says: "For a year or two past there has been a great deal of talk concerning the worship of Satan, which a certain class of writers declares has been exclusively practised in modern France. Mr. Waite in this volume of 300 pages subjects the evidence that is adduced to prove the existence of this worship of Satan to a crucical examination. . . . There is ample room for the careful and destructive analysis. . . . Mr. Waite has done his work with much painstaking and great care."